NO CASE TO ANSWER

NO CASE TO ANSWER

THE MEN WHO GOT AWAY WITH THE
GREAT TRAIN ROBBERY

ANDREW COOK

Jacket illustrations
Front: MI5 report, 13 January 1964 (The National Archives); an Identikit picture of 'Old Alf' (Thames Valley Police); Danny Pembroke CRO photograph (Metropolitan Police); Harry Smith CRO photograph (Metropolitan Police); Police at the scene of the Great Train Robbery (Evening Standard/Getty Images).

Back: MI5 folder (The National Archives); postcard from Cannes, allegedly from Terry Hogan (Police & Gendarmerie Records, High Court of Grasse, France); Danny Pembroke criminal intelligence file (BPMA); Danny Pembroke in the army (Danny Pembroke Jnr).

Back cover quote from Ronnie Biggs' serialisation in *The Sun*, 20–28 April 1970, reproduced from the Metropolitan Police Files.

First published 2022

The History Press
97 St George's Place, Cheltenham,
Gloucestershire, GL50 3QB
www.thehistorypress.co.uk

© Andrew Cook, 2022

The right of Andrew Cook to be identified as the Author of this work has been asserted in accordance with the Copyright, Designs and Patents Act 1988.

British Library Cataloguing in Publication Data.
A catalogue record for this book is available from the British Library.

ISBN 978 0 7509 9386 9

Typesetting and origination by The History Press
Printed and bound in Great Britain by TJ Books Limited, Padstow, Cornwall.

MIX
Paper from responsible sources
FSC® C013056
www.fsc.org

Trees for L🌱fe

CONTENTS

APPENDICES

ACKNOWLEDGEMENTS

IT IS UNFORTUNATELY NOT possible in a book of this kind to acknowledge, properly and by name, certain individuals who have provided extensive help, documentation and assistance in the researching of key aspects of this story. Those individuals do, however, know who they are, and have been privately thanked for the information and cooperation they provided, and indeed for the fascinating hours of their time they spent with me.

Audrey and Diana in South Africa, Bill Adams, Jill Adams, Sue Adcock (Hampshire Police), Anne Archer (BT Archive), Jordan Auslander (USA), Colin Boyes (Thames Valley Police), Garry Forsyth (Chief Constable Bedfordshire Constabulary), Philippe Chapelin (France), Daksha Chauhan, Alia Cook, Neeta Davda, Jim Davies (British Airways Heritage Collection/Archive), Garry Forsyth (Chief Constable Bedfordshire Constabulary), Gina Hynard (Hampshire Archives & Local Studies Centre), Mary Jursazek, Colin Kendall, Dick Kirby, Suhalia Liaquat, Michelle McConnell, Gavin McGuffie (Royal Mail Archive), Andrew Minney, Jade Pawaar, Danny Pembroke Jnr, Amanda Rossiter, Dr Tim Ryan, Yagnesh Shah, Lindsay Siviter, Sue Smith (Metropolitan Police), Lionel Stewart (Bedfordshire Police), Phil Tomaselli, Steve Walsh, Kevin Welch, Ken Wells (Thames Valley Police), Richard West, Alisa Wickens (Wiltshire Police)

PREFACE

THIS BOOK IS BASED on several years of carefully documented research, studying over a thousand pages of new material. Much of the detail recorded here has never before seen the light of day, being from closed, redacted, unfiled or retained sources.

My earlier book, published in 2013, *The Great Train Robbery: The Untold Story from the Closed Investigation Files*, was essentially the story of the robbery itself. It was based, on the whole, on over 1,000 pages of documents from investigation files that had been opened as a result of Freedom of Information (FOI) requests. The book was later used as a source for two television documentaries on the robbery, and the 2013 two-part World Productions/BBC1 television movie *The Great Train Robbery: A Robber's Tale & A Copper's Tale*. It was a great privilege to work with scriptwriter Chris Chibnall, and to watch the stars of the film, Jim Broadbent, Luke Evans, Robert Glenister, James Fox, Paul Anderson, Martin Compston, and a whole host of other great actors, bring the story to life during filming.

This second book, however, is about something very different. It is not really about the robbery itself, although inevitably its thread runs throughout the book. Almost anyone who has ever heard of the Great Train Robbery knows the names of those who will forever be associated with it – Bruce Reynolds, Buster Edwards, Gordon Goody, Ronnie Biggs, and so forth. They are virtually household names today. However, from the moment I first read Colin McKenzie's book *The Most Wanted Man* over forty years ago, I was intrigued more by the untold story of the robbers who had no need to go on the run, were not handed down thirty-year sentences, and did not live their lives out of suitcases, forever looking over their shoulders. This book is about how and why they remained at liberty, and why the Director of Public Prosecutions deemed in 1964 that they had 'no case to answer' as far as the British judicial system was concerned.

Neither this book, nor the previous one, could ever have been written without the advent of Freedom of Information legislation in this country, and other countries around the world, during the past two decades. That in itself has not been a panacea, for a whole host of new obstacles and barriers have sprung up to counter it during the same period of time.

The ball really started rolling when the Chancellor of the Duchy of Lancaster, William Waldegrave, announced on 25 June 1992 the first tentative steps on the long and rocky road that would eventually lead to the UK's Freedom of Information Act: 'I would like to invite serious historians to write to me … those who want to write serious historical works will know, probably better than we do, of blocks of papers that could be of help to them which we could consider releasing.'

The response from historians, serious and otherwise, came a close second to rivalling the sacks of mail addressed to Santa Claus received every Christmas in sorting offices up and down the country. Thankfully, unlike Santa's mountain of mail, the Post Office had a Whitehall address to which Waldegrave's missives could be delivered.

Very few of those who put pen to paper were to receive much more than a cursory letter of acknowledgement. Still fewer were to get the green light to embark on the process of submitting references, a curriculum vitae and a list of previous publications. I was one of the fortunate few. My initial request was in respect to the MI6 spy Sidney Reilly and his activities in Russia shortly after the 1917 Revolution. Having successfully navigated my way through the vetting process, I eventually received a letter setting out the conditions for granting me access to the files I had requested. Suffice to say that none of these were found by myself to be in the least bit unreasonable or objectionable, and I was more than happy to sign a declaration acknowledging my obligations under the Official Secrets Acts, an undertaking I have abided by to this day.

I was fortunate, over the following two decades, to have been granted further access to other closed files on a range of topics. During that time, the Freedom of Information Act was passed in 2000 and came into effect on 1 January 2005. The Act gave citizens the right to access information held by public authorities. The intention of the Act was to try to make government more transparent and to increase public confidence in political institutions. Some have argued, over the past fifteen years or so, that this has either failed to achieve its objective or, in some cases, has actually achieved the opposite.

The percentage of Freedom of Information requests granted in full has apparently fallen from 62 per cent in 2010 to 44 per cent in 2019. Requests flatly denied have grown from 21 per cent to 35 per cent in the same period. The Ministry of Justice, the Treasury, the Health Department and the Home Office all have high rates of rejecting FOIs. The department with the highest number of FOI rejections is the Cabinet Office, which declined 60 per cent of FOI requests in 2019. The Information Commissioner's Office (ICO), the regulator for the Freedom of Information Act, has seen its funding fall by 41 per cent in real terms in a decade, while the number of FOI complaints have grown significantly.

According to Katherine Gunderson of the Campaign for Freedom of Information, 'Authorities have learnt that they can breach FOI deadlines and even ignore the ICO's interventions without repercussions.' Jon Baines, an FOI expert at the law firm Mishcon de Reya, has highlighted a tactic known as 'stonewalling', which involves public bodies, who are required to respond to Freedom of Information Requests within twenty working days, simply ignoring the request. Without a formal refusal, requesters cannot appeal to the Information Commissioner.

While I have certainly experienced a number of tactics over recent years to avoid responding to FOI requests or to release information, it has to be said that in some instances, funding cuts in the public sector have led to diminishing staff numbers handling such requests. This, in the view of some, has led directly to more FOI requests being rejected out of hand on tenuous grounds. Because of lack of search time, some are resorting to this tactic purely out of practicality, rather than seeking to deliberately withhold information from the public. The fact that files are now closed for a minimum period of twenty years, under the 2010 Constitutional Reform and Governance Act, and not thirty as before, has also dramatically upped the workload of those whose job it is to prepare files for release and consider FOI requests.

It could also be argued, however, that Freedom of Information access, or lack of access, has become a distraction in terms of locating critical source material from the past.

The National Archives has a major clue within its name. The National Archives are, generally speaking, a repository for national records, not local or regional ones. While the Metropolitan Police, for example, is theoretically a police force covering the Greater London area, it is, to all intents and purposes, an unofficial national force. Its detectives, in particular, have more often than not been called in to assist on cases the length and breadth of the country for over 150 years. The Great Train Robbery, a crime that occurred in rural Buckinghamshire, is but one case in point.

Being a national archive, the records of provincial forces involved in the Great Train Robbery investigation, such as Surrey, Hertfordshire, Bedfordshire, Buckinghamshire, City of London and Sussex constabularies, for example, are not to be found at The National Archives. Instead, these 'provincial forces' are responsible for their own record keeping, archiving, storage and policy, as is Royal Mail, who hold the records of the world's oldest criminal investigation department, the Post Office Investigation Branch.

When I first began researching intelligence records well over twenty years ago, I quickly realised that, as with all hierarchical bureaucratic organisations, intelligence departments such as MI5 and MI6 will periodically copy in other government departments, such as the Ministry of Defence, Home Office, Foreign Office, Board of Trade, etc., with documents, particularly if they have a shared interest or are undertaking an assignment from one of them. When, decades later, the departmental weeders are going through files prior to releasing them to The National Archives, they will occasionally miss the significance of a document emanating from an intelligence department, and sign off the entire file as 'open' for the purposes of public access. In this way, a copy document, the original of which will never see the light of day, will enter the public domain.

When researching the Royal Mail's train robbery investigation files, I soon spotted a similar pattern, i.e. the Flying Squad would periodically supply the IB with investigation reports, and vice versa. The same picture emerged when I examined the records of some of the provincial police forces, particularly those in close proximity to London and/or the scene of the crime. They were receiving almost daily reports and telexes from Scotland Yard. Unlike the Metropolitan Police originals, which are mostly closed and inaccessible to the public, these provincial force copies are, on the whole, accessible to the discerning researcher.

Another researching 'loophole' that can sometimes be found is in the fact that while a file on a particular individual or event might be closed to the public in the UK, in another connected country where that individual may have visited or operated, open files might exist. Even if such a file is closed in that country, the process for applying for its release may well be less demanding and onerous than in the UK. This has certainly been my experience in a good many cases.

As with organisational records generally, some police files, or individual documents within them, are occasionally thought to be lost. Among the possible reasons that they are not initially locatable might be that material within a case file has been lost while on loan to other departments, other constabularies or other government departments. Equally, documents and files that were returned might not have been put back in the right file or location. Other records may have been accidently attached to, or subsumed by, another investigation file that involved the same detective or offender. Records might also have been separated when a department was split, reorganised, amalgamated or ceased to exist. In a very small minority of cases, some records might not have been catalogued in the first place and therefore do not show up on indexes or databases. The same story is routinely repeated in other law enforcement organisations abroad, including Interpol. An awareness of these possible pitfalls can, after much foraging, result in the unearthing of material previously thought to be off the radar.

There are, of course, other contemporary or near contemporary sources that can, with the aid of the births, deaths and marriage records at the General Register Office, be accessed. While published memoirs are of great value and interest to the researcher, of more interest still are those either never published, never finished or, indeed, never started. The never started variety often comprise copious handwritten background notes that require the patience of a saint to decipher. Those that were never finished are usually legible, and often typed, in hope and anticipation of being published. The unpublished variety are typically those that have either been rejected by a publishing house or written as a personal record for the writer themselves, or as a memento for their children. Of the three, the unfinished memoir, started in a fit of enthusiasm, but stopped dead in its tracks by ill health, boredom or the inability to stick at it, is without doubt the majority experience.

While the popular assumption is that journalists and FOI researchers are primarily focused on contemporary issues, this rather overlooks the fact that past events often impact on the present and the future. Again, the Great Train Robbery is a case in point.

It was, after all, the emergence of the tabloid 'scoop' culture in the late 1960s, led by Rupert Murdoch's newspaper stable, that finally blew the lid off the Great Train Robbery cover-up. Despite the line taken by two successive governments, and Scotland Yard's top brass, who had told the British public that all those involved in the robbery had been arrested and convicted and, with the exception of the escaped Ronnie Biggs, were now safely under lock and key – the truth was, in fact, quite the opposite.

PART 1

ONCE UPON A CRIME

SCOOP OF THE CENTURY

APRIL 1970

THE ENORMOUS CONCRETE AND glass slab in Holborn Circus was Cecil King's idea of a futuristic headquarters to match his ambition to be Britain's number one media mogul. With the *Daily Mirror*, then Britain's biggest-selling daily newspaper, enjoying bumper profits, King had money to spend, and went on an acquisition spree. By buying up a collection of over 200 newspapers and magazines, he created, in 1963, the International Publishing Corporation (IPC), which instantly became the largest publishing conglomerate in the country.

While the *Daily Mirror* was the jewel in IPC's crown, its *Daily Herald* newspaper was, by contrast, on its last legs. However, the vainglorious King was convinced that he had the Midas touch, and appointed market researchers to devise a strategy to give the paper a phoenix-like rebirth.

The report to the IPC board was, if nothing else, a bold one. He proposed to replace the *Daily Herald*, whose nose-diving circulation among working-class readers was seen as terminal, with a new bold, modernist broadsheet paper called *The Sun*. The new paper would, he argued, appeal to middle-class social radicals, who would unite with the *Herald*'s working-class political radicals to create a new mass readership for the paper. King's board endorsed the plan, and the first edition of *The Sun* rolled off the presses to a fanfare of optimism on 15 September 1964.

However, like so many other examples of sixties utopian optimism, the *Sun* project soon became embroiled in the mires of reality. By 1969, *The Sun* was losing around £2 million a year and had a circulation of only 800,000, which was lower than the *Herald*'s readership when it closed five years earlier. By this time, too, the IPC board had fired King himself and resolved to sell *The Sun* to stem growing losses.

Publisher and Labour MP Robert Maxwell was quick off the mark in putting in an offer and promised to retain *The Sun*'s commitment to the Labour Party. However, under close questioning from the print unions, he was forced to concede that there would need to be wide-scale redundancies at *The Sun* in order to turn around its fortunes.[1]

It was at this point that the Australian media magnate Rupert Murdoch saw his chance. He had recently bought the *News of the World* Sunday newspaper and was ambitious to own a UK daily paper.

Murdoch craftily bypassed the IPC board and approached the print unions directly, emphasising not only his Australian papers' support for the ALP (Australian Labor Party), but more significantly, his commitment to make far fewer redundancies than those being touted by Maxwell, if he were to purchase *The Sun*. To IPC he promised that he would publish a 'straightforward, honest newspaper' that would continue to support Labour. IPC, under pressure from the unions, reluctantly rejected Maxwell's higher offer, and Murdoch bought the paper for a steal at £800,000. This was to be paid over a period of years, which effectively reduced the cost of the purchase still further, as he was then able to use *The Sun's* revenue stream to repay IPC.

Murdoch quickly appointed former *Mirror* sub-editor Larry Lamb as *The Sun's* new editor. Lamb was scathing in his opinion of the *Daily Mirror*, its antiquated work practices and its overstaffed operation. He shared Murdoch's view that, 'a paper's quality is best measured by its sales'.

Lamb immediately set about recruiting 120 new journalists (fewer than half the number employed on the *Mirror*), who were signed up forthwith and promptly reported for work at 30 Bouverie Street, *The Sun's* new premises. One of these new signings was Brian McConnell, Lamb's choice for *The Sun's* news editor, whom he had previously worked with at the *Mirror*.

Murdoch's vision of *The Sun* was to prove a very different one from IPC's. While *The Sun* copied the *Daily Mirror* in several ways – it was, from this point on, tabloid size with the paper's name in white against a red rectangle. It was also, without doubt, much livelier and punchier, centring itself on human interest stories, exclusive scoops and sex.

The first edition of the Murdoch *Sun* on 17 November 1969 proclaimed: 'Today's *Sun* is a new newspaper. It has a new shape, new writers, new ideas. But it inherits all that is best from the great traditions of its predecessors.' While *The Sun's* first front page headline was 'Horse Dope Sensation', Murdoch knew full well that this was hardly the type of scoop that would be required if *The Sun* was to topple the *Daily Mirror* from its perch as the UK's number one newspaper. The heavy responsibility for finding and exploiting news scoops was to fall on the shoulders of Brian McConnell.

It was often said of McConnell that his greatest claim to fame came from embodying a headline rather than penning one, thanks to a series of events that occured on the evening of 20 March 1974:

> McConnell ... happened to be in a taxi travelling down the Mall ahead of a royal limousine carrying the princess and her then husband, Captain Mark Phillips, when a car swerved into it and forced it off the road.

Hearing the crash, the cab driver screeched to a halt, and McConnell jumped out to discover the gunman threatening the princess's bodyguard. Instead of running for cover, McConnell stepped between the royal party and the gunman and tried to reason with him, famously saying: 'Don't be silly, old boy, put the gun down.'

The man responded by shooting McConnell in the chest and opening fire on several others, wounding two policemen and the chauffeur before being overpowered … He was later honoured with the Queen's Gallantry Medal, while the gunman, who had a history of mental illness … ended up in Rampton hospital.[2]

Throughout his Fleet Street career, McConnell was acknowledged as a Fleet Street character and an instinctive newshound. Known too as 'a heroic drinker', he spent many hours entertaining members of the Press Club in Salisbury Court. It was following one such night out in April 1970 that he arrived home rather late. He had not been in long when the phone rang. It was a Scotland Yard officer he had known for some time, responding to a message he had left earlier in the day. Initially making the excuse that he was trying to find out more about a recent bank robbery in the West End, McConnell eventually showed his hand and asked who *The Sun* should contact at Scotland Yard if, by chance, they ever came across information about an undisclosed high-profile robbery from some years ago? The officer at first sounded a little surprised, but after a few failed attempts to elicit more from McConnell, finally gave in and volunteered the Scotland Yard phone extension number for the private secretary of Assistant Commissioner (Crime) Peter Brodie.[3]

The following day, McConnell phoned the Yard:

Memo to Mr H Hudson, A/A.C.C. – 14.4.70

At 12.20 p.m. I received a telephone call from a Mr McConnell, News Editor of 'The Sun' newspaper. He informed me that his editor Mr Larry Lamb, had in his possession a document regarding a crime of major importance – McConnell himself does not know what the document contains – he wishes to hand a copy of it to Mr Brodie or his Deputy. I informed him that Mr Brodie was on leave and that you were A/A.C.C. and was not at present available. This message would be passed on and that he would hear from us later today. Mr McConnell's tel. no. 353-3030 extn. 337.[4]

At 2.40 p.m., Deputy Assistant Commissioner Crime Harold Hudson spoke to McConnell's secretary, and at 3.40 p.m. it was arranged that he, Deputy Assistant Commissioner Bernard Halliday and Commander Wally Virgo would meet Larry

Lamb at 2 p.m. the following day at his Bouverie Street office. However, this was postponed at the last minute by Lamb, as *The Sun's* legal representative was not available until later in the afternoon. As a result, the meeting eventually took place at 3.40 p.m., when Lamb and McConnell were flanked by not one, but two lawyers.[5]

Larry Lamb wasted little time in pleasantries and apparently handed the Yard men two sealed envelopes the moment they sat down, saying that he thought the contents would be helpful to the police in the investigation of the 'Biggs Case'. He asked that the police read the documents and offer any comment they might think fit. He also pointed out that each page bore a fingerprint and a signature, and wondered if the Yard could oblige by authenticating them. Lamb went on to say that he realised some parts of the manuscript were libellous, but having taken legal advice, *The Sun* would not publish anything detrimental to the police.

The Sun's lawyers then emphasised that neither Lamb, McConnell, nor indeed anyone else connected to *The Sun*, had at any time any personal contact with either Biggs or anyone else who might be considered his agent. Rather than be drawn on the spot, Hudson told Lamb that they would give him a receipt for the two envelopes and take them back to the Yard to study. They would then get back to him as soon as they could.

On arrival back at the Yard, the three officers, along with Deputy Assistant Commissioner Crime (HQ Operations) Richard Chitty, eagerly tore open the envelopes. In the smaller of the two were copies of two letters addressed to J.T. Hassett Esq., c/o Walter & Hassett, Solicitors, 178 Queen Street, Melbourne, and signed 'R.A. Biggs' and 'Ronald A. Biggs'. In the second, much larger envelope they discovered seventy-seven pages of typescript, each of which bore a fingerprint and the signature 'R.A. Biggs' and one page that bore two fingerprints and the signature 'R.A. Biggs'.[6]

The seventy-seven pages of typescript were apparently Biggs's life story, from his birth in August 1930 to present, detailing in particular his involvement in the planning and execution of the 'Great Train Robbery', the events that immediately followed his arrest, remands in prison, his committal, trial and sentence, and finally his escape from the prison. It was immediately agreed that the documents should be handed over to Commander Peat of C.3 (fingerprints), and Reginald Frydd in the Yard's Forensic Science Laboratory.

The following day, Peat reported that he had identified the clearest of the fingerprints as being identical with the left forefinger print of Biggs. While this was clear, he also made clear that it was not possible to say that Biggs had actually made the impression himself on each page of the typescript and, in fact, his guess was that these prints were probably made from a cast or stamp. Frydd's report stated that in his opinion the signatures appearing on the documents had been traced or copied from ten or twelve specimen signatures, and were therefore 'not the true signature of Biggs'. Frydd further speculated that he felt the signatures had certain female characteristics, and arrangements were now in hand to compare these with samples of Charmian Biggs's handwriting.[7]

After reporting the findings to the Commissioner, Sir John Waldron, the advice of the Solicitor to the Metropolitan Police was then sought, and he gave his opinion that *The Sun* could and should be told of the findings and opinions respecting the fingerprints and the signatures. He also pointed out that not to do so would obviously not prevent publication, and could, in certain circumstances, lead to unfavourable comment about the police in any subsequent publication of the story by *The Sun*. It was also agreed, in a meeting between Waldron, Chitty, Halliday and Hudson, that over and above this, the police would make no comment at all on the content of the seventy-seven-page document, its validity, or indeed on any other aspect of it. As a result, Commander Wally Virgo was deputed to return to Bouvourie Street to return the contents of the two envelopes to Larry Lamb, which he did on the afternoon of 16 April.

The serialisation of Biggs's story, billed as the 'Scoop of the Century' by *The Sun*, began four days after Virgo returned the envelopes to Lamb and McConnell. Spread over several full pages each and every day between 20 and 28 April, the story certainly succeeded in selling papers.

Appearing under the banner headline 'Ronald Biggs Talks', the first instalment of the story began as it intended to proceed – with fanfare and hyperbole:

THE SCOOP of the century. From a secret hide-out Ronald Biggs, one of the Great Train Robbers, writes his own story of the crime, of his dramatic jail break and of his life on the run ever since. Every page of the manuscript bears his thumbprint and signature.[8]

The eight double-page instalments ran as follows:

April 20 – Day 1:	We Wait at the Farm
April 21 – Day 2:	Ambush!
April 22 – Day 3:	Things Begin to go Wrong
April 23 – Day 4:	On Trial: And already we talk of a crash out
April 24 – Day 5:	Going Down Fighting
April 27 – Day 6:	Wandsworth! And hell-bent for a break
April 28 – Day 7:	At Last: Over the Wall
April 29 – Day 8:	A New Face[9]

At the foot of each day's instalment was a strap-line to bait readers for the next day's revelations. Following the first day's double-page spread on pages 17 and 18 was a box headline: 'Tomorrow: Who Really Hit Driver Mills?' Biggs's apparent willingness to point the finger on this issue was one of a number of matters that would cause a degree of rancour between him and a number of the other train robbers over the decades to come. Was Biggs in fact pointing the finger? Was he actually even there at the moment when the attack on the locomotive cab took place at Sears Crossing at approximately 3.05 a.m.? This and other issues surrounding the accuracy of recollections and testimony by a number of those present that night will be examined in detail later on in this book. In the meantime, suffice to say this was not something hotly debated in April 1970.

As a result of what was a genuine and dramatic scoop that Larry Lamb had pulled out all the stops to publicise in the wider media, *The Sun* literally flew off the newsagents' shelves that week, giving Murdoch his best circulation figures since issue number one on 17 November 1969. For the mass of readers who opened their copies of *The Sun* over breakfast on 20 April 1970, the story of the train robbery was as fresh, vivid and compelling as it had been on that August morning seven years previously, when it came over on the early morning BBC radio news.

Tommy Butler, the man who had led the train robbery investigation, and who had arguably misled the public about the outcome of the hunt, never lived to see Biggs's story in print. He died on the very day it hit the presses at *The Sun's* Bouverie Street printworks. True to form, he had kept his cards close to his chest one last time. Virtually no one knew that he had been diagnosed with terminal cancer a year earlier.

Not unexpectedly, *The Sun's* 'scoop of the century' created a storm. Apart from the expected backlash from other Fleet Street papers that *The Sun* was giving cash and a public platform to a major criminal, the serialisation resulted in several major blow-backs for the Metropolitan Police. While the Yard had already battened down the hatches for the expected awkward questions and criticism that was bound to arise from Biggs's revelations, they were certainly not expecting the fury that hit them on the first day of publication, in the shape of a full-on broadside from the Commissioner of the New South Wales Police in Sydney, Australia, Norman Allan. The New South Wales Police already had a degree of egg on their faces for letting Biggs slip through their fingers following a raid by fourteen armed officers on his Melbourne home on 17 October the previous year, only to find he had left the property only hours before. Now, to add insult to injury, the London police seemed to be hand-in-glove with *The Sun*, as far as the Biggs scoop was concerned.

Allan rang the Yard an hour before he was due to attend a meeting with the Australian Attorney-General, and demanded to be put through to the Commissioner, Sir John Waldron. Having been told that Waldron was unavailable, the call was put through instead to Commander Don Adams, on whom Allan let rip.[10]

In an apparently expletive-filled tirade, Allan expressed his amazement that New Scotland Yard 'had supported this newspaper venture', and felt that 'it was holding the New South Wales force and the Metropolitan Police up to ridicule'. He promptly followed this up with a letter telexed over to Sir John Waldron, in which he:

> pointed out that whilst police in both countries could not find Biggs, a solicitor had been able to receive from him his story with his fingerprints and signature. He felt that the police, by confirming the authenticity of the fingerprints were, in fact, enabling Biggs to obtain further money to assist his escape. He did not for one moment believe that any of the money from the story would be placed in a trust fund for Biggs' children.[11]

Allan went on to lay into the Murdoch press, in both Britain and Australia, for 'giving comfort and aid to an escaped prisoner', and implied that Waldron's force was aiding and abetting *The Sun* in doing so. While the Metropolitan Police file containing the account of Allan's correspondence and telephone conversation was not to be opened for another three decades, the British public were able to hear, at first hand, a similar tirade raised by Members of Parliament from all parties on the floor of the House of Commons. The Home Secretary, James Callaghan, was subjected to a string of questions about the Biggs story at Question Time on 22 April 1970. Arthur Lewis, the Labour MP for West Ham North, waded in first, following up on two written questions he had submitted earlier that day. The first was:

> To ask the Secretary of State for the Home Department, whether he has considered the information supplied to him by the honourable Member for West Ham North, showing that a newspaper has paid, either Ronald Biggs or his agents, money in relation to the mail bag robbery; whether he will take action against the newspaper concerned for aiding and abetting a convicted criminal; and whether he will make a statement.[12]

Lewis's second question was as follows:

> To ask the Secretary of State for the Home Department, whether he will now make a further statement on action taken to bring about the apprehension of

Ronald Biggs, an escaped prisoner; and whether he will institute proceedings against Biggs and others connected with the great train robbery for the murder of the train driver.[13]

Papers in the closed police file show that the Home Office immediately requested that the Yard provide the Home Secretary with background notes to assist him in answering these and related questions from MPs later that day. Commander Don Adams of C2 was deputed to write briefing notes for James Callaghan:

The first question can be answered quite shortly but most authoritatively. Police efforts to locate and rearrest Biggs are as intense now as they ever were. No effort is spared to achieve this object and the authorities and indeed the general public may be assured that police activity in this direction is of a very high and persistent order.

The second question can be answered quite shortly but factually. No proceedings for murder can be taken against any of the of the persons involved in the 'Great Train Robbery' in relation to the subsequent death of the train driver. It is clearly defined in law that before such proceedings can ensue, the victim of violence must die within a year and a day of the infliction of same.[14]

Adams's notes, drawn up with the aid of the Metropolitan Police Solicitor, were both concise and politically astute. Adams could just as easily and accurately have stated that Lewis was mistaken in asserting that the train driver had been murdered. Mills had died only a short while before, on 4 February 1970, at Barony Hospital in Nantwich. The West Cheshire Coroner had confirmed that:

Leukaemia with complications due to bronchial pneumonia was the cause of death. I am aware that Mr Mills sustained a head injury during the course of the train robbery in 1963. In my opinion, there is nothing to connect this incident with the cause of death.[15]

However, Lewis was a Labour MP, and Callaghan, as a Labour Home Secretary, would certainly not have wished to embarrass him on the floor of the House of Commons; neither would Callaghan have wanted to appear soft on crime in the eyes on the public by pointing out that the train robbers were not, according to the coroner's report, responsible for Mills's death. By answering the question on a point of law, both of these potential pitfalls were avoided.

The Yard had, of course, taken photographic copies of the envelopes they had been given by Larry Lamb, and these had then been sent to DCI Powell of the

Yard's Criminal Intelligence Section, C11, for their thoughts and analysis. Was Biggs's vivid and descriptive tale of the train robbery and how it was planned and executed the truth, the whole truth and nothing but the truth? Or was Biggs, now down on his luck and next to penniless, simply spinning a cock-and-bull story to cash in on Murdoch's famed willingness to write big cheques for big scoop stories?

What did C11 make of his account once they had the chance to line it up against the intelligence and closed file information they had at their disposal? The manuscript had, of course, been carefully scrutinised by *The Sun's* lawyers prior to publication in order to avoid any obvious pitfalls that might land the paper in the hot waters of potential litigation. One example was the removing of the numerous mentions of John Daly's name from the story. Daly had been found not guilty in February 1964 and was, therefore, in the eyes of the law, an innocent man and not a train robber.

As a result of this deletion, and a few other legal and editorial tweaks, the version that appeared in *The Sun's* serialisation was somewhat shorter than the original manuscript. It was therefore the original, unedited version that C11 set about analysing.

The first thing that the Yard's intelligence gatherers did was to pull out Biggs's CRO file. Among the material that had been accumulated since 1963 was a copy of Mr Justice Edmund Davies's sentencing statement:

> Ronald Arthur Biggs, yesterday you were convicted of both the first and second counts of this indictment. Your learned Counsel has urged that you had no special talent and you were plainly not an originator of the conspiracy. Those and all other submissions I bear in mind, but the truth is that I do not know when you entered the conspiracy or what part you played. What I do know is that you are a specious and facile liar and you have this week, in this court, perjured yourself time and again, but I add not a day to your sentence on that account. Your previous record qualifies you to be sentenced to preventative detention; that I shall not do. Instead, the sentence of the court upon you in respect of the first count, is one of 25 years' imprisonment, and in respect to the second account, 30 years' imprisonment. Those sentences to be served concurrently.[16]

Of course, Biggs was no more or less of a 'specious and facile liar' than arguably anyone else in the dock of the Buckinghamshire Assize Court on 16 April 1964. However, it did underline the obvious point in C11's mind that nothing Biggs said in his memoir could be taken at face value, without prior and established corroboration from other reliable sources. The validity of Biggs's manuscript was hardly helped by the fact that the very first paragraph of his account of the robbery read by C11 was clearly a massive embellishment of the truth at best, and a wild tale at worst:

> The fact that British Railways transport great sums of money for the General Post Office has been common knowledge to London's criminal fraternity for many years. I first heard about it in 1949, at which time I was doing half a stretch in Lewes Prison, Sussex, for shop-breaking. I palled up with an ex-GPO sorter named Albert, who came from Middlesex – it was from him that I heard and inwardly digested practically everything there was to know about Post Office procedure.[17]

Biggs goes on to mention that the following year, while in Wormwood Scrubs Prison, he met for the first time another prisoner by the name of Bruce Reynolds:

> During conversations with Bruce, I mentioned my friend Albert and the information he passed on to me regarding the mail train, and we discussed the possibilities of 'having it off' at great length ... I became good friends with Bruce and our paths crossed frequently – we often spoke about 'the train'.[18]

When C11 cross-referenced Biggs's account of Albert with information on file at the Yard, and consulted Lewes Prison records, they found that Albert was:

Albert George Kitson
Born: 21 March 1928, Marylebone, London
Address: 8 Goshawk Gardens, Hayes, Middlesex.[19]

Far from being 'an old post office sorter', Kitson was in fact a 20-year-old juvenile offender, who had been sentenced to eighteen months' imprisonment for being an accessory to a break-in at Hayes Post Office, where he worked as a clerk. According to his file, Kitson had fallen under the influence of one Cyril Edward Maunders, a 32-year-old habitual criminal known to local police and Southall parents as 'Daddy Fagin'. Described in a report by Detective Inspector Robinson as 'a very bad influence in the district and known as a corrupter of youths', Maunders, together with an associate, Alan Victor Parnell (alias 'Alan the Screwsman'), had planned to rob Hayes Post Office. Maunders had always been skilful with tools, and especially at making false keys. In the prison workshop he had developed this skill. On his release in August 1948, he sought out Parnell, and the pair 'picked out Kitson, bought him drinks, flattered him and finally persuaded him to make impressions in modelling wax of the keys of the main post office door and the safe'. False keys were then made, and on 1 January 1949, Parnell and an 18-year-old youth named Roy Douglas Atkins entered the post office and robbed the safe of £2,760.

Albert Kitson would, it was concluded, have had no knowledge of Travelling Post Offices or TPO procedures, and it was therefore considered that Biggs's claim to have first learned about TPOs, the amounts of money carried by them, and their lack of security could not be viewed with any great degree of credibility.

Of course, in writing his story, Biggs was stuck between a rock and a hard place. If his account reflected too much the minor role he had actually played in the robbery, there was little chance that a major newspaper would be interested in buying the manuscript for any sizeable sum of money. Alternatively, if he overplayed his hand and embellished his role too heavily, he ran the risk that on being recaptured (as he then believed was only a matter of time), a court could look more harshly on him if it was thought that he was one of the more senior members of the gang. In fact, it could be said that, if anything, his attempt at a fine balancing act possibly leant too far in the wrong direction. The recently retired Chief Superintendent Frank Williams (who had been Tommy Butler's Flying Squad deputy) was, by 1971, Head of Security at Qantas Airlines at Heathrow Airport. He was among those who avidly read the *Sun* serialisation. As a result of what he read, he later commented that: 'I admit that during the earlier part of the robbery investigation, after the fingerprints were found, I thought Biggs had been used by the gang as a reliable labourer, but I know now that he and Reynolds were two of the leading members.'[20]

Despite the Kitson embellishment, and a few other red herrings thrown in for good measure, did the manuscript contribute anything meaningful to C11's already significant knowledge of the train robbery and the identities of those who took part in its planning and execution, and who had so far evaded arrest?

THE MISTER MEN

November 1969

IN 1834, EUROPEAN SETTLERS landed on the banks of the Yarra River in Australia, declaring the area congenial enough for a village. Soon after, the Yarra flowed through a small, haphazard settlement, surrounded by swamps and undulating countryside. In record time, a grand, well-planned city grew on its banks.

By 1969, the city of Melbourne had a population of just under 2 million. It was located at the apex of one of the world's great natural seaports, Port Phillip Bay; southward to the horizon in both directions, the peninsulas practically joined to form an inland sea. Surrounded by 200km of beaches, this seaside playground provided almost unlimited work and opportunity for anyone seeking to make their way in the world. To the east, the Mornington Peninsula stretched like a rolling carpet of green, ending in coastal holiday communities that had been popular for generations.

Graham Kennedy, the compère and comedian, ruled the TV screens, with *In Melbourne Tonight* (the IMT Show) on Channel Nine, the nation's highest-rating channel, owned by the *Daily Telegraph* proprietor Sir Frank Packer. Kennedy's show, based on the US *Tonight Show* format, went out live every week from Channel Nine's Bendigo Street studios, a few blocks away from the Old Melbourne Gaol, where outlaw Ned Kelly had been hanged in 1880. As Kennedy often said on the show, 'Australians love a rogue.'

Among the workers making and dismantling the Channel Nine studio sets was a carpenter by the name of Terry Cook. Kennedy had been pressing the IMT producers for a bigger dressing room for some time; such frivolities were rarely agreed to by Sir Frank Packer's mandarins, but eventually they grudgingly agreed. Terry Cook and three others were deputed to build the new dressing room close to the IMT set.

After Terry had left Channel Nine the following year for a better-paid job with an air-conditioning company, he had apparently disappeared. It later came out that Terry was in fact none other than Great Train Robber Ronald Biggs. Graham Kennedy made this his lead story on 17 October 1969, announcing that he was having the dressing room torn to pieces in case 'Terry' had hidden any of the train robbery money in the walls.

'Terry' saw the IMT show from the back room of a small bungalow, belonging to friends Mike and Jesse Haynes, in the Melbourne suburb of Noble Park. It was here, during the months of October and November 1969, while in hiding, that he decided to write his story. It was not the result of a considered or planned effort to write a first-hand, fly-on-the-wall account, nor was it written with the luxury of time. It did help, however, to while away the long days and weeks holed up there, while the Commonwealth Police searched high and low for him.

His plan was to finish the story of his life and have it delivered to a lawyer by Mike Haynes before the police eventually caught up with him, as he fully believed they inevitably would. The idea had sprung from the fact that his wife, Charmian, had been offered the sum of A$60,000 for her story by Sir Frank Packer's Sydney-based *Daily Telegraph* tabloid. Biggs wagered that if Charmian's story could fetch A$60,000, his own story must surely count for a whole lot more.

The most revelatory aspect of the story was that it shot down in flames a claim that had hit newspaper headlines all over the world less than twelve months before. On 15 January 1969, Chief Superintendent Tommy Butler, the man who had headed the train robbery investigation, held a press conference following the sentencing of Bruce Reynolds to twenty-five years' imprisonment at Aylesbury Assizes. Butler opened his remarks by telling the assembled journalists that 'Reynolds is the last of the fifteen men who robbed the train'. With the exception of Biggs, he added, all those who had committed Britain's biggest cash robbery were now under lock and key. 'Does this mean that this is the end so far as the Train Robbery is concerned?' asked the *Daily Mirror*'s Tom Tullett. 'No,' Butler replied. 'Got to catch Biggs first.'

However, according to the Biggs's manuscript, four mystery men who had taken part in the hold-up at Bridego Bridge on 8 August 1963 were in fact still at liberty.

While we now know, from a number of Butler's still closed written reports, that he knew full well that some of the gang had slipped through his fingers, this remained his public stance until the day he died. More mysterious is the decision by the former Deputy Assistant Commissioner, Ernest Millen, to attack Biggs in writing shortly after the publication of *The Sun*'s serialisation: 'As for Biggs's claim that four members of the robbery gang are still free men, this is sheer bunkum.' As we shall see later on in this book, both Butler and Millen may have had other motives for trying to obscure the truth about those who got away.

For obvious reasons, Biggs chose to use aliases for the four mystery men. Recalling his first meeting with the gang in June 1963, at Roy James's flat in Nell Gwyn Court, Chelsea, he wrote:

There I met and was introduced to 13 men, one of whom I already knew. Three of these men and another who joined the group later have never, to my knowledge, been wanted by the police in connection with the train robbery so, for their protection, I will refer to them as, Joe, Bert, Sid, and Fred.[1]

These four men would, in 1978, be given four new aliases in the Piers Paul Read book, *The Train Robbers*.[2] Thanks to a later book by Ronnie Biggs & Chris Packard, this would eventually evolve into 'The Mister Men', i.e. Mister 1, Mister 2, etc.

While Biggs's account was written six short years after the robbery, the events of 1963 were still relatively fresh and clear in his mind. The original seventy-seven handwritten pages were typed up by Jesse Haynes and eventually sold to Rupert Murdoch's Australian tabloid, the *Daily Mirror*, and syndicated to *The Sun* in London.

By late 1969 the other convicted robbers were already six years into their sentences. There had been no collusion or contact between Biggs and the other robbers since their Court of Appeal hearings held between 10 and 14 July 1964. The manuscript was therefore based entirely on Biggs's unaided and uninfluenced recollection of events, albeit with a few changes here and there to avoid getting himself into even hotter water should he be arrested in the near future.

As noted in the previous chapter, for understandable reasons Biggs had walked a tightrope in not over- or underplaying his role in the robbery, so far as the manuscript was concerned. He therefore sought to airbrush out the role he had played in recruiting an alternative train driver, and maintained that he had joined the gang before the decision to find another driver had been taken in June 1963. Recalling a planning meeting held at Roy James's flat in Chelsea, Biggs recalls the debate:

'As we stand at the moment, our only problem is pulling the train after we've stopped it,' said Reynolds.

'I still say we can make the driver do it,' broke in Goody.

'Suppose he refuses,' objected Buster.

'Make him.'

'How?'

'Frighten him!'

'Suppose he doesn't frighten – suppose he has a heart attack!'

'Why don't we get our own driver?' Bert asked. 'I know an old bloke who, I think, might be interested.'

'Even if he was interested and brought in,' Roy protested, 'he would still be an "outsider" and a danger to all of us. Apart from that, do you really think a straight man would have the nerve? You must be joking!'

The point was debated until, once again on a show of hands it was decided that Bert should go ahead and, if possible, procure the railway man's services and, at a subsequent 'meet' we were introduced to a cheerful, old (sixtyish) train-driver named Fred. He had been approached at his local pub by Bert, who had offered him £20,000 to drive a diesel train for a short distance 'sometime in the future'. Fred had been only too pleased to oblige, and he intimated he would drive a train to Land's End for £20,000.[3]

Having shifted his responsibility for recruiting Fred the driver from himself to Bert, Biggs, from there on in, tells the story pretty much in line with other subsequently corroborated sources.

What, then, does Biggs's manuscript tell us about Joe, Bert, Sid and Fred and the respective roles they played in the robbery?

According to the original manuscript:

It was decided, that our arrival at the farm should be staggered so as not to arouse suspicion. It was arranged that Bruce, Jim White, John Daly, Bert, Fred and myself would travel in one of the Land Rovers early on the morning of the sixth of August. Buster, Jim Hussey, Tom Wisbey, Bob Welch and Joe would arrive in the truck about 9.00 p.m., and Charlie Wilson, Roy James and Sid in the second Land Rover about 10.00 p.m. Goody was to remain at the house of Brian Field in Pangbourne for a telephone message from our 'man up North' which would tell us when the 'holiday money' was on its way to London.

At 9.00 a.m that same day, Biggs recalled:

I climbed into the back of one of the Land Rover which was parked near Victoria Station; the others were already there, and with Jim White driving we set off for the farm in Buckinghamshire. The journey was a cheerful one. We were in good spirits and my 'windfall' of the previous day was regarded by all as a good omen.

'You'll be able to buy us all a beer on the way back!' laughed Fred.

The many moments of humour provided by Fred were mostly unintentional and often he would ask, 'What are you laughing at?' Strictly speaking, he was an honest man and he was extremely naïve about the magnitude of the operation he had entered into. During the journey he asked who the Land Rover belonged to, and when he was informed that it had been stolen, he exclaimed, 'My lord! I hope we don't get pinched!'[4]

As Biggs indicates, Fred was not a career criminal; in fact, he was not a criminal at all, but a former British Railways engine driver. Already there are telltale clues early on in the manuscript that Fred is exceptionally naïve at best, or at worst, a man with possible mental health issues.

As we shall discover later in this book, a previous bad experience of taking on an 'expert' from outside the criminal fraternity may well have been one of the reasons why the gang thought twice about taking Fred on the job in the first place. However, as with Buster Edwards's previous difficulty the year before with an alarm engineer who later turned 'Queen's evidence' against the gang, necessity outweighed the risks, in that without the 'expert', the job could not be undertaken in the first place.

Biggs then discusses their arrival at Leatherslade Farm on Tuesday, 6 August:

> We arrived at the farm about 11.00 a.m. There was no sign of life anywhere and we had entered the lane leading to the farmhouse without being observed. We unloaded the contents of the Land Rover into the kitchen – food, sleeping bags, cups and eating utensils and several pick-axe handles.[5]

Biggs then introduces us to Bert:

> I explored the farmhouse and the outbuildings with Bert. Thick bushes provided good cover at ground level and from the upstairs windows there was a good view of the surrounding countryside. We were of the opinion that the farm had been well chosen.
>
> 'Couldn't be better,' Bert said, as he closed the door of one of the larger outbuildings. 'Old Bill would have to go some to find this place!'[6]

In another passage, the relevance of which will become apparent later in this book, Biggs alludes to the time of Gordon Goody's arrival at the farm:

> At eleven thirty, or thereabouts, Goody was dropped off at the bottom of the lane by Brian Field. Gordon greeted us with the news that we wouldn't be doing anything until the following night, as he had been informed that there was only a very small number of registered sacks on the train. This was by no means a serious setback – it simply meant a delay of twenty-four hours before we went to work. We sat around talking and joking, drinking warm beer and eating sausage sandwiches prepared by Fred, who had volunteered to be our 'tea boy'.

On the following page we are told a little more about Fred's disposition:

> All the men, with the exception of Fred, were experienced determined thieves with reputations for gameness, loyalty and ability. The only one who might possibly go to pieces was Fred, but at no time did the old man show any signs of fear or alarm before or during the robbery. He did, however, receive a bit of a scare afterwards, but more of that later.

Around eleven o'clock the next night, the gang began preparing to leave the farm to journey to the railway track:

> We got into our army uniforms and moved the Land Rovers and truck out of their sheds. Gordon had gone to a 'phone box' in the nearby village and had received the glad tidings that the big load was on the way. 'At least a hundred bags!' Goody had announced elatedly. 'Almost five each!'[7]

At 12.30 a.m., the convoy left the farm, arriving at the track an hour later. The big angular, canvas-topped ex-army truck was tucked into the darkness at the bottom of the embankment below Bridego Bridge. Phone lines to the district had been cut on arrival. Some of the robbers stayed with the vehicles when they got close to Sears Crossing, but others got out and headed across country to the railway line, wearing blue railway 'slop' jackets and trousers over their combat gear. They were variously tasked with re-jigging the signals, uncoupling the train, overcoming the driver and gaining entry to the HVP coach and the driver's cab:

> I was with Charlie, Sid and Fred, talking quietly waiting for the train to arrive. Suddenly the red signal came on overhead for about ten seconds, and then went out again. Fred was very interested in this and said admiringly, 'You buggers! You think of everything.'
>
> 'Well, it wouldn't have been much good standing on the line waving a red flag, would it?' said Charlie.
>
> Fred took his pipe out of his mouth, lit it and settled back on his elbow puffing contentedly.
>
> 'Look at him,' said Sid, 'Would think he was on his [fucking] holidays!'[8]

The Glasgow mail train was a diesel locomotive hauling twelve coaches. The first coach next to the engine was the parcels van, which had no communication with the coaches behind it. High Value Packets of money were transported in the second coach, and this was connected by corridor to the ten mail coaches behind.

The train had left Glasgow at 6.50 p.m., hauling parcels, the HVP coach and only the first three coaches; the other nine would join at Carstairs and Crewe. By 2.30 a.m. the train was speeding through a clear night on its run to Euston, with seventy-seven GPO men aboard in addition to the driver, fireman and guard.

At 2.53 a.m. it passed through Bletchley. Shortly after 3.00 a.m., the driver, Jack Mills, saw a warning signal ahead. A 'caution' lamp from a dwarf signal (i.e. a lamp at ground level, not on a gantry) made him apply the brakes and the red 'Stop' signal nearly a mile further on made him bring the train to a halt yards from the signal gantry at Sears Crossing.

The train was now less than 30 miles from Euston, stationary above flat fields on a raised embankment. The fireman, David Whitby, jumped down from his seat beside the driver and headed over the rails to the trackside telephone, but quickly realised that something was wrong. He shouted: 'The wires have been cut.' According to Biggs:

> Jack Mills, the driver, promptly grabbed Bert and was succeeding in pushing him off the steps when Bert put his arm around the driver and hit him twice on the head with a cosh. Mr Mills, dazed, fell back from the doorway. Bert climbed in followed by Gordon who opened the other door which was on our side of the train. Charlie climbed into the cab then Fred, then myself, Sid was one of the 'shunters' and he joined Buster and Roy at the rear of the High Value Package coach where the rest of the train was to be uncoupled.
>
> Fred was hustled into the driver's seat and I leaned out of the cab waiting for Roy to give me the sign that the disconnection had been made. Then moments later he came running towards the cab. 'It's done,' he called softly. 'Let's go!'
>
> 'Pull away!' I told Fred giving him a nudge.
>
> 'I can't until I get my brake pressure!' he announced calmly, watching the instruments.
>
> 'Drive it!' Gordon shouted.
>
> 'I'm waiting for my brake,' the old man shouted back. 'I must have twenty-one inches!'
>
> Goody grabbed Fred's shoulder and hauled him out of the driver's seat. 'Get the driver up here!' Goody fumed. 'Where's the [fucking] driver?'[9]

'Fred' was shoved out of the driver's seat and Jack Mills was shouted for and instructed to drive – they were off. The five GPO men in the HVP coach knew they'd come adrift from the rest of the train, but had no communicating door with the parcels van or driver ahead, so they pulled the communication cord; it was all they could do. The train kept moving forward. Then it stopped. They could hear muffled voices ahead. Then, within feet of them, the loud smash of glass.

A window crashed inwards. A GPO assistant inspector yelled, 'It's a raid!'

He and another postman raced to secure the rear corridor door, where already half a dozen robbers were trying to break in. They could hear shouting outside, and somebody yelling what they thought was 'Get the guns!' and then robbers swarmed in through the doors, in through the windows. They obeyed the message: 'Lie still and you won't get hurt.' They were kept under guard on the floor at the front of the coach while they listened to mailbags being unloaded. The driver and fireman were shoved in to join them. Everyone present was told to keep still, or else. Timing was crucial. The robbers needed the cover of darkness, so the money had to be unloaded fast. Sagging, heavy sacks were lobbed from man to man down the embankment and hurled into the army truck. At 3.30 a.m. they had to go:

> The truck was almost full, barely room for any passengers and the word passed up from below that we had as much as we could carry. As the three exhausted off-loaders got down from the coach, Joe said to the GPO men, 'Don't move for half an hour; we've got a man posted just outside and you'll be sorry if you try to make a move.'[10]

Although it was not known at the time, so confident were the banks that no one could ever or would ever successfully hold up and rob a Travelling Post Office train, that the majority of them not only decided against insuring the money against loss or theft, but more bafflingly neglected to keep a list of banknote serial numbers. To them it was pointless – why go to all the time and trouble of listing and recording the numbers of so many notes when there was virtually no chance at all of anything untoward ever happening to them? This was one of the major reasons why, ultimately, less than one seventh of the stolen money was ever recovered.

And so it was that all but 1,579 of the stolen banknotes effectively became untraceable. The robbers, too, would have remained untraceable had it not been for their speedy departure from Leatherslade Farm and the incriminating evidence found later at the farm by the police. Joe, Bert, Sid and Fred did, however, remain untraceable, at least in the eyes of the public.

Evading prosecution is, of course, a very different thing from the police not knowing who had pulled off Britain's biggest ever cash robbery to date. Even if every single member of the gang had not been arrested, charged or prosecuted,

C11 had a pretty comprehensive idea of who was involved almost from day one, if not prior to day one. Had it not been for the evidence found at the farm, the robbers' names would have remained locked away, gathering dust in a file that would have been unlikely to have seen the light of day for at least a century. In the meantime, the named men would have gone about their everyday lives, no doubt starting or expanding legitimate businesses, buying new homes and enrolling their children at private schools.

Biggs, for example, was already running a fledgling building firm in Redhill that had, shortly before the robbery, been promised a carpentry and painting contract for fifty houses on a new estate that was to be built shortly on the outskirts of the town. The contract was apparently his, so long as he could guarantee to have twelve men on site at all times. This was the snag: without the money to invest in his business, he would be hard pressed to acquire the additional men and equipment needed to take on bigger projects. With his new-found wealth, he now planned to 'gradually start feeding the money into the business'. As a result, 'the firm would go from strength to strength'.[11]

In this alternative universe, some of the men would no doubt have spent their money quicker than others, or as was actually the case, had money taken from them by other criminals, or sunk their money into bad investments. Others would, no doubt, have been galvanised to move on to further high-profile crimes that may, or may not, have resulted in their arrest and prosecution.

As it was, in the real world, only four men, not fifteen, along with a small supporting cast, remained at liberty. Commenting on these men in his 2008 National Archives publication on the robbery files, Peter Gutteridge astutely observed that: 'it is possible that we know these men for crimes committed later. But it is also possible that they took their whacks – which, if it was a relatively equal split, would been around £3,000,000 in today's money, and lived happily ever after. Doubtful though.'[12]

Despite a number of misgivings about certain aspects of the Biggs manuscript and reservations relating to the authenticity of the signatures and fingerprints, the Xeroxed copy of Biggs's magnum opus was studied with fascination by C11, the Criminal Intelligence Section at New Scotland Yard. Of course, they had always been aware, as the late Detective Chief Superintendent Tommy Butler had been, that a number of men directly involved in the planning and execution of the train robbery had 'no case to answer' in the eyes of the Director of Public Prosecutions. Their existence had been publicly hushed up for seven long years now. What did surprise C11 most, though, was that Biggs had decided to reveal this aspect of the story that, as a result, would ignite endless guessing games, theories and wild-goose chases over the coming decades.

Biggs, whose name would be associated with multiple retellings of the story published between 1970 and his death in 2013, would eventually rename Joe, Bert, Sid and Fred firstly by letters, then by numbers, i.e. Mister One, Mister Two, Mister Three, etc.

In 1971, children's author Roger Hargreaves created the first in a series of children's books called the Mr Men. Over the ensuing fifty years, the number of names mentioned in books and articles speculating on the identities of the mystery train robbers would not only rival Hargreaves's characters in number, but would also compete with the other literary fixations that took hold in the 1960s and '70s: 'Who was Jack the Ripper?' and 'Who killed JFK?'

C11 may not have had the foggiest idea who Jack the Ripper was, or whether Lee Harvey Oswald had actually assassinated President Kennedy, but they did know a thing or two about was organised crime in London, and in particular, who had avoided conviction for the mail train robbery. In fact, they knew who 'Bert' and 'Sid' were, almost immediately after the robbery took place.

Set up only three years before the Great Train Robbery, C11 aimed to mirror the criminal intelligence capabilities the FBI were effectively using to counter top-drawer criminals in the United States. As it turned out, in many respects C11 actually knew a great deal more about the background to the Great Train Robbery than Ronald Biggs did, although a number of things he divulged in *The Sun* were found to be of great interest to their intelligence gatherers.

What do the closed files that C11 had at their disposal tell us about the advance awareness of the main players in the train robbery, and how this helped them identify Bert, Sid and so many of the others before Leatherslade Farm had even been found?

A LITTLE CLOAK
AND DAGGER

THE ASSISTANT COMMISSIONER OF the Metropolitan Police, Sir Richard Jackson, known to friends as Joe, was a portly man in his late fifties, with horn-rimmed spectacles and ice-blue eyes, who walked with a curious gait that some attributed to his considerable weight. He was balding on top, with strands of black hair heavily oiled and brushed fiercely away from the temples and meeting at the back of his head, in a sort of spiked ruffle, like the tip of the tail of an exotic flamingo.

While Jackson played a comparatively minor, almost insignificant, role in the actual train robbery investigation (he retired on 1 October 1963), he was without doubt the person who cast the largest unseen shadow over the whole affair. Four years previously he had begun a series of fundamental, almost revolutionary, police reforms at Scotland Yard that would make a major impact on the methods used to identify the men who robbed the Travelling Post Office train at Bridego Bridge on 8 August 1963.

Born in India in 1902, he attended Eton College, where he made the acquaintance of a number of influential friends, including the future Prime Minister, Sir Alec Douglas-Home. At Trinity College, Cambridge, he read Law and was called to the Bar at Middle Temple in 1927. Six years later, in 1933, he joined the Department for the Director of Public Prosecutions,[1] and at the end of the Second World War was appointed to a senior civilian post at Scotland Yard. Soon after, he was seconded to Malaya as a member of the Police Mission. As an advisor to the colonial administration on counter-insurgency policing methods, Jackson was directly involved in what was to be one of the few post-war successes against jungle guerrilla campaigns.

On his return to London in August 1953, Jackson was promoted to the plum job of Assistant Commissioner in charge of the Yard's Criminal Investigation Department. Not long afterwards, he struck up what would soon become a strong relationship with another former barrister, Joseph Simpson, the Assistant Commissioner for Traffic. Interested in international policing methods, Jackson was appointed British representative to Interpol in 1957. When, in that same year, Simpson was promoted to Commissioner of the Metropolitan Police, with a mandate from the new Home

Secretary, Rab Butler, to combat the growing menace of organised crime, Jackson wasn't slow to spot a gift horse when he saw one.

Shortly after Simpson's appointment, a government White Paper was published, outlining Butler's plans to tackle organised crime on a variety of levels. Simpson immediately took up Butler's suggestion that he should visit the FBI headquarters in Washington DC to find out more about how they were responding to the growth of organised crime there. Butler, as it turned out, was preaching to the converted as Simpson was already sold on the idea that so far as policing methods were concerned, America was the future.[2]

He returned from his visit to Washington DC with glowing reports about the FBI's criminal intelligence capability, introduced following the passage of anti-organised crime legislation in 1953. This was later expanded in 1957 with the creation of the 'Top Hoodlum Program', which sought to gather intelligence on the top fifty organised crime figures through an array of legal and semi-legal methods, including physical surveillance, phone tapping and electronic surveillance. At a meeting with CID's top brass, shortly after his report back to the Home Secretary, Simpson gave Jackson the go-ahead to begin a full feasibility study on how Scotland Yard could develop for themselves the criminal intelligence strategies being employed by the FBI.

Written by Jackson, Reginald Spooner, William Rawlings, George Hatherill and Ernie Millen,[3] the report was ready in double-quick time. In its introduction, Jackson set out his belief that the nature and organisation of crime was changing and new tools were needed to counter it:

> Criminal gangs nowadays are less likely to be permanent entities than teams selected for a particular operation. Drivers and strong-arm men are readily available, but crime has become so much more mobile, so much less local. Once the new pattern was established its development was cumulative. Each successful operation provided capital for the next. This is where the raw crime statistics are deceptive.[4]

Jackson went on to observe that:

> Overt robbery is not the only type of crime in which the new generation of criminals indulge, but it is the fastest growing, for the simple reason that it produces the largest reward for the minimum number of incidents.[5]

The report proposed that an ongoing campaign against criminals of this calibre ought to be waged 'like a military campaign against jungle terrorists'.[6]

Its recommendations to the Commissioner centred around the proposal that a new unit, the Criminal Intelligence Section, 'would obtain, collate, and disseminate information exclusively about hard-core professional criminals and their associates'.[7]

Sir Joseph Simpson and the Home Secretary both welcomed the report and endorsed its findings. The Commissioner gave Jackson the authority to go ahead, and it was agreed that the new Criminal Intelligence Section would begin its work in March 1960, with carefully chosen, hand-picked staff.[8] From the off, Jackson was keen to ensure that the new intelligence section should work hand in glove with Scotland Yard's Criminal Record Office (CRO), known as C4.[9] The CRO maintained a number of separate indexes: a register of all convicted criminals; an index of crimes reported but not solved; and an index of wanted persons. In addition, there was a method index in which criminals were grouped by modus operandi.

There was, however, to be a fundamental difference between the two sections. While the Criminal Record Office listed only the names of those who had actually been convicted of a criminal offence, the criminal intelligence department, on the other hand, would keep records on those individuals who had either never been caught, or had only been apprehended for one or two trivial offences, when the suspicion was that they were, in reality, much bigger fish. The new intelligence section, given the official title of C11, would therefore compile information about a criminal's associates, their background, and the offences they were suspected of, but not to date convicted of. According to Jackson:

> The Intelligence section would follow a new way of thinking about London's crime. The pattern, as we had been made painfully to realize, was not static; as circumstances changed, the pieces shifted like a kaleidoscope, but they were still the same pieces, with a few being added and a few subtracted. The Intelligence section was designed to present a complete current picture of what the major professional criminals were doing, where they were, and with whom they were associating. The official records could contribute to this picture but were not enough in themselves. Other sources had to be constantly tapped.[10]

Between 1960 and 1963, C11 significantly increased its manpower and extended its tentacles. Its intelligence reach was also greatly enhanced by Jackson's election to the post of President of Interpol, at its Washington DC Congress in 1960. While there, Jackson met not only the FBI Director, J. Edgar Hoover, but also his rival and counterpart, the CIA Director, Allen Dulles. The bespectacled Dulles made an interesting contrast to the bombastic Hoover, and was, to Jackson's mind, 'quieter and less forceful' than Hoover – 'much more like an Englishman in his manner and appearance'. Jackson's interest in the 'cloak and dagger' made the agency's espionage work something of a fascination for him.[11]

Jackson's belief in the virtues of cooperation with Interpol, and other police forces on the Continent, was in sharp contrast to the 'Euro-sceptic' approach to policing that prevailed at Scotland Yard at the time. Closer cooperation with Interpol allowed C11 to tap into an even greater criminal data base than the one they were already building. Interpol boasted a huge, cross-referenced filing system containing more than a million entries detailing the descriptions and aliases of some 350,000 criminals.

Another innovation that would be introduced at the Yard, and from there to Interpol, had been picked up by Jackson shortly before the creation of C11, when:

> At a lunch one day in the Café Royal, I met a huge genial giant of a man, called Pete Pitchess. He had been in the FBI and was now Sheriff of Los Angeles County. After lunch he came back to see the Black Museum and the Information Room at Scotland Yard. When we were having a drink in my room afterwards with a few senior officers I'd invited to meet him, he showed us a piece of equipment which had been invented by his deputy, Hugh McDonald. It was a book of interchangeable transparent flaps, each with some part of a face, eyes, eyebrows, hairline, nose, mouth.[12]

The making of pictures from eyewitness descriptions was not new in Britain. However, the police artist didn't normally work with the witness and merely followed a description that had been given to him by the investigating officer. All too often, witnesses who had later been shown the completed drawing were all too willing to accept it. The Identikit picture, however, was put together by a trained police officer working directly with the witness, and could be continually altered until the witness was totally satisfied that it represented the face they had seen:

> I showed the Identikit to the Commissioner, and we both expressed interest in the possibility of acquiring it. A week or so later I received a letter from the American company which manufactured the equipment. Pitchess had told them of our interest, they said. They were willing to consider leasing it to us, and offered to send a representative to Scotland Yard, to run a course of instruction.[13]

One of the major advantages, if Identikit were widely adopted, was made clear to the Commissioner by Jackson:

A telephone call to a central index, the Criminal Records Office, perhaps could, by using a code of numbers and figures, pass a likeness to other forces without any need to transmit the actual picture. It could be useful for the Chief Superintendents of C1 which includes the Interpol Office and the Criminal Records Office. The possibility of using Identikit internationally was debated at length during the Interpol General Assembly in 1962.[14]

Apart from innovations such as these, Jackson believed that being guided by the intelligence coming into C11 would enable the Yard to be able to target more effectively its resources and efforts. Once a month, Millan, as Head of the Flying Squad, prepared a crime report for Jackson's office. Jackson's priority was robbery, housebreaking and burglary, the crimes that, in his view, 'really affect the public'. Of these, robbery was the number one target Jackson set for C11 and the Flying Squad. He reasoned that the activities of criminals:

> tend to go in cycles – that is, they concentrate on one sort of theft until mounting opposition renders it too dangerous; whereupon they move on to something else; and then to something else again, until their original victims have grown slack enough to invite another assault. Banks have always been targets. A few years ago, the fashion was for breaking into strong-rooms during the week-end, usually by tunnelling through from adjoining premises. The safes, locks and alarms were often extraordinarily primitive, and most banks didn't regard it as worthwhile to employ watchmen. As banks eventually took more effective steps in response, the fashionable technique switched to hold-ups during banking hours, and to wage-snatches as the money was carried from the banks on pay-day. A wage-snatch in the street may look to bystanders like a sudden act of spontaneous violence, but in fact it is usually the climax to weeks of careful preparation and observation; weeks in which the gang will have familiarized themselves with the faces and habits of the wage-collectors, with routes and vehicles customarily employed, and with avenues of escape for use afterwards.[15]

Within a year of C11's formation, wage snatches had become so frequent in certain parts of London that the Flying Squad were tasked with mounting a counter-attack by the Commissioner, Sir Joseph Simpson. He believed that the strength of the Metropolitan Police was 5,000 or 6,000 below requirement. Given this shortage of manpower, the question facing Simpson and Jackson was how to best deploy the men they had available in the most effective way.

When the issue was discussed at senior level within the Flying Squad, some officers were of the view that the primary reason for the increase in violence was the use of younger, more reckless criminals. CID statistics indicated that the development of crime during the period 1959–61 showed that the teams that attacked mail vans, raided banks and rammed cars carrying wages no longer consisted of only two or three men. Instead, between five and eight robbers was now the norm: 'These larger teams are more effective because they are more terrifying. Eight men uniformly masked and armed, moving with speed and purpose, exercising deliberate violence, are a spectacle frightening enough to paralyze opposition. The planners use violence scientifically, like a tool.'[16]

In view of the Commissioner's assessment of available police numbers, the impact that C11 could make was particularly critical. Jackson's perspective all along had been to see C11 in the same terms as military intelligence – the more you knew about the enemy's strength, intentions and strategy, the more you could marshall your resources and manpower in a concentrated way that was best placed to maximise results.

The Commissioner's wage-snatch campaign was therefore seen by Jackson as the first major test for C11 and a welcome opportunity to demonstrate the impact that criminal intelligence could have on the success of such an operation. The first step was to analyse the problem, and look in particular at 41 of the 196 robberies that took place in 1960 and 1961:

CONFIDENTIAL

The majority of cases occurred in Nos. 2 and 3 Districts, whereas in the 18 months Nos. 1 and 4 Districts were comparatively clear. It cannot be that the money is concentrated in the north-eastern quadrant of the MPD. There are, presumably, as many large firms in the south and west with large payrolls collected each week from banks and no doubt as many criminals capable of planning and executing such robberies. Why is it then that the bulk of these robberies have taken place in only a limited area of the MPD, and why are Central London, the south, the west and the whole outer periphery studiously avoided? We do not know the answer to these questions and cannot even hazard a guess. These questions are inevitably linked with another – why are there so few of these robberies when every week there must be scores of opportunities for thieves to steal payrolls or over £1,000 in cash? We suspect the answer to these questions is closely tied up with the number of teams who specialize in this method of robbery but we cannot say what is the exact relationship.

The time of day of the 41 robberies is of interest. It would seem obvious that cash must be collected from banks in the morning in time for wage packets to be made up for distribution in the afternoon, and that the time must be limited to bank hours of business. This is true to some extent, but the table below shows a large proportion as having occurred before banks are open to the public, i.e., before 10 a.m. The answer to this lies in the fact that for the mutual convenience of bank and customers arrangements are often made for large payrolls to be collected before 10 a.m. What usually happens is that the customer notifies the bank the day before collection of the amount of cash required and its breakdown (£ notes, 10/- notes and silver and copper). The payroll is made up in advance by the bank so that collection on the following day takes place in a matter of minutes.[17]

Of these forty-one cases, it was decided to focus on thirty in particular that not only yielded some of the largest sums stolen, but more significantly involved the halting of the vehicle carrying the money either by deliberate ramming or by forcing it to stop in another way. It was immediately apparent that in all the cases involving the deliberate ramming of the cash-carrying vehicle the method was similar.

While the thirty cases were clearly the work of a number of different gangs, patterns began to emerge. One of the first features noted was that the cars stolen to order for jobs, in a variety of London neighbourhoods, were being stolen from a limited number of locations. The following examples of hold-ups during the first six months of 1961 show the robbery locations and the Metropolitan Police Divisions in which the cars were stolen:

13/1/61	Lockfield Avenue, Enfield	1 vehicle stolen in H Division
16/2/61	Carpenters Road, Stratford	2 vehicles stolen in K Division
30/3/61	Vale Road, Finsbury Park	2 vehicles stolen in D Division
7/4/61	River Way, Palmers Green	3 vehicles stolen in D Division
21/4/61	North Road, Holloway	2 vehicles stolen in N & D Divisions
26/4/61	Longley Avenue, Alperton	2 vehicles stolen in D Division
28/4/61	Hillside Road, Stamford Hill	1 vehicle stolen in G Division
5/5/61	Steele Road, West Ham	2 vehicles stolen in J Division
12/5/61	New Barn Street, Plaistow	2 vehicles stolen from K Division
23/6/61	Queensway, Enfield	2 vehicles stolen in N & D Divisions[18]

Of the nineteen cars stolen in connection with the ten robberies listed during the first six months of 1961, nine of the vehicles had been stolen in one division:

D Division (Marylebone). Other similarities were noted in terms of the way the robberies were executed:

At about 9.30 a.m. on Friday, 7 April, 1961, the Assistant Accountant, a clerk and a driver, employees of the Metal Box Company, Chequers Way, Palmers Green, N15, left the factory in Chequers Way in the firm's car (a grey Austin A55 saloon) to collect the weekly wages from the Midland Bank Branch at Alderman's Hill, Palmer's Green. On arrival at the bank at about 9.40 a.m. the driver waited outside in the car. The accountant and the clerk were joined by another employee who had arranged to meet them at the bank. The three men entered the bank (at a time when it was not open for public business) and collected the company's wages amounting to £6,767 4s. 9d., mostly in notes. The money was placed in four brown leather Gladstone bags, and the men re-entered the car and were driven away, heading back for the factory by a route chosen by the driver, viz., Green Lanes, Lodge Drive, River Way, Hazelwood Lane, Connaught Gardens and across the North Circular Road into Chequers Way. The time was then about 9.40 a.m. At about 9.45 a.m., while travelling in River Way towards Hazelwood Lane, a dark blue Ford Zephyr pulled out sharply from the nearside kerb in front of the Austin, causing the driver to brake sharply. He could not, however, stop in time and the two cars collided head on.

Parked on the opposite side of the road were a blue Ford Thames van and a light blue Ford Zephyr. Behind the ramming car, on the nearside of the road and nearer Hazelwood Lane, was a maroon Ford Zephyr. As the Austin came to a standstill four men with stocking masks over their faces jumped out of the back of the blue Ford Thames van. They brandished short wooden clubs and adopted a menacing attitude. One of them, carrying a vehicle starting handle, shattered the Austin's windscreen and then the driver's window. He pushed the driver down on to the passenger seat and withdrew the ignition key from its lock on the dashboard. In the meantime, the three employees got out of the car, leaving the doors open. Two of the robbers snatched the four Gladstone bags from the floor – two from in front and two from the rear.

The robbers ran to the light blue Ford Zephyr, whose engine was switched on by one of the men during the raid, and drove off at high speed down River Way towards Lodge Drive. The maroon Zephyr pulled away from the nearside kerb, and followed the light blue car. The dark blue Zephyr and the Ford Thames van were left abandoned on the spot.[19]

The Palmers Green robbery was one of a number of hold-ups in the north-east area of London. The other area that experienced a disproportionate number of raids was north-west London. Two raids in particular are worthy of note:

At 10.20 am on Wednesday 26 April a wages car was slowed down and rammed at the junction of Longley Avenue and Queensberry Road in Alperton. Another car passing by stopped, as they thought that the collision was an accident. One raider then smashed the windscreen of this car. There may have been five or more men engaged in this attack. There seems to be some doubt about how they were dressed, but it seems reasonably certain that they were all masked and carried iron bars. It also seems that one of these men stood out from the others in that he was dressed in a white boiler suit and was about 6' tall and well built. It was this man who smashed in windscreen. One of the stolen cars, a Ford Consul, was abandoned at the scene, the other vehicle, a Ford Zephyr, was abandoned in Ealing.[20]

Three months later, on Friday, 28 July 1961, in nearby Chiswick, a Securicor van set off from its depot on the Great West Road, London W4. It had collected £57,563 from the Midland Bank at 281 Chiswick High Road, and was on its way to deliver weekly wages to the nearby Gillette factory, the Firestone Tyre Company, Macleans Toothpaste, Rambler Motors Ltd, and Smith's Potato Crisps Ltd. The Securicor van never made its first call:

At 7.05 am on Friday 28 July a Securicor armoured van was rammed by a Ford Zodiac in Syon Lane, Brentford, having been diverted from its original route by road signage that had been stolen earlier in nearby Acacia Avenue. Five men, dressed in overalls, were thought be involved, all masked apart from the driver. The Zodiac was abandoned afterwards in Hanwell.[21]

The analysis then turned its attention to the thieves who were known or thought to have taken part in the raids. The number of men taking part was always difficult to establish, owing to the confusion of victims and eyewitnesses. C11 were of the view that some members of certain teams suspected of having taken part in earlier raids had broken away and formed their own teams for one job, and then rejoined the main team for another raid. Some teams were loose-knit associations of thieves who would be called upon for a particular job; others were believed to be more or less permanent associations of men born and bred in the same area and given a local name, e.g. the 'Hoxton Boys'.

Of all the patterns identified, one of the most practical to follow up on was the source of the stolen vehicles used in the raids. As approximately 50 per cent of the vehicles were stolen in D Division (Marylebone), further enquiries were taken up with divisional CID officers to find out what intelligence they might be able to offer.

It soon became clear that as far as D Division officers were concerned, there were several names and associates who, according to informants, were responsible for a 'theft to order' approach to car crime. In fact, the name mentioned more often than not by D Division officers was a man appropriately nicknamed 'The Coachman' by his peers for his ability to quickly acquire exactly the make and type of vehicle required. According to his CRO file, 'The Coachman' was identified as one Michael John Ball of 100A Finborough Road, London SW10.[22] Although born and raised in Fulham, Ball had a number of associations with the Marylebone area. Of particular note was his membership of a karting club in Marylebone, where he had shown great potential as a driver and had greatly honed his racing skills. Karting was a relatively new sport in the UK in the early 1960s, having jumped the Atlantic in 1959 from its inception in California three years earlier, and was commonly perceived to be a stepping stone to the higher ranks of motor sport. Together with a close friend, Roy John James, who was also an active member of the Marylebone club, Ball was an early subscriber to the KKC Club's typewritten magazine *The Go-Karter*. Ball's C11 file also reproduces details of his past criminal record:

Lambeth Juvenile Court	27/8/48	Stealing a jack knife
Stamford Juvenile Court	30/10/52	Taking & driving away a motor car without consent
Acton Magistrates Court	8/6/56	Stealing a motor vehicle & contents, value £900
Bow St. Magistrates Court	19/6/57	Taking & driving away a motor car, no insurance
Country of London Sessions	19/1/59	Stealing cigarettes value £1,205

C11's intelligence trawl led them to draw up a list of criminals strongly suspected of involvement in wage robberies and ram-raids in the metropolitan area:

Edward Thomas Hearn, CRO No. 45440-48, b. Shoreditch 1-11-30
John William Dunlop, CRO No. 15795-45, b. Shoreditch 20-5-32
James Thomas Spinks, CRO No. 1132-46, b. Shoreditch 24-11-31
John Charles Isaacs, CRO No. 32516-48, b. London 24-3-32
Alfred Hines, CRO No. 9082-40, b. Shoreditch 16-11-25

John Edward Hines, CRO No. 21533-47, b. Hoxton 2-9-27
Bruce Richard Reynolds, CRO No. 41212-48, b. St. Martin 7-9-31
Douglas Gordon Goody, CRO No. 4290-46, b. Oxford 11-3-30
Charles Frederick Wilson, CRO No. 5010-54, b. Battersea 30-6-32
Terence Hogan, CRO No. 38593-45, b. Chelsea 19-6-31
Jeremiah Callaghan, CRO No. 9303-40, b. Bermondsey 21-9-24
William David Ambrose, CRO No. 21598-52, b. Stepney 21-9-29[24]

While Ball was clearly playing an important role in procuring the means to carry out a good number of wage snatches, it is clear from the files that he was still seen, at this point, as a peripheral accessory. It would not be too long, however, before C11 were to reassess their view of 'The Coachman' in light of new and revelatory intelligence that would shortly be landing in their in-tray from the Mediterranean shores of the French Riviera.

THAT RIVIERA TOUCH

September 1962

IN 1962, THE NUEVO Chamartín Stadium, recently renamed the Santiago Bernabéu Stadium in honour of the Real Madrid stadium architect and club president, was universally acknowledged to be the finest club stadium in football. Recent improvements to the iconic ground had raised its capacity to 125,000 and given Real Madrid what they claimed to be the best floodlighting in the world.

It was hardly surprising, then, that on Wednesday, 19 September, the football-obsessed Spanish press was full of stories about the highly anticipated visit of Matt Busby's Manchester United team, who were to play Real Madrid that evening in what promised to be the biggest showpiece so far under Bernabéu's new flood-lighting. Much to the chagrin of Interpol, whose 1962 General Assembly was to open in Madrid on the same day, there was hardly a word to be found about their gathering, which had been relegated to the inside pages and was virtually eclipsed by features on Matt Busby, Bobby Charlton and Denis Law.

For Interpol President Richard Jackson, the disappointment was soothed some-what by an envelope of free tickets for the United game, courtesy of the Spanish police. Jackson, accompanied by his wife, daughter and two old friends attending the Interpol General Assembly (*Daily Express* crime correspondent Percy Hoskins and the *Daily Mirror*'s Tom Tullett), had the additional consolation of witnessing first hand the shock 2–0 defeat of the five-time European champions by United strikers David Herd and Mark Pearson.[1]

It was apparently after the game that Jackson confided in Hoskins that as a result of closer Interpol cooperation, Scotland Yard were on the verge of tightening the net on several cases involving British criminal enterprises on the Continent.

While Prime Minister Harold Macmillan was, at that very moment, endeavour-ing to negotiate membership of the European Common Market to enable British industry to exploit new opportunities abroad, the British criminal fraternity were already one step ahead. For some time, it had been apparent to high-end British criminals that horizons and ambitions needed to be raised, and that Continental Europe was a place where opportunity knocked.

One of the first big cases that bore fruit for Jackson's Eurocentric Interpol approach was a big-league smuggling operation that was to involve the police forces and customs of three countries. Suspicions first came to the ears of C11 in August 1961, when an Interpol bulletin was issued about large consignments of Swiss watches that were apparently being smuggled through France to Britain, via the Channel ports. On top of that, whispers from the streets of South London began to filter through to the Flying Squad and C11 that bargain-basement Swiss watches were appearing in growing numbers in the pubs, clubs and street markets.

Customs and Excise were alerted by the Met and a joint operation was set up, working in cooperation with the French and Swiss authorities. It would appear that this investigation was one of the first on record to employ a tactic that Jackson was particularly keen to utilise in what he saw as 'a war against organised crime' – telephone tapping. As a result of listening in to calls, tip-offs from informants, shadowing suspects and information gleaned through French and Swiss police, a modus operandi slowly began to emerge. The watches, in kit bags, were taken from Switzerland to the Normandy coast by courier, where the bags were transferred to a small French fishing boat. The boat then waited for nightfall before leaving port to rendezvous with a British fishing boat anchored off the French coast. The two boats alerted each other to their presence by red flashing lights. The contraband was then transferred from one boat to the other by a small rubber dinghy, and the British boat returned to the port of Newhaven in Sussex. From there they were offloaded and taken out of the port without reporting to customs.

An early mystery to the authorities was how the watches were being paid for. From 1939 to 1979, the ability of British citizens to take or transfer money out of the country was severely limited by law. So called Exchange Controls were originally introduced at the outbreak of war in 1939 by the Emergency Powers Act. This was aimed to prevent a run on sterling and to stop any panic outflow of cash or capital from the country. These emergency restrictions were formalised into law by the Exchange Control Act 1947. While the amount of money that British holidaymakers, for example, could take abroad was varied from time to time by the Chancellor of the Exchequer, the limit rarely exceeded £100.

The mystery was eventually solved by customs officers at Dover quite by chance, when they noticed a car that was well down on its suspension springs, despite the fact that there were no passengers on the back seat. Officers then searched the back of the car, where they found twenty-two brown paper parcels wrapped in hessian, tied to the springs of the rear seat.

The mystery deepened further when customs officers unwrapped the parcels, only to find what appeared to be valueless soot in them. The driver, John Robbins, a 49-year-old London docker of East Street, Walworth, was arrested pending further enquiries. Customs and Excise scientists were soon on the case and quickly reported back that the packets contained not soot, but black platinum dust worth £13,717 (£244,574 in today's money).

According to C11 files, Robbins was, as a result, charged with attempting to export platinum without an export licence. On 21 March 1962, he was found guilty at Kent Assizes and given a three-year prison sentence. But where was Robbins taking the platinum to? Had he succeeded in crossing the Channel?[2]

The only lead was the platinum dust itself. Were there any clues within the packets themselves? Without further ado, they were taken by Kent Police from the custody of Customs and Excise to Scotland Yard. There, the Forensic Laboratory (C7) and Fingerprint Department (C3), closely examined every aspect of the packets. According to a C3 report, a fingerprint belonging to a Brian Loughran was found on one of the parcels. A copy of the print was then forwarded to the Criminal Record Office (C4), who reported that 27-year-old Loughran of Shroffold Road, Downham, South London, had a criminal record dating back to 1951 and a long list of associates with criminal records.[3]

It was from this list of associates that the Flying Squad began their investigations. As a result of subsequent telephone tapping and shadowing of suspects, up to a dozen men were suspected of involvement in what would eventually be revealed to be a £500,000 (£8,915,000 in today's money) Swiss watch smuggling racket. Those eventually arrested and convicted were, according to the file:

Patrick O'Nions, age 32, Shorncliffe Row, Southwark
Peter Loughran, age 27, Reedworth Street, Kennington
Brian Loughran, age 28, Shroffold Road, Downham
Alfred Robert Gerrard, age 38, Barking Road, Canning Town
Maurice Francis Herr, age 30, Spurstowe Road, Hackney
John Michael Murphy, age 28, Albert Terrace, Stockwell[4]

According to the file, it was later established that the car concealing the twenty-two packets of platinum dust was to have been taken to a bridge in a largely unpopulated area of countryside on the French–Spanish border, where it was to be left. The vehicle was then to be collected some hours later and driven back to England. How the consignment of watches was actually paid for, following the confiscation of the platinum dust, is not revealed by the file. However, we are told that on 24 September 1961, at a Customs and Excise shed at Dover, a Commer van driven by Anthony John Cavanagh was found to be fitted with a steel floor. Customs officers ripped up the floor of the van and under it found 4,328 new Swiss watches.

Patrick O'Nions was believed to be the main contact with the Swiss end of the operation. He was shadowed on several occasions while making clandestine trips to Zurich and Basle. It was later ascertained that John Robbins was, in fact, O'Nions's father-in-law.

Maurice Herr and John Murphy were both identified as carriers, taking consignments to and from Switzerland. Herr had, on several occasions, driven to Zurich in a caravan with his wife, where he met O'Nions and put the containers of watches in a concealed compartment inside the bed fitting of the caravan. He then drove to the Normandy coast near Dieppe, where he met up again with O'Nions, who had travelled there separately, and took the containers to the beach.

Brian Hill, a Newhaven fisherman, was alleged to have been paid by Alfred Gerrard and Peter Loughran to ferry them to and from the French coast. On 5 November 1961, Gerrard, James Loughran and Hill were waiting in a small fishing boat off the Normandy coast until a red light was flashed on the beach by Patrick O'Nions. James Loughran then rowed to the beach in an inflatable rubber dinghy. There the containers were put into the dinghy, rowed back to the fishing boat, and taken to Newhaven.

A Customs and Excise report states that customs officers were fully aware of the fishing boat and its contraband cargo, and observed it as it arrived in harbour. Once the boat was tied up:

> Gerrard, who was the first to get out of the boat, went off and came back to the quayside in a Jaguar motor vehicle which he backed up to the quayside. The boot was open and into the boot were put three heavy containers. Customs officers then made themselves known to Gerrard, who was in the driving seat, with James Loughran by his side and Hill in the back. He ignored their attempts to get the ignition key and to stop the car, and very nearly killed one of the investigating officers at whom he rode, who managed to jump out of the way. In due course they threw the containers out into a ditch at Southease, near Lewes, Sussex, where they were found to contain over 4,000 new Swiss watches of a value of about £33,500.[5]

When the Jaguar was ultimately recovered, it was discovered that the splash plates had been removed from underneath the front wings, revealing spaces in which contraband could be concealed. Hill was later found and arrested, and appeared at Lewes Magistrates Court on 24 April 1962. Alfred Gerrard was arrested a short while later in London, and like Hill was charged with fraudulently evading customs duty on 4,300 Swiss-made watches. It was not until 28 July 1963 that Loughran was arrested at 27 Burton Road, Didsbury, where 438 watches were found. He had been living at the address under the alias of Pitt. He appeared at Lewes on 19 August 1963 charged with the same offences as Hill and Gerrard.

Interestingly, the file also refers to an incident that occurred during the course of the earlier trial at Lewes Magistrates Court, on 10 October 1962. A newspaper photographer by the name of Peter Burges was taking photographs on the pavement outside the court as those attending the case arrived. One of those whose photograph was taken took exception to Burges's efforts to get a full-on photo, and punched him. Burges fell over and dropped his camera. The man then proceeded to smash it. He was promptly arrested, and appeared in court on 20 November 1962 charged with assaulting Burges and doing £36 worth of damage to his camera. The man in the dock was named as Daniel Pembroke of 22 Hood House, Elmington Estate, Camberwell. In his defence, Pembroke told magistrates that Burges had persisted in taking his photograph after being asked to stop. He was found guilty and given a six-month prison sentence. Pembroke later gave notice of appeal against the sentence and was released on bail. His name and C11 file will figure later in our story, as will Patrick O'Nions and John 'Spud' Murphy.[6]

While the cross-Channel smuggling of Swiss watches and other contraband was a lucrative trade, the richer and indeed more plentiful pickings were to be had in the South of France on the Cote d'Azur, or as the British preferred to call it, the French Riviera. The 70km stretch of coast between Cannes and the Italian border was once an inhospitable shore with few natural harbours, its tiny local communities preferring to cluster around feudal castles high above the sea. It is now an almost uninterrupted promenade, lined with palm trees and megabucks hotels, with speeding sports cars on the corniche roads and yachts like minor ocean liners moored at each resort.

The Riviera's largest city, Nice, became fashionable as a winter resort in the eighteenth century. The fishing village of Cannes was discovered in the 1830s by a retired British chancellor who couldn't get to Nice because of a cholera epidemic. Up until the First World War, aristocrats and royals from all over Europe came here to build their Riviera mansions. The inter-war years saw the advent of more artists – Picasso, Matisse, Dufy, Bonnard and Miro – come to the town.

By the mid-1950s, mass tourism started to take off and the real transformation began. A general increase in prosperity throughout Europe after the war meant that people could now afford to visit the region in large numbers. Rich pickings had been on hand for some time, but the fifties ushered in a new land of plenty – jewellery stores, banks, casinos and exclusive shops appeared and multiplied like rabbits. Five-star hotels appeared on the Promenade and De La Croisette, which were a magnetic attraction to the rich and nouveau riche from Europe and the United States. Much to the consternation of the civic authorities on the Riviera, Alfred Hitchcock's classic cat-burglar movie *To Catch a Thief*, starring Cary Grant and Grace Kelly, hit the screens in 1955, further cementing the Riviera's reputation as the glamourous playground of the rich and famous, not to mention 'gentleman thieves' and cat burglars.

Of equal frustration to the French forces of law and order was the fact that, in addition to their own home-grown criminal fraternity, a small but growing band of top professional British criminals were now making the Riviera their location of choice. The British authorities, too, were similarly conscious of the Riviera's illicit attraction to a number of their target criminals. This mutual concern in turn kindled a spirit of cooperation between Scotland Yard and the Sûreté Nationale, through the offices of Interpol.

From the moment of his appointment as President of Interpol in September 1960 and the creation of C11 that same year, Richard Jackson had set out to make criminal intelligence gathering an international venture, and lost no time in fostering links between the Metropolitan Police and their international counterparts. This was by no means an easy task, bearing in mind that there was a significant core of 'Eurosceptic' officers at Scotland Yard, who saw little or no reason to be working in tandem with foreigners. However, against the tide, Jackson's mantra of harmonisation of systems and detection methods slowly began to rub off, particularly his contention that top-drawer crime was not only becoming more organised, but was becoming more internationalised too.

In the summer of 1961, a lucky break provided by the Sûreté Nationale would not only lead to the breaking up of an international jewel robbery syndicate, but would help C11 lift the lid on big-time 'project' crime in London.

The Wollés jewellery shop was a smart, upmarket store located at 19 Boulevard de la Croisette, on the corner junction with Boulevard des Etats-Unis. On 9 August 1961, not long after the staff reopened the store after lunch, an armed robbery relieved the proprietors of an estimated £217,000 of jewellery.

According to Mr M. Gally, Chief Commissar and Head of the Criminal Section, Sûreté Nationale:

> The store opened at about 2.20 p.m. Immediately afterwards, Mr Wollés, who is secretary-general of the Yacht-Club de Cannes, left to go to the post office. A few minutes later, a blue-grey DS 19 with a ram roof stopped in front of the window. Three men got out. They were young and dressed like all tourists in shorts or canvas pants and shirts. They were masked and one of them was brandishing a machine

gun. One of the young men leaned against the door to block it. Mrs Wollés said; 'Another came up to me and threatened me.' He shouted, 'Lie down on the floor and don't move.' Meanwhile, the third was calmly beginning to help himself from among the jewellery in the display cases. Mrs Wollés began to shout, 'Then a bandit slapped me violently and hit me with his fist. I kept screaming.'

The three men then ran from the store. The shouts of the victim attracted the attention of a passer-by, Louis Rosemarie, a 53-year-old newspaper seller from Lancashire, who was passing through Cannes. He tried to block the way of the fleeing raiders, but was struck violently in the face by one of them. The raiders made their getaway in the blue-grey DS 19 car that headed east and turned at the first street on the right. Witnesses, Miss Marcelle Sennecy, 29, and Emmanuel Leonardy, 28, both noted the license number 1471 4E 75, and that it was a Citroen. The car was found the same day on Rue Amouretti in Cannes at 6.00 p.m. It had been stolen during the night of 7/8 August in Juan-les-Pins. A false registration plate had been made.[7]

Sûreté Nationale sources in Cannes suggested that the perpetrators might well be English. The names of four men who may have been involved in either organising, executing or disposing of the jewellery are recorded in a Sûreté Nationale report dated 26 August: 'Benjamin Selby, born February 8, 1913, Duncan Smith, nick-named 'Bombo', born 9 February 1923, Graham Evans, born February 18, 1932, and Michael John Ball, born 21 February 1936.'[8]

A search for the men began that same day:

Smith resided at the Palais Miramar, Rue Pasteur, in Cannes. Ball had rented an apartment through the Tessier agency, at 15, Rue de Bivouac Napoléon. Ball was found, however, at 47 Avenue de Grasse in Cannes. No trace of Selby was found; Smith had apparently left Cannes for England 48 hours before the search.[9]

Ball was placed under arrest, which is recorded in the case file:

Michael John Ball, born 21 February 1936 in London, son of Michael and Rose Kelly. Profession: credit agent. On holiday in Cannes, Palais Le Chenonceaux, 47 Avenue de Grasse. Usually 111A Lambrook Terrace, Fulham SW6, London. Single, British Passport 30917. Does not understand French. Sentenced twice: first for driving without a license, then 18 months in prison for stealing cigarettes in 1958. Arrived in Cannes on 1 June 1961 for a vacation. Rented this apartment from Tessier agency for the price of 180 NF per week. Had £1,000. Remained

£35 and NF 250. Arrived from England with Roy John James and Graham Evans, another friend.

At the home of M.J. Ball, Palais Le Chenonceaux, second floor, apartment B. The door is opened by the interested party. The apartment has two bedrooms, a kitchen, a bathroom and a toilet. Present in the apartment is Roy John James, born August 30, 1935 in Stepney, London … [and] Graham Rodrigue Jim Evans, born February 18, 1932 in Christchurch Bournemouth, England. No documents or objects have been found that might be relevant to the present case.[10]

Under questioning, Ball denied that he was in Cannes on the day of the robbery, and lacking any firm evidence, either in terms of personal identification or the lack of anything tangible found at Ball's apartment, the Sûreté Nationale reluctantly released him.

That was not, however, the end of the matter. Convinced of their suspicions, the Sûreté worked closely with C11 and the Flying Squad, asking them to keep those under suspicion of the Cannes jewel robbery under close scrutiny.

Scotland Yard cabled the Sûreté a list of Ball's London associates who were known to have travelled to the South of France during July/August 1961:

Roy John James
Bruce Reynolds
John Daly
Graham Evans
Gordon Goody
Charles Wilson
Terence Hogan
Benjamin Selby
Duncan Smith[11]

As a result of surveillance in London of those suspected of the Wollés jewellery store robbery in Cannes, the Flying Squad had only one successful result:

Duncan John Smith, a 38 year old automatic machine vendor of King's Road, Chelsea, was arrested following a search of his flat. Det. Insp. Lewis found a pearl necklace, a brooch and a ring, which have since been positively identified as part of the proceeds of a jewellery robbery in the South of France in August.[12]

In an interview at Scotland Yard, following his arrest, Smith claimed that he had visited the South of France during the summer, but knew nothing of the robbery.

At his home he claimed that he was approached by a man who asked him to dispose of two articles of jewellery. At Wimbledon Greyhound Stadium, he claimed that another man had handed him the other piece.

The police report further notes that Smith had nineteen previous convictions, twelve of which were for gaming. When he appeared at the Surrey Quarter Sessions at Kingston upon Thames on 28 November 1961, Smith told the court that he had gone to France for pleasure and had taken an interest in the casino in Cannes in view of the recent change in the gambling laws in Britain, and thought that he might be able to open a casino or gambling club in London. In Smith's defence, his solicitor, Miss Nicola Lethbridge, said that only a small proportion of the proceeds of the Cannes robbery had found its way to Smith, who was very much on the fringe of the affair and knew nothing about the robbery. Smith's wife, Rebecca, was called to give evidence, and told the court that her husband had been taking a course of slimming pills that might well have had an effect on him mentally.

The Chairman of the Magistrates, Brigadier A.C.C. Willway, was clearly unconvinced by the story and sentenced Smith to three years' imprisonment for receiving stolen goods.

According to C11 files, the following summer when Ball and his confederates were again in Cannes, another high-profile jewel robbery took place. A closed-file French Sûreté report states that:

On 24 August 1962 at about 7 p.m., Miss Armande Dellamaria, employed as a saleswoman at the Martin Jewellery Store in Nice, Cap d'Antibes branch, closed the store after having put away in a suitcase the collection of valuable jewellery that was in the display cases. She carried out this operation, which lasted about 40 minutes each time. Each piece of jewellery was wrapped in tissue paper and boxes. She then placed the suitcase in her car on the rear floor of her 4cv Renault and sat behind the wheel, having at her side on the front seat a young saleswoman employed in a luxury hosiery store of Eden Roc. She used to go home every evening, or almost every evening so as not to be alone.

Having started the engine, she drove in the direction of the park exit to reach the Hotel du Parc, a hundred metres away, where the jewellery is stored every evening in the safe. No sooner had she gone fifty metres than she saw a car parked on the right side of the driveway that was reversing at an angle towards her own car. Miss Dellamaria stopped and applied her handbrake. However, the other driver continued to back up until he touched the front bumper of the 4cv with his rear bumper. A young man then got out of the car and quickly made for the rear left door which he opened and took the suitcase. The man left immediately without saying a word or making any threats. This took only a few seconds. The individual returned to his car, an olive-green Jaguar with a British registration plate 642 JW GB, which started abruptly and made its way out of the Eden Roc Park. Surprised and realizing what had just happened, Miss Dellamaria got out of the car while shouting, and ran towards the Eden Roc pavilion to alert the Police Station of Antibes. The approximate value of the jewels and watches was estimated at some £1.4 million.[13]

A French investigation was reported on 22 October by Police High Commissioner Mr M. Robert:

Initial findings. Jaguar belonging to Mr Leyton, British, olive green, stolen in the afternoon of the same day from the Garage de l'Esterel in Juan les Pins and was recovered around 9.00 p.m. that same day near Boulevard de la Garouupe in Cap d'Antibes. No clues found. Monsieur Lucein Martin, the owner of the jewellery store, filed a complaint. Mrs Dellamaria was heard at length by a Police Officer. Inquiry with the staff of the Eden Roc Lodge regarding the comings and goings of doubtful customers in the days preceding 24 August.[14]

Miss Dellamaria, as well as the other two occupants of the 4cv, were shown a police line-up of the individuals. Despite a slight similarity between the physical appearance of Graham Evans and that of the individual recognised, no element appeared likely to guide the case. However, Ball, during the hearing, gave the names of two other Englishmen who had come on holiday with him: Sidney Yass and Roy John James. The latter left rather abruptly the day after the flight of Eden Roc, on the night of 24–25 August 1962. Appearing somewhat suspicious, he was thus reported to the authorities at New Scotland Yard. These British men led a luxurious lifestyle and were known to the British Police as thieves, burglars and notorious swindlers. They had already been convicted in Britain on numerous occasions.[15]

Again as a result of information supplied by the French Sûreté Nationale and Interpol, Scotland Yard were aware of the return to Britain of Micky Ball, Roy James, Graham Evans and Gordon Goody during mid-October 1962. They were also aware that they might have in their possession items of jewellery stolen in Cannes on 24 August. The Flying Squad therefore resolved to visit and search their respective homes.

Detective Inspector Winston Gardner of the Flying Squad took out a search warrant for Mickey Ball's flat at 100a Finborough Road, SW10, and, accompanied by Detective Sergeant John Loakman and Detective Sergeant Roy Wilmshurst, arrived at 7.45 p.m. on Monday, 22 October. During the course of their search items of jewellery were found, along with three chauffeurs' caps.

Gardner also searched a Mercedes, registration number 600 JKM, outside the flat, which was owned and registered in Ball's name. On the rear seat was found another chauffeur's cap. The jewellery and chauffeurs' caps were taken by the police, who also arrested Ball and took him to Cannon Row Police Station for further questioning. He was charged with being in possession of stolen property soon after.[16]

Four days later, Gardner undertook a search of Goody's address:

On Friday 26 October 1962, at around 8.20 a.m., in company with DS Wilmshurst and other officers, I went to 6 Common Dale Road SW15, where I saw Gordon Goody. I said to him, 'We have a warrant to search your flat for stolen jewellery.' I showed the warrant to Goody and he said, 'You won't find any gear like that here.'

We searched his bedroom, where in a dressing table drawer, between two sheets, DS Wilmshurst found two grotesque rubber masks. In another dressing table drawer was a cigar box containing 3 sticks of green paint, false moustaches and sideboards. I said to Goody, 'What have you got this equipment for?' He said, 'I bought that lot for a party we had last Christmas.'

In the kitchen, DS Wilmshurst found a postman's hat. He said to Goody, 'What is this doing here?' and Goody said, 'It belonged to my father. He used to work for the Post Office.' In the hallway, above a gas meter, we found a chauffeur's cap. DS Wilmshurst asked Goody where it had come from. He replied, 'It has been here for some time now.' We found no stolen property in the flat; none of the property mentioned was seized by us and we left the premises at approximately 9.15 a.m.[17]

While the police had found jewellery in the possession of Micky Ball, nothing had been found at the homes of Goody, James or Evans. Despite this limited success, the detectives' interest had been aroused by the chauffeurs' caps, Post Office hat, theatrical make-up and false moustaches found in the possession of Ball and Goody. This led to the suspicion that they and others may well be planning a big job in London in the not too distant future.

What was being planned and who else was involved? C11 were tasked with finding out. In the meantime, Ball was released on bail, and summoned to appear on 4 January 1963 before a jury at the Old Bailey on a charge of receiving stolen property.

AN INSPECTOR CALLS

Tuesday, 27 November 1962

THE DAY BEGAN AS any other day at Comet House, the headquarters of the British Overseas Airways Corporation (BOAC), on the outer perimeter of London Airport.[1] However, in the gents' toilet on the top floor of the building, something a little odd was occurring, and had attracted the attention of Herbert Turner:

> I am employed by BOAC. Part of my duties are to look after the toilets in Comet House. On the morning of 27 November, I was just coming out of the toilets on the third floor of the South West Wing of Comet House. It was approximately 9.33–9.40 a.m. then. As I went across the corridor, I saw four men in twos walking slowly up the stairs. They were dressed pretty decent. They went into the toilets. After I had been to the other side, I came back again in two or three minutes. The toilet doors were all shut. Two were still at the urinals. I didn't see anyone coming out of the toilets or what happened to the two men at the urinals. As I let the door go, I saw some men getting into the lift.[2]

The men who had spent so long in the top-floor toilets had been looking out the window, from which they had direct sight of the Hatton Cross branch of Barclays Bank, 400 yards away. They had watched intently as three guards emerged from the bank with a black metal box, followed by BOAC accountant Arthur Grey. Grey would later recall that:

> I went with another accountant to Barclays Bank in London Airport to draw wages. Having got to the bank, I handed in a cheque for £62,500. I received the money in notes of various denominations, packed it into the box and returned to Comet House in a car whilst the box went in a bullion van. I arrived back at Comet House at about 10.00 a.m.
>
> The box was then unloaded and carried into the foyer and put on a trolley which was waiting by the door. I rang for the lift. The lift was delayed. While I was waiting for the lift the only two people I saw were a man and a woman, who work in the Data Processing Centre, who came down the stairs. We waited half a minute at the outside before the lift started to move. We could see it on

the locator above the lift door. When the lift arrived on the ground floor the doors opened and I was overwhelmed by a number of men. I realized the man immediately in front of me was masked by a blue woollen mask around his face. I realized we were being attacked. The only thing I remember after that was that I received a blow on the head. The blow dazed me and caused blood to run in my eyes. When I came to, I saw Brian Howe lying on the floor also injured. The only impression I had was that the men were well dressed. I only saw the one man who came at me. He was masked. I only had an impression of the others. I was taken to hospital with a wound to my head and I was detained in hospital. I wouldn't recognize the man who came straight at me. The box was gone when I came to.[3]

Outside Comet House, parking his car, was BOAC Communication Officer Cyril Birkinshaw:

I was parking my car in No. 3 Car Park at Comet House at about ten o'clock. I noticed a blue Jaguar car in the fairway, practically in line with the entrance to Comet House. There was a driver in the car. He was wearing a chauffeur's cap. The driver looked very agitated. He was looking over his left shoulder continuously. There was a second car behind and a smaller third car. I was suddenly aware of the fact that there was a fight going on in the doorway of Comet House. The men appeared to be wearing some type of mask. I thought it was a blue stocking.

I saw two men with a large black box coming towards me in the car park. It then appeared to be on the ground. I saw a third small car. I don't know if it was a van or a saloon. It was smallish and grey. It stopped immediately behind the second car. The driver got out of the car and walked towards the black box. That's the last I saw of the box. I got the starting handle out of my car with the idea of throwing it through the windows of the cars when they left. The cars proceeded along the service road out of the car park and turned left into the Eastern Perimeter Road and set off eastwards along that road. I thought they would go the other way, so I couldn't get near the cars. I ran back through the car park to the telephone. I didn't see the grey vehicle go.[4]

Having driven at speed along the Eastern Perimeter Road, the two Jaguars came to a halt at a padlocked double gate leading out to the Great South West Road. This chain was quickly severed by a pair of bolt cutters, and the two cars turned left onto the main road in the direction of Hounslow.

Around five minutes later, in nearby Faggs Road, several witnesses, including George Jacks, a bus passenger, saw two men get out of a grey van. The men had moustaches, and were wearing dark suits, bowler hats and both carried umbrellas. At approximately the same time, Thomas Cook and his wife were walking south down Corban Road, when they saw a blue Jaguar containing five men, the majority wearing bowler hats, moving at speed before turning sharply right into a service road. Moments later, as they turned into Bath Road, they saw two men 'walking towards Bulstrode Road. They were walking separately, one some distance from the other and both had come out of the service road. They were two of the men in the car. I did not see which way they went when they reached Bulstrode Road.'[5]

Within minutes of the wages raid taking place, airport security had phoned the nearby 'T Division' at Harlington Police Station, less than a mile away, where they were put through to Detective Inspector Robert Field. As a result, CID officers were immediately dispatched to Comet House, where they found the London Ambulance Service already in attendance. Field also sent word to the Flying Squad and promised a full incident report in due course. T Division officers then begun the task of seeking out and taking statements from individual witnesses. The process would take some weeks and eventually amounted to over seventy sworn statements.

Over at Scotland Yard, it took the Flying Squad only a matter of hours to make the connection between the reports of the previous month concerning the searches of the homes of Micky Ball and Gordon Goody, and the airport robbery. DI Winston Gardner in particular recalled the chauffeurs' caps found in Ball's Mercedes, and the false moustaches and make-up found in Goody's bedroom:

On Wednesday 28 November 1962, again with Detective Sergeant Wilmshurst, I went to Goody's flat. As a result of what I was told, I went to his business at Lower Richmond Road, a hairdressers, and saw Goody. I said to him, 'You know who we are. You answer the description of one of the men who took part in the robbery at London Airport yesterday morning.' He said, 'How did you know this was my place?' Detective Sergeant Wilmshurst said, 'Your Mother told us that this is yours.' I said to him, 'You are being taken to Cannon Row Police Station where you will be put up for identification with a number of witnesses.' He said, 'That's a laugh, I wasn't anywhere near there.' I said to him, 'Where is your car?' He said, 'In a side street.' I said to him, 'We would like to search it.' I then went to a Jaguar index 9811 UB which he indicated was his: I didn't find anything in it. I then said, 'Before we go to Cannon Row Police Station, we would like to search your home address.' He said, 'Certainly.' We searched the address but we could not find the masks, make-up kit or two caps. He said, 'I got rid of those. Other coppers might get the wrong impression if they found them here.' He was taken to Cannon Row Police Station.[6]

C11, in the meantime, were focusing on the known associates of Goody and Ball, and in particular a potential connection with a robbery that had taken place some three months earlier at the National Provincial Bank in Clapham, when bank clerk Ronald Powell was robbed of £9,460 by three raiders:

> I was sitting at a stool behind the counter and the first thing I noticed was a loud banging against the screen partition to the right of me. I looked up and saw the head and shoulders of a man who was carrying a white stick. He began to attack me with the stick, and as I ducked, to avoid the blow, I fell off the stool.[7]

The raider with the white stick then climbed over the partition and stole the money from Powell's cash drawer.

The suspects were Charles Wilson, Gordon Goody, Joseph Hartfield, Micky Ball and Roy James. The police were sure either Ball or James had been the getaway driver, but had no real evidence on either. As a result of the subsequent interviews with the bank staff, who were also shown several books of mugshots, Wilson and Hartfield were arrested and appeared at the South Western Magistrates Court on 29 November, two days after the London Airport raid. Both men were remanded in custody, pending a trial at the Old Bailey set for 13 December 1962. A third man, James Edward Rose, who the police were satisfied had not taken part in the robbery, was also charged with receiving the sum of £601 10s, knowing it to have been stolen.

On the basis that Hartfield was clearly a close associate of Wilson and Goody, his name was also placed on the airport suspects list. By now the suspects list – or to be more precise, the two airport suspects lists – had grown somewhat. According to the various eyewitnesses inside and outside Comet House, the gang had divided themselves into three separate units. The first secreted themselves in the men's toilets on the third floor of Comet House, the second on the first floor landing, at the top of the stairs leading down to the lobby, and the third outside Comet House, who entered the building close behind the pay clerks. The consensus of the various eyewitness accounts suggested to the police that eight, possibly nine men had been involved in the raid. The two suspect lists, one emanating from C11 and the other from DI Gardner, contained the following names:

Roy James	Wilson
Michael Ball	Reynolds
Gordon Goody	Edwards
Bruce Reynolds	Goody

Ronald Edwards	Hammond
Charles Wilson	Hartfield
Terence Hogan	James
Derek Ruddell	Ball
Jimmy Collins	Hogan
John Daly	Wilson[8]

C11 had also picked up word from 'reliable' sources information to the effect that the raid had been postponed on two occasions prior to 27 November. On the first occasion, a routine police escort accompanied the money from Barclays Bank to Comet House that day, which was spotted from the toilet window at Comet House. As a result, the gang quietly walked out of the building and rearranged the raid. On the second occasion, two members of the gang had apparently failed to turn up, and the raid was again postponed due to their absence. The consensus among the gang was that the two men had 'lost their bottle'. One claimed that his car had broken down on the way, and the other said he'd simply 'been late' and didn't bother turning up. A vote was taken, and one of the two men, Jimmy Collins, was voted out of the team. The other unnamed member, despite some scepticism, was given the benefit of the doubt by a narrow margin.

Despite the wealth of 'information received', in terms of hard evidence there was very little was to be had, apart from circumstantial evidence, i.e. the items seen at the homes of Goody and Ball. The only other resort open to the police was to hold identification parades.

The first was held at Canon Row Police Station on 28 November, attended by Brian Howe, Arthur Smith and Herbert Turner, three BOAC employees, in which Ball, Goody and Wilson were picked out. Joseph Hartfield was not picked out, and it was therefore ruled that there was insufficient evidence to charge him with the London Airport robbery. He was, however, picked out in another separate identification parade by bank clerk Rose Cawley, along with Charles Wilson, and as a result both men were charged with the National Provincial Bank robbery in Clapham. After the first parade, DI Field re-interviewed Ball:

You know three witnesses have picked you out on the parade today. I am now going to take you to Harlington Police Station where you will be charged with robbery with violence at London Airport. I am sure your solicitor has advised you but let me remind you that you need not say anything, but what you do say could be used as evidence. Ball said, 'All right Mr Field.' He was placed in the back of a police car with PC Lancaster. The car was driven by Detective Constable

Wildman and I was in the front with him. After a few minutes Ball said to me, 'Well it looks as though I'm in it. My hair has got me into trouble again but I can't complain that was a straight ident. The fellow standing next to me was a dead ringer for me.' After a pause he said, 'What's the sentence for this sort of job?' I said, 'That's a matter for the court.' He said, 'How are the blokes who got hit?' I said, 'One of them was in hospital for a few days and had about 10 stitches. The others had cut heads but I think they are all on the way to recovery.' Ball said, 'Thank Christ for that. I want you to believe me I never hit anybody. I couldn't even fight myself. It's my Mum I worry about. I promised her and now I'm mixed up with this. If it wasn't for her I'd plead guilty but this would kill her.' He then got very emotional and after a minute or two he said, 'Will you get in touch with my Mum and Dad.' I said, 'Yes, when we get to the Police Station.'[9]

As the next few weeks went by, it began to dawn on Micky Ball that he was in bigger trouble than even he'd at first thought. While driving a getaway car in robbery with violence was serious enough, it now seemed that a number of witnesses were identifying him as one of the main players who had actually assaulted the security staff in the lobby at Comet House. Strangely, so far no one had actually come forward and identified Ball as sitting in the blue Jaguar outside Comet House, chauffeur's hat on head, although, in fact, several people had walked past in close proximity to the car.

While he was beginning to suspect that he was a victim of mistaken identity, this was hardly something he could volunteer to DI Field without giving Field the scent of a lead. After all, to disclose that there was another member of the gang whose general physical description could be mistaken for his would be seen as 'grassing' so far as the rest of the gang was concerned. Realising that he was stuck between a rock and a hard place, the mental pressure began to take its toll. Finally, he snapped after being interviewed by DI Field for probably the umpteenth time. Field was canny enough to recognise that little, if anything, was going to be squeezed out of Goody or Wilson. Ball, on the other hand, was a different case, or so he thought. Field clearly thought that putting pressure on Ball might lead to some further disclosures. According to Reginald Sillwood, one of Field's DSs, the following conversation took place on 1 December, as he was taking Ball back to the cells at Harlington Police Station after an interview in the CID offices with DI Field:

He said to me, 'There is something I want to tell you, just you. I have been wanting to talk to you all the evening. Can you get me a cup of tea.' I locked the cell door and returned shortly afterwards with the tea. I gave it to him. I said, 'You'll have to drink it while I'm here. I can't leave you with a cup. I also want your tie and belt.' Ball was drinking the tea. Between sips he said to me, 'I keep saying I'm finished but here I am mixed up in his job. Why can't I get an ordinary job?' I said to him, 'That's up to you.' He said, 'You know I wasn't in at the blagging don't you. Honest Mr Sillwood, I just can't stand a fight. I'm sure Mr Field knows I wasn't in the blag. I've told him and I'll tell the Court and all the world. I got the spoof plates for the Jags and was in on the job but don't blame me for the coshes and crow bars.' I said to him, 'I know you've had a talk with Mr Field. Have you told him this?' Ball said, 'Yes, he's coming to see me in the morning, but when you're with a team like this, a bloke like me has to do as he's told.' He started to cry again and sob and said, 'You know what I did in the job don't you. You might not believe this Mr Sillwood, but I have spent thousands this year and I'm ashamed of it. When this is all over, I'm going to get a real job and keep away from the hooks. I don't really fit in. It's just that I wanted to be somebody and not be pushed around. My Dad has always been straight.' He then mentioned the name of the footballer Johnny Haynes, [10] the person who his Dad worked for. I said to him, 'Now understand this: you have been charged and I want to get home. If you want to say anything about this, I'll write down a statement. If you want to give me an alibi, we will get it checked, but I'm not stopping here all night.' Ball said, 'I can't give an alibi because it would show out the others in the job. Mr Sillwood, you know I'm in this but I'll never give the others away. I'm only talking to you now because there are no witnesses. I really want to get away from all this and get an £8 per week job. That's a laugh, don't you know. I'm shown on the books as working for my brother-in-law as a credit agent but even that's false. It's all rigged the same as everything about me.' The conversation then ceased. He had a headache and I got him something for it. [11]

Ball is, on the whole, quite candid in insisting that while he drove one of the Jaguars, he was never inside Comet House and consequently did not take part in the wage snatch in the lobby. He was equally truthful about obtaining the false registration plates for the two stolen Jaguars used in the robbery. Ironically, when questioned by the police, the individuals at the two companies that sold Ball the plates had no recollection of the person who bought them and were thus unable to give a description:

Arthur Wynyard of Bluemel Brothers Ltd, 216, Great Portland Street, W1, took an order for the index plates 457 EXO over the telephone from a man giving the name 'Walters' of 57 Hyde Park Mansions, W2. Wynyard has no recollection of the person who collected these plates.

The index plates 165 DUV were made by Hills (Patents) Ltd, 5 Everton Buildings, Stanhope Street, NW1 on 17 October 1962. Mrs Gloria Frost, who was then employed by Hills, dealt with this transaction. She says she took an order from a man giving the name of 'Naylor', 26 Sussex Gardens for a pair of index plates, No. 165 DUV for a Jaguar motor car. She cannot remember whether this order was made personally or by phone. She says a man dressed in a bowler hat, black overcoat, striped trousers and carrying either an umbrella or walking stick called for the plates. She has not identified this man.[12]

The police investigation file also reveals that:

In spite of widespread enquiries, the source of the bolt cutters cannot be traced. These enquiries, however, revealed that on 23 November 1962 at about 12.45 p.m. a man called at the premises of Buck & Ryan Ltd, Tool Merchants, 310 Euston Road, NW1, and asked for a pair of 24" bolt cutters. He was dealt with by Mr Denis Walton, a Director of the firm. As no bolt cutters of that size were in stock at that time, he offered the customer a pair of 30" cutters which were refused. He had by this time become suspicious, as this man was wearing a boiler suit over which was a jacket of expensive cut. He therefore instructed one of his salesmen, Mr Frank Alderman, to wait outside the shop and follow this man. Alderman did this, and followed as the man walked into Stanhope Street, and turned left into Longford Street. At that time, he saw a Jaguar car, Index No. 9811 UB drive out of Drummond Street, turn left into Stanhope Street, and right into Longford Street. Here the man Mr Alderman had seen in the shop, got into the front passenger seat of the car and drove off.[13]

While Ball admitted obtaining the false plates, he was adamant that he was not the person who attempted to buy the bolt cutters at Buck & Ryan. He was equally correct in asserting he had not at any time been inside Comet House, either in the top-floor toilets or taking part in the attack in the ground-floor lobby. How, then, could several witnesses claim, in all sincerity, to have seen him at Buck & Ryan and inside Comet House?

On 11 and 17 December 1962, at Twickenham Police Station, Wilson, Goody and Ball were again picked out by six witnesses who had been at the airport in various locations, although all of them at some point picked out people other than the three suspects. According to Inspector Ian Richardson, who was supervising the parades, 'Mr Herbert Turner was quite adamant that the man Ball is one of the men he saw in the toilets in Comet House.'[14] Likewise, Peter Exford, a BOAC surveyor, who had seen between three and five 'city gents' in the toilets the week before, also identified Ball and Goody as being among them.

At the Buck & Ryan identify parades, Denis Walton, the Buck & Ryan director, said of Ball, 'this is the man that asked for the croppers'.[15] However, on the same parade, his colleague Mr Frank Alderman picked out a member of the public taking part in the line-up, and not Micky Ball.

Contrary to the claim made in several previous books on the Great Train Robbery,[16] Ball at no point pleaded guilty or offered to plead guilty to the charges of conspiracy to rob and robbery. He pleaded innocent at his Old Bailey trial, and his counsel did their best to contest the Crown's assertions in the face of what appeared to be exceptionally strong prosecution evidence.

While Ball maintained all along that he had played no direct part in the robbery itself and the violence in particular, being in the blue Jaguar before, during and after the raid, the jury, on the strength of the identifications at Comet House and Buck & Ryan, decided that he was indeed guilty as charged. He was sentenced to five years' imprisonment. Goody was eventually found not guilty after a retrial. In Wilson's case, the judge directed the jury to find him not guilty on the basis of insufficient evidence.

If, as seems highly likely, Ball was telling the truth all along, who was the man tasked with buying the bolt cutters and identified in the top-floor toilets moments before the raid? His identity would later prove to be key in unravelling the mysterious 'Mister Men' conundrum a decade later.

6

THE BIG JOB

WITHIN WEEKS OF THE London Airport raid, Britain, almost overnight, descended into one of the worst winters on record. Within living memory, only the winter of 1947 had rivalled it for sheer misery. In 1963, just eighteen years after the war, most people still did not have central heating or cars, and shortages of fuel and power made life grim.

It started unremarkably enough. The first few days of December saw temperatures fall below freezing, despite the sunshine, which was followed by thick, often freezing, fog. On the afternoon of Boxing Day snow drifted down in huge flakes and began to settle. By early evening, frozen points at Crewe were delaying trains from the north, creating a tailback of trains at signals further up the line; the Glasgow–London train was among them. When signals forced it to wait in the dark at a point some way past Winslow, the driver found that the phone didn't work at the Coppenhall signal-box ahead and chose to ignore a red light. What he could not see, in darkness through swirling snow, was a stationary train ahead: the 16.45 from Liverpool to Birmingham. He collided with the back of it at about 20mph; its rear coaches were telescoped, killing eighteen and injuring thirty-four.[1]

More thick snow fell every day until 29 December, when blizzards began. Local councils up and down the country were kept busy salting the roads; snowdrifts were 3ft deep and in most places travel by car was impossible. People postponed journeys by road, but the weather didn't improve; trains were delayed all over the country. Pipes were frozen and local authorities had to open standpipes in the street.

The freezing temperatures did not abate. Snow blanketed the whole of Britain until the end of January, and lay thick until March in some areas. Power cuts closed cinemas and theatres, and prevented floodlit football fixtures, not that many matches could have been played; most were called off because of frozen pitches. Street lighting flickered and traffic lights stopped working. The roads were dangerous already, with people falling over and cars skidding or getting stuck. A country accustomed to using public transport found it too cold to wait for a bus. Trains were constantly delayed by frozen points. To keep roads open at all, councils had frozen snow shovelled onto lorries and piled up on open land. Salting the roads became ineffective as it required a certain amount of traffic to mix it in and melt the ice and snow; this traffic failed to arrive, especially at night and at weekends when temperatures were very low.

It was during the first few days of the new year that an informant began pass-ing on a series of snippets to Chief Inspector Walker of C11 about several 'target criminals' currently on Walker's observation list – Bruce Reynolds, John Daly and Roy James. Two weeks later, Walker received further information to the effect that these three names, together with a number of others, were planning a big robbery that was imminent, and a train leaving Weymouth was the target:

> The train was said to travel to London via Woking, that it made four to six stops en-route and at each stop collected surplus monies received at banks. According to the informant, each bank carried a certain float and when the bank tak-ings exceeded this float the balance was conveyed on the same train each day. At Woking, this surplus money was conveyed from the railway platform onto the train itself by two men who wore yellow around a uniform cap. The precise point of the alleged attack was not known, but it was expected that it would occur en-route and that Woking was the probable point.

Further enquiries by C11, via British Railways Southern Region and Royal Mail, eventually identified the train mentioned by the informant as being the South West Travelling Post Office 'Night Up'. As a result, Walker liaised with W.J. Edwards, the Assistant Controller of the Post Office Investigation Branch, with a view to strengthening security on the train. Walker also sent out a warning message to all chief constables, who increased the number of police officers present at each of the stations where the train stopped and additional High Value Packages sacks were put on the train.

During the course of these enquiries, C11 learnt from Edwards just how much money was being moved from points all over the country to central banks in London by rail – in round figures, a staggering £4 billion a year. By the beginning of February, intelligence about a possible attack on the South West Travelling Post Office train had gone cold. Little more was heard from the informant and the paperwork was filed away.

By this point, the cold weather had returned with a vengeance. Throughout the first fortnight of February there was heavy snow and storms, with gale-force winds reaching force 8 on the Beaufort scale. While C11 and the Post Office Investigation Branch still had their ears open for any further talk about a Weymouth–Waterloo hold-up, a mail train robbery on the opposite side of London, on British Railways London Midland Region, took the authorities, and indeed the police, by total surprise. Unlike the Southern Region, for example, there had been no history of hold-ups or of stopping trains north of London. Despite the freezing fog, snow and storms, eight masked men held up the Euston–Holyhead Irish Mail train on the outskirts of Hemel Hempstead on 20 February 1963, at around 9.25 p.m., some forty-five minutes after it had left London. While this was a mail train, the majority of those on board were passengers. The incident made the front pages in most of the next day's newspapers. According to the *Daily Express*, 'Bandits battled with dining car attendants along the corridors of the Irish Mail express last night after overpowering a guard and ransacking the mail van. The fight spilled over into first class compartments.'[2]

Apparently, the train had been brought to a halt when the communication cord was pulled as the train neared Boxmoor Station, Hemel Hempstead. According to the *Express*, it had been one of the raiders. Their correspondent, Edward Laxton, also alluded to the robbers jumping down onto the track and 'scrambling up a snow-covered embankment'. In a Hertfordshire Constabulary report,[3] an attendant who claimed to have chased them stated that he saw a car waiting on the road and heard doors banging and a second car move off. He may have been mistaken, however, for reasons we shall see shortly.

The next morning, a British Railways spokesman said: 'We do not know yet just what is missing, but I think it must be a fair haul.' Compared to the Hertfordshire Police and British Railways reports that are somewhat precise and matter of fact, Laxton's story adds a little more colour and detail:

White-coated attendants prepared to serve the first sitting of dinner. The bandits, who are thought to have split up among other passengers when they boarded the train at Euston, converged on the guard's van. Six of the gang wore nylon stockings over their faces and carried coshes. They attacked the guard, Mr Howel Owen from Holyhead, and tied him up. They began to rifle the 50 bags of mail. The ticket collector was called into an empty compartment further along the train and coshed. But his cries for help were heard by two dining car attendants. They fought with the bandits in compartments and along the corridor and were joined by two more waiters. But the six bandits barred the way to the guard's van at the rear where two accomplices were steadily going through the mail. Bags were ripped open. A detective said, 'They obviously knew what they were looking for.'[4]

According to the Hertfordshire Constabulary, the communication cord was pulled at Boxmoor by a passenger, although that person is not identified. Night duty porter Peter George, of Ridgeley, Hemel Hempstead, said:

I had the shock of my life when I saw the Irish Mail train pulling up. There was a terrible hollering and shouting. I ran across the line and the guard, ticket collector and dining car men were tumbling out of the train. A couple of them had blood streaming down their faces and one yelled to the foreman to call the police.[5]

Five of the train crew had cuts and bruises, but refused to go to hospital for treatment. Police sealed off surrounding roads. Patrol cars throughout the area – West Herts, Bedfordshire and Buckinghamshire – were alerted by radio. The mail van was de-coupled from the mail train further up the line in Bletchley. After an hour's delay, the train was permitted to continue to Holyhead – with guard Howel Owen, the dining car men and local detectives.

The Post Office Investigation Branch were of the view that the Irish Mail train hold-up might possibly be the work of the gang who, for the past three years, had been involved in comparatively small scale but highly effective raids on the London–Brighton line.[6] These had been characterised by cunning, boldness and a good degree of technical knowledge. C11, too, had intelligence that a Brighton florist by the name of Roger Cordrey was possibly involved in the Brighton line robberies. Cordrey, according to information received, was a boffin-like character who had developed the know-how to manipulate and override the signalling system to stop trains at will. While the Irish Mail robbery had not involved the train being halted by a manipulation of the signalling system, C11 strongly suspected that the robbery had not gone entirely to plan. The pulling of the communication cord was, it was speculated, an unplanned response to the fight that broke out between the robbers and some of the waiters and passengers as the train neared Hemel Hempstead. It may well have been originally intended to halt the train to the north-west of Tring, several minutes after Hemel Hempstead. Information received by C11 after the robbery suggested that, contrary to the claim of a dining car attendant, who stated that he had tried chasing the raiders and saw a getaway car waiting for them, there had not, in fact, been a such a car – or at least there had not been one anywhere near Boxmoor Station.

The Post Office Investigation Branch had on record reports of two trains that had been brought to an unscheduled and mysterious halt at signals on the Parkhill Farm–Folly Bridge section of the line during the previous month. In one case, the signal quickly changed back from red to green before the fireman had the chance to leave the cab and call the signalman. On the second occasion, the fireman had called the nearest signal box, only for the signalman to angrily deny that he had changed the signal from green to red. Both incidents were quickly forgotten about and the cause put down to unexplained signal failures. Later on, it was speculated that these two incidents may well have been 'dry runs' to see if an express train could be successfully halted at the Parkfield Farm signal gantry. If this hypothesis is correct, it would suggest that the original plan was to halt the train at the signal gantry and for the raiders to then jump from the train and head up the embankment, presumably to where getaway vehicles were waiting in Marshcroft Lane. If this was the case, the halting of two trains on the Parkfield Farm section of the Euston mainline was the first known use of Roger Cordrey's newly perfected 'battery and glove' technique that would be used again six months later, 3 miles north of Tring, at Sears Crossing in Buckinghamshire.

The new approach was necessary, as the London Midland Region was very different to the Southern Region, where Cordrey had gained much of his previous railway experience. Apart from the fact that the locomotives were self-powered diesel electrics, as opposed to being powered by a third electrified rail, the signal system too was totally different. It ran on a similar basis to road traffic lights – green, amber and red light bulbs. If a gantry signal was red, the driver would be warned well before reaching it by a smaller ground-mounted 'dwarf signal', which would display an amber light bulb, telling him that the next signal would be red, thus giving him plenty of time to reduce speed and come to a halt at the next gantry.

For a period, Cordrey's telephone line, Molesey 6100, had been tapped in the hope this might give some clue to the identity of his associates and to the degree that he may or may not be involved in mail robbery offences.

C11 and certain Flying Squad officers were also, at this time, beginning to pick up word that a 'big job' was being planned by a specially assembled gang. Other than that, they had little to go on and resolved to keep their respective ears to the ground.

Not long after, information came to Inspector Walker in C11 that several of their target criminals who had been in the frame for the aborted Weymouth job, and also suspected of involvement in the London Airport robbery, were actively involved in the planning of this 'big job'.

The Flying Squad were therefore brought in to carry out observation on Gordon Goody, Charlie Wilson and Bruce Reynolds. To all intents and purposes, Goody and Wilson seemed to be going about their normal, everyday business without raising the least suspicion. Reynolds's movements, however, raised an eyebrow with members of the 5-Squad observation team, not particularly because of what they saw him doing, but more to the point, what they couldn't see him doing. In the words of Detective Inspector Frank Williams, head of 5-Squad, 'observation on his flat in Putney was difficult, made more so by the fact that Reynolds often used a motorcycle on his reconnoitring excursions'.[7] C11 and the Flying Squad did not have to wait long to find out more about the 'big job' ... it was a matter of when rather than if.

When the news broke, on Thursday, 8 August, that 'over £2 million' in used notes had been stolen from a mail train, the British public were first astonished – and then amazed that it had never happened before.

In 1963, £2 million was a dizzying amount of money, which – according to posters on the sides of double-decker buses – you could win on Vernons' Football Pools any Saturday. You could buy ten four-bedroomed freehold houses in London's leafy Holland Park for that. Over £2 million! It was unimaginable.

Cash was required for all but the largest transactions in 1963. British people had no plastic cards; in fact, the vast majority had no bank accounts. Up and down the country, thousands of small traders carried their takings in cash to local bank branches. If they hadn't made it by 3.30 p.m. when the bank shut, they deposited their money in the night safe in the wall. The following day, bank staff counted and bagged the deposits.

These hundreds of thousands of banknotes were dispatched to a main railway station, from which they were sent every night to the City of London for distribution to the relevant clearing banks. Since the days of the stagecoach, 'up' lines had been routes into London. For instance, parcels, letters and banknotes from towns around Glasgow, Aberdeen and Carlisle, and points south, would travel up the line to Euston. From a starting point at Glasgow, more coaches and mailbags would be coupled onto the train at a few big stations en route. Money and mail were separated, and sorted, on the train by scores of Post Office employees as they hurtled through the night.

After a bank holiday, such as that on Monday, 5 August 1963, there would be extra money aboard. In fact, the exact amount of money on the train that night has never been officially published. Bearing in mind that £2.6 million was actually stolen and seven sacks were left behind by the robbers, the likely estimated total would be in the region of £3 million.[8]

Much has been written since about how the police supposedly cracked the case as a result of a telephone call from a herdsman by the name of John Maris, who lived at Glencoe House in Oakley. At 9.00 a.m. on 12 August 1963, he had telephoned Buckinghamshire Constabulary's incident room and reported his suspicions about nearby Leatherslade Farm. He told the officer who took the call, PC 145 Peter Collins, that having read in his morning paper that the police were interested in isolated farms in connection with the mail train investigation, he had gone up the lane to the farm to take a look for himself.

He noticed immediately that curtain and sacking material covered all of the windows as if they were blacked out, and more mysteriously, he saw small triangular-shaped peepholes at the corners of each window. More intriguing, he saw a large army-type lorry parked in one of the outbuildings, similar to the one that had been mentioned on the radio news the day before.

Collins apparently passed on this message to Bucks CID, although it appears to have gone astray, as no action was taken as a result. What finally triggered Aylesbury HQ to send out someone to take a look at the farm was a telephone call from Detective Inspector Densham of Oxfordshire CID. On the evening of Sunday, 11 August, he had met a man by the name of Thomas Sheppard at a golf club. Sheppard had told him about Leatherslade Farm and the fact that, to the best of his knowledge, it was currently empty. Densham therefore phoned this through to the Aylesbury incident room the following morning. Having heard nothing back, he called Aylesbury again on Tuesday morning, which appears to have been the decisive call that finally elicited a response. As a result, Aylesbury incident room phoned Sergeant Ronald Blackman in Waddesdon, requesting that the farm be checked out pronto.

Blackman in turn wasted no time in contacting John Woolley, the Brill village beat constable. They left Brill Police Station together at 10.50 a.m. that same morning on Blackman's Triumph 250cc police motorcycle. As they were later to testify, they had no radio with them, and only their truncheons to hand. Had the gang still been in situ, they would have been in dire straits. What they found was pretty much what Maris had reported. The farmhouse was locked, but Woolley managed to effect an entry through a ground-floor window, and then let Sergeant Blackman in through the front door. Detective Superintendent Malcolm Fewtrell, Head of Bucks CID, later described the ground-floor rooms of the house as resembling 'a hastily abandoned camping site', due to the amount of self-catering paraphernalia left lying around. Ever a man with a turn of phrase, it was a comment he made later when the press eventually arrived at the farm in droves, that is best remembered today – 'the whole place is one big clue'. Indeed it was, but that's another story entirely.

While the tale of John Maris and his phone call was repeated umpteen times in press stories the length and breadth of the country, the police and Post Office remained tight-lipped about how they had come to the view that the robbers possibly had a farmhouse hideaway.

Later on in 1964, the Postmaster-General and the Post Office Solicitor had a dilemma on their hands in trying to decide how and in what way to disperse the reward that had been offered to the person whose information led to the arrest and conviction of the robbers. Among a list of claimants were John Maris and Thomas Sheppard.

Eight months later, the question of who it actually was that first alerted the police in such a way as to lead directly to the apprehension and conviction of those robbers in custody at that time was debated at Post Office headquarters. While there were four claimants to the reward, it seemed at that point that it was really a choice between two of them – John Maris and Thomas Sheppard. The Post Office file covering the legal issues surrounding this dilemma was only opened in 2019, and highlights from it can be found in Appendix 4.

When the Post Office wrote to the Chief Constable of Buckinghamshire for guidance, he responded with a very non-committal letter, dodging the question entirely. The Post Office then invited Detective Superintendent McArthur of Scotland Yard to a confidential meeting at GPO Headquarters, to discuss the matter in more depth. McArthur turned out to be a disappointment, indicating that the police did not wish to be publicly drawn into the matter of the division of the reward.

McArthur did say, however, that the police took the position that none of the four claimants provided information that led directly to the discovery of the farm, and by implication to the conviction of a number of the robbers. While they were not prepared to say this publicly, they were happy for the Post Office to say that in making their decision on the reward, they had consulted the police.

McArthur at no point explained why the police took the view they did, and clearly was not prepared to enter into such a conversation. For their part, the Post Office really did not want to find themselves between a rock and a hard place. They therefore opted for a good old-fashioned compromise, and avoided the question altogether by sharing the reward between the four individuals.

What did McArthur mean? If none of the four claimants was directly responsible for leading the police to Leatherslade Farm, did he mean that one or more of them was indirectly responsible, or was he implying that the intelligence that put the police on the scent came from an entirely different source?

While McArthur's statement and the background to the allocation of the reward only came to light in 2019, through a previously closed Post Office file, the definitive answer to this conundrum lies within the records of the Metropolitan Police. Although this jigsaw is still far from complete, there are sufficient pieces now in place to give us a reasonable idea as to what was going on at Scotland Yard.

From the very off, C11 already had a rough idea who the main runners and riders might be in terms of suspects, but they needed more to go on. The Home Secretary, Sir Henry Brooke, was therefore called upon to authorise a number of phone taps. It would seem, however, that the sheer number of lines tapped somewhat exceeded the number of warrants Brooke had authorised. This is not only corroborated by sources who were involved, but in telltale remarks in Post Office

Investigation Branch records. For example, on 27 August 1963, we learn that as the result of information supplied by C11 that same day, which was sent to both Tommy Butler and IB Controller Clifford Osmond, three individuals in London had immediate taps placed on their phones. Leo Heller, Doris May Golding and Edith Simon's homes were suspected of 'being linked to Bruce Reynolds support network'. This raises the question of proportion. If such minor individuals, some distance down the chain from those actually suspected of playing a direct part in the robbery, are being tapped, how many others above and below them were also having their conversations monitored? One comment in particular from this IB report stands out: 'As a result of information received from DI Pickles, C11, I arranged for the Supervisor, Wanstead Exchange, to trace calls incoming to Wanstead 5078.'[8]

The tap appears to be virtually instantaneous, and there is no mention or even hint of contacting the Home Office for a warrant before instructing the Wanstead Exchange supervisor. It is also clear from the IB report that typed transcripts relating to these three taps were being made and placed on file.

A previously closed Post Office file on telephone tapping, released in 2019, gives a very firm indication of the extent to which unauthorised and semi-authorised tapping had been taking place in the years before 1963. Highlights from the file appear in Appendix 2.

DI Wilf Pickles had previously been a member of the Flying Squad's 1–Squad, under Tommy Butler, and by 1963 headed C11's Intercept Room. Nicknamed 'Deafy' at the Yard, it was apparently considered a hilarious irony that someone with a hearing impediment should be in charge of overhearing telephone conversations. Telephone intercepts almost certainly assisted C11's work on suspect lists just as much as 'information received' from informants. While such intercepts could not be used as evidence and were therefore inadmissible in court, word from 'the horse's mouth' was often considered more reliable, as those being tapped were generally unaware that their calls were being listened in to, and therefore spoke more freely.

From such intercepts immediately after the robbery, a number of conversations yielded references to the nicknames of those they were talking about or talking to, and a list of nicknames was compiled. Most of these names were garnered by C11, who managed to come up with the names most associated with each nickname. Butler then told the Fingerprint Department (C3) 'to try these names first' when comparing the fingerprints they had found at Leatherslade Farm with those catalogued in their vast records. The nicknames they had included:

Buster
Little Jock
Weasel
Checker
Chas
Big Jim
Harry Boy
Old Alf
Shooting Break
Blue
Ding Dong
Pug
Paddy
Danny
Tel[9]

The following list, which appears to be one of a number, also tells a story of its own:

Bruce Reynolds	WIM 6293
Harry Browne	SHOR 5584
Richard G. Cahill	ALB 1050
Brian Field	PANG 585
Douglas G. Goody	REN 3816
Doris Golding	REN 3592
Leo Heller	PRI 0218
Charles Lilley	HIT 7067
Kenneth Shakeshaft	CUN 0901
Harry Smith	BIS 5235
Billy Still	WIM 6393
Ronald Biggs	REDHILL 1299
Robert Welch	CLI 0329
Roy J. James	FLA 2198
Michael Kehoe	TRA 6776
Edith Simon	WAN 5078
Thomas Wisbey	ROD 6229/HOP 4581
Charles Alexander	WAT 4602
M. & M. Regan	MON 5843/TER 7603
Terence Hogan	EAL 0811[10]

Knowing that telephone tapping was widely used during August 1963, and that the conversations recorded on tape were then typed up and filed, I made a Freedom of Information Request to the Metropolitan Police on 27 May 2019, asking if 'the intercept transcripts are held in one of the few remaining closed files on the robbery and will the Metropolitan Police make available these transcripts now that the subjects of the intercepts are dead?'

On 23 August 2019, the Metropolitan Police responded to the FOI, refusing to provide the requested information, citing section 12 of the Freedom of Information Act, i.e. the cost of compliance. That same day, I wrote to the Metropolitan Police, offering to personally pay the costs incurred in searching for and supplying copies of the transcripts. On 28 August, I received a reply, effectively refusing my offer. After requesting an internal review, which also rejected the request, I referred the matter to the Information Commissioner on 8 December 2019. When approached by the Information Commissioner, the Metropolitan Police stated that they 'could neither confirm nor deny' that they still held the transcripts. On 6 April 2020, the Commissioner ruled that, 'the MPS was entitled to neither confirm nor deny whether it held the requested information in accordance with section 12(2) of the FOIA'.

While a considerable amount of information received during the days and weeks after the robbery did indeed come from a network of informants, it was equally known to be standard practice, in certain circumstances, to state that particularly sensitive information that had come to light through telephone tapping had been received through a nameless informant. That way, such information could then be recorded in official reports without having to disclose that its true source was an unauthorised phone tap.

A case in point might very well apply to information that was deemed to have been received from an informant on 9 August 1963. This informant apparently gave the names of ten men who had taken part in the robbery, and stated that the gang were using a 'remote Buckinghamshire farm' as a hideout. This was two days before DI Densham reported what he had heard about Leatherslade Farm at an Oxford golf vlub, and three days before John Maris put his head through the hedge in Newtons Lane.

Any potential intelligence gleaned by telephone taps could well have found its way into an account given by Commander Hatherill on 29 August, when he related the story of a mystery informant who had named names to the IB's Clifford Osmond and Richard Yates. While he originally claimed that it came from a single source, i.e. a prisoner that he and Chief Superintendent Ernie Millen had visited in prison on 26 August, he would later concede in a private conversation with Osmond on 2 September that, 'some of the information concerned had reached him second-hand and it could have lost some of its accuracy on the way'. We will be returning to Hatherill's source later in this book.

Information from telephone taps may well have been the reason for Detective Superintendent McArthur's cryptic words at the meeting with the Post Office in the summer of 1964, when hairs were split over who could justifiably claim to have provided the information that led the police to Leatherslade Farm. We may never know for sure.

Whatever the realities of the train robbery story, contrary to all expectation, it was a narrative that would run and run for years to come. Unanswered questions surrounding those who had taken part did not go away. Some of these key questions were to be reignited a decade later by another major crime that would engross not only the Metropolitan Police, but umpteen other police forces abroad, not to mention the UK's intelligence services.

PART 2

FISH OFF THE HOOK

During the course of this book, well over 100 names mentioned in official files and records are referred to. In only three instances are the real names of individuals either not used or withheld. In each of these three cases, on first mention, I have explained the reason for not doing so. In the case of 'Hugh',[1] a retired member of the Security Service (also known as MI5), the reason is national security.

NIGHT OWLS

Tuesday, 6 July 1976

THE THREE MEN, WHO had left the Log Cabin Club in Wardour Street a few minutes previously, were coming in his direction. Hugh let them pass him, pretending to be studying the latest fashions from Harry Fenton,[2] while at the same time watching them in the shop window reflection. They strolled on a few yards, crossed the road, and turned into Broadwick Street. By the time Hugh had reached the corner, they were turning right into Marshall Street. He went down Broadwick Street on the other side, staying back 15 yards behind them. Suddenly, they changed their minds and came back into Broadwick Street and crossed over to a betting shop. They disappeared into the betting shop; Hugh estimated they were in there for some fifteen minutes. When they eventually came out, they headed back up Marshall Street, then left into Great Marlborough Street, crossing the road opposite the junction with Argyle Street.

For a moment, Hugh thought they were about to shout down a cab; instead, they carried on walking. He quickened his pace to get closer as the crowds thickened, which was just as well as the three men quickly slipped down the stairs into Oxford Circus Station.

Following them down the big escalator and along the tunnel to the Victoria Line platforms, he was half expecting the men to be going north, but they turned left onto the other platform just as the train was pulling in. Hugh kept well away from them until the train stopped. While they sat down, he stood by the double doors, occasionally risking a sideways glance.

They all got out at the next station, Green Park. Coming up into the ticket hall, Hugh stayed as close as he could in the circumstances and hung back while one of them was buying an *Evening News*. Once outside in the street, the three crossed the road and walked into the Ritz Hotel. It was now 12.25 p.m. and it looked like they were heading for a liquid lunch, if not something a little more substantial, in the Rivoli Bar.

By the mid-1970s the Ritz was a little down at heel, having fallen into a turbulent period. Terrorist threats from the IRA became the chief concern, and bomb scares were not uncommon. The oil crisis in the early seventies directly affected business and prompted the Bracewell–Smith family, who owned the hotel, to sell it to Trafalgar House on 5 April 1976 for £2.75 million.

By that point, the hotel's occupancy rate had apparently dropped to 45 per cent – as a result, the Grill Room had been closed and the hotel was losing money. The Ritz was synonymous with the glamour of a bygone age. The Rivoli Bar was stylishly designed to create the impression of walking into a glittering jewellery box, although it too was also looking a little jaded.

Rather than push his luck and follow them into the hotel, Hugh decided to report their current position and hand over to another watcher. Just as he was about to turn around and cross Arlington Street, he noticed a face on the opposite side of the street that he was sure he'd seen earlier on, while waiting for the trio to emerge from the betting shop in Broadwick Street. Unless he was very much mistaken, this meant competition – but who else could possibly be following his three targets?

Saturday, 24 July 1976

The pizza restaurant in Notting Hill Gate was full to the brim that evening. It was 9.46 p.m. when a short, tubby man in his 50s, positively identified as one Henry Oberlander, arrived and was shown to a table where two others, later identified as Ricardo Guz and Francisco Fiocca, were already seated.

At 11.15 p.m., all three men paid their bill, headed out of the restaurant, spoke a few words on the pavement, and then went their separate ways. Oberlander drove west along Holland Park Avenue, arriving at his Clarendon Road flat ten minutes later, while Guz and Fiocca walked a short distance to a parked car and headed in the opposite direction.

At 11.21 I saw the white Mercedes, index number GGC 456J at the junction of Pembridge Gardens and Bayswater Road. There were two men aboard. The driver was identified as Francisco Fiocca. On receiving information that the vehicle was proceeding to an unknown destination, we took up the pursuit position and followed it east along Bayswater Road for a distance of ½ a mile. The vehicle then turned left into Inverness Terrace, where it proceeded north to 8 Westbourne Gardens W2.[3]

Monday, 26 July 1976

Westbourne Gardens, like so many other Georgian streets west of Marble Arch, had a vaguely Italianate elegance about it, or at least it had at one time. By the mid-1970s its white, cake-icing stucco houses had seen better days. Vere Court at no. 8, though, had no such pedigree, being a characterless, four-storey 1930s apartment building at the junction with Porchester Road. The flat under observation by officers of the Security Service, MI5, was on the third floor of Vere Court, directly opposite 5 Westbourne Gardens on the other side of the street. Hugh noted with some irony that the Russian spy Alexander Tudor-Hart had once lived in a flat at no. 5, four decades earlier; now, in 1976, it was acting as host to those keeping a watchful eye on the comings and goings at Vere Court.

The Security Service were not alone so far as interest in Vere Court was concerned. On the night of Monday, 26 July 1976, it was also under observation from a Serious Crime Squad team, taking photographs from a location unintentionally close to where the Security Service observers were operating at no. 5. The Serious Crime Squad officers soon sensed that something was going on and challenged one of the men: 'DS Trevor Cloughley had a word with one of our co-watchers; his explanation was neither satisfactory nor convincing and a huge row developed. It later transpired that the man was from MI5.'[4]

As a result of this unintentional blowing of each other's cover, senior officers at Scotland Yard and the Security Service briefly conferred and the two operations, from there on in, ensured that they did not tread on each other's toes.

The Serious Crime Squad's involvement in the affair sprung from an intelligence lead referred to them by C11 in May 1976. This suggested there was reason to believe that a man with a long criminal record, now running an engineering company in the East End of London, was involved in the fraudulent trading of stolen and forged cheques. As a result, it was decided to place him under close observation pending a review of the results.

The target, William David 'Billy' Ambrose, was followed from his home at 496 Barking Road, Plaistow, E13, to W. Cahill and Son Engineering Ltd, situated two streets away at 13 Prince Regent Lane, E13.

From a covert location on the opposite side of the street, those coming and going from no. 13 were noted, photographed and logged. One of the many observers working in shifts at Prince Regent Lane, DS Hilda Harris, noticed that one individual who appeared at Cahills quite often was a 'funny, fat little foreigner'. Before too long, he became the subject of surveillance himself. Originally thought to be a man named Weisser, he was later identified by Interpol as Henry Oberlander, age 51. The picture slowly developing was that Oberlander and Ambrose appeared to be involved in a web of international fraud. The bulk of Oberlander's contacts and associates were other foreign nationals. Long-distance cameras were therefore employed, along with bugging devices, telephone taps and interceptions. Apart from the surveillance placed on W. Cahill & Son Engineering Ltd, Billy Ambrose would also be followed and whoever he came into contact with, often at meetings in the West End, would also be recorded and photographed.

As a result of the bungled Vere Court observation, the Security Service decided that the time had come to find out exactly what Francisco Fiocca was up to in his flat at Vere Court. In so doing, they had a distinctive advantage over the Metropolitan Police. In the basement workshop of their headquarters at Leconfield House, in Curzon Street, Mayfair, the Security Service had an enormous collection of thousands of keys, all carefully numbered, indexed and individually hung on small hooks on the walls. They had, over the years, acquired or made secret imprints of keys of offices, hotels, private houses and flats, and in this way had gained access to premises all over the country. It had always been emphasised in service training that the first rule, if you were endeavouring to enter premises, was only pick the lock as a last resort. The logic being that it was virtually impossible to pick a lock without scratching it, and that would almost certainly give the game away to a trained intelligence officer.

The question, so far as Vere Court was concerned, was that they were not sure at this point whether or not one or more of the targets were connected with a foreign or East European intelligence agency. Was Francisco Fiocca, the resident of the Vere Court flat, sufficiently worldly-wise to know or guess that his flat might have been entered if they picked the lock? His door lock was a Yale, which consisted of a series of pins sitting in various positions inside the barrel. The bites in the key acted on the pins, to push them upwards and allow the key to be turned in the barrel. A hooked implement could therefore be inserted into the keyhole and the barrel 'stroked' in a steady rhythmic action, one pin at a time, until all the pins were up.

The view was that it was best not to take the chance. A key was therefore purloined and the premises entered at a time of day when observation records suggested it was regularly empty. They were also anticipating the possibility of having to open a safe. Burmah safes were regarded as by far the most difficult to open. The pins moved horizontally through the lock and it was virtually impossible to pick. A Chubb, on the other hand, while advertised as being unpickable, was not, apparently, such a hard task for a skilled man.

What the Security Service found in the third-floor flat at Vere Court was to change the entire course of the enquiry. Once a report had been made to the officer managing the case, the decision was made to open what the Service called a List File. The Secret Intelligence Service (also known as MI6) was also updated, for it was their section in Switzerland who had first raised a query on suspicious international dealings involving some of the protagonists.

The List File on the case was then recorded in the Registry. The Registry was the nerve centre of the Security Service and was spread across the whole ground floor of Leconfield House. It housed the main file index and the files themselves. The rooms leading off from the central concourse held the other specialist card indexes. Duplicate copies of all files and indexes were routinely made on microfilm and sent for storage in a specially protected Security Service warehouse in Cheltenham.

Prior to the early 1970s, the Security Service held around 2 million Personal Files, or PFs, which were buff coloured and arranged in alphabetical order. However, the number of PFs began to increase dramatically as the seventies wore on with the onset of student and industrial militancy. Then there were Subject Files, or organisational files, such as the Communist Party of Great Britain and the National Front. Subject files often ran into several volumes and were elaborately cross-referenced with the PFs. The final main category of file was the duck-egg-blue List File. These comprised material gathered during a particular case that could not be placed within either of the two previous categories.

Files were located by using card indexes. A system had been devised many years before whereby each card was classified with a series of punched holes to identify the category of files; for instance, to find an individual using several aliases, an officer had to draw out a master card corresponding to that category. Long needles were placed through the holes in the master card to locate any other cards that fitted the same constellation. These could then be searched by hand.

The concourse of the Registry was always busy with trolleys transporting files from the Registry shelves to special lifts. The trolleys ran on tracks so that files could be shifted at great speed up to the case officers working on the floors above – F Branch on the first floor, E branch on the second, D on the third and fourth, and A branch on the fifth. It was the case officers in A Branch (Intelligence Resources & Operations), and F Branch (Counter Espionage), who were the principal receivers and depositors of files on the Ambrose, Oberlander et al. case.

As the case rolled on, it seemed to raise more questions than answers. While it was reasonably clear to see what was happening on the surface, in terms of a mass international fraud it remained far from clear what, apart from the amassing of cash, was the ultimate objective, and whether there was a nation state, agency or organisation behind the whole plot. Switzerland seemed to be the common denominator, which hardly helped matters due to its secretive and private banking system. Indeed, Swiss bankers were known colloquially, and perhaps not without justification, as 'the Gnomes of Zurich'.

As catchphrases go, 'The Gnomes of Zurich' was both a colourful and evocative one while it lasted. It certainly sparked the public's imagination: In fairy tales, gnomes live underground, secretly counting their riches; in newspaper cartoons, Swiss bankers did the same. The Swiss Banking Law of 1934 codified banking secrecy. Many banks offered clients numbered bank accounts, where the identity of the account holder was replaced by a multi-digit number known only to the client and to the bank. Some Swiss banks supplemented the number with a code name that identified the client. Along with protecting Jewish assets in the war, Swiss banks collaborated with the Nazis and their allies by storing gold and cash. Adolf Hitler maintained a personal account at the Union Bank of Switzerland (UBS), believed to have a balance of 1.1 billion Reichsmarks in 1945.

Swiss bankers and Swiss bank accounts had for some time been associated in the public mind with dodgy dealing, currency speculation, secrecy and tax evasion, not to mention allegedly providing a safe haven for Nazi war plunder, on a no-questions-asked basis. The birth of the 'Gnomes of Zurich' phase has often been credited to Britain's deputy prime minister, George Brown, who laid into Swiss bankers at a Cabinet meeting in November 1964, blaming them for speculating against the pound. During the meeting he said, 'the gnomes of Zurich are at work again'. Ever the political opportunist, it didn't take Prime Minister Harold Wilson long to jump on the bandwagon. Several weeks later he vowed to the press that he would 'resist the gnomes' sinister power'.

By that time, the Soviet Union and a number of its Eastern Bloc allies had established outposts of their state banks in Switzerland, leading to western suspicions that the Soviets were either using this as a cover for other purposes or to potentially destabilise western nations or allies. Of equal concern was the potential for the Soviet Union to use the international banking system to channel funds to sympathetic political groups abroad, as well as to terrorist organisations.

All in all, by the end of the Serious Crime Squad's observation operation, some 2,000 photographs had been taken. Finally, once C11 and senior officers at Scotland Yard were sure that they had all the names in the frame they needed, word was given to begin the mass arrest of suspects. Shortly after dawn on Friday, 13 August 1976, over 100 police officers assembled in the gymnasium at Limehouse Police Station for a short notice operational briefing. All available members of the Serious Crime Squad were present – numbers were further swelled by the calling in of officers from other CID departments at the Yard, as well as members of the SPG (the Special Patrol Group). The objective: to arrest a host of names thought to be the 'big fish' involved in a fraud conspiracy dating back to January 1972. Officers were then broken up into teams and separately briefed about the individual they had been assigned to arrest. Synchronised timing would be imperative: the arrests were to take place at exactly the same time, to avoid the possibility of any of the targets alerting others.

DC Tony Goss was one of the team assigned to arrest Francisco Fiocca, who according to the briefing was a 48-year-old Argentinian national. At precisely the allotted time, Goss kicked in the front door of his Vere Court flat. As he and the other officers piled in, they were momentarily stunned by what they saw. Goss immediately grabbed the phone in the flat to call Detective Superintendent Len Gilbert at the Yard: 'Fucking hell Guv'nor! Fucking hell! You'd better come down here quick and see for yourself!'[5]

The flat was without doubt an Aladdin's cave of evidence. When the haul had been taken back to the Yard, examined and logged, it was established that there were:

1,500 forged bank drafts drawn on 39 banks with a face value of £3 million;

Engraving equipment;

Rubber stamps for visas, which appeared to have been stolen from embassies and consulates;

340 stolen airline tickets;

Type-faces from different countries;

A machine for printing in amounts on bank drafts;

120 forged passports along with stolen birth certificates, baptism certificates and travel documents;

4 million pesetas;

$50,000 in forged currency;

An 'escapers' kit of forged papers for gaining entry to a variety of Eastern Bloc countries.[6]

On 18 August 1976, *The Times* reported that:

Twelve men and two women were charged yesterday after investigations by Scotland Yard. All but one were remanded at Thames Magistrates' Court in custody until August 25 on charges including plotting to defraud and conspiracy to obtain cash by possessing forged bank notes.

They are: Tomislav Butigan, aged 31, care of Guards Hotel, Lancaster Gate; William Frederick Anthony Voss, aged 36, of Bewley Street, Shadwell, East London; Carl Albert Lempertz, aged 56, of James Street, Westminster; Jorge Grunfeld, aged 52, and Mrs Irene Grunfeld aged 28, both of Clarendon Road, Notting Hill.

William David Ambrose, aged 46, of Sandown Road, Esher, Surrey; Henry Oberlander, aged 50, of Clarendon Road, Notting Hill; Mrs Monica Ellison, aged 44, of Vane Close, Rosslyn Hill, Hampstead; André Biro, 51, also of Vane Close; Emile Fleischman, aged 57, of Ladbroke Mews, Notting Hill; Francisco Fiocca, of Westbourne Gardens, Bayswater.

Patrick Bloggs, aged 57, of Highbury New Park, Islington; Sidney Harold Solomans, aged 38, of Clark Street, Stepney, and Roberto Maddalena, aged 32, of King Street, West London.

All were charged with conspiracy to cheat and defraud except Mr Maddalena, who is charged with dishonestly handling a watch. He was given bail in £2,000, with one surety of the same amount, until September 7. Mr Lempertz, Mr Ambrose, Mr Oberlander and Mr Fleischman are charged with conspiracy to obtain $360,000 from Dr Peter Livingston Bilder, by means of criminal deception by falsely stating that certain drafts were good and valid.

Mr Oberlander, Mr Fleischman, Mr Grunfeld and Mrs Grunfeld were charged with conspiracy to defraud the Israeli Discount Bank Ltd by possessing forged bank drafts drawn on the bank with intent to defraud.

Mr Voss, Mr Lempertz, Mr Ambrose, Mr Oberlander, Mrs Biro, Mr Fleischman and Mrs Ellison are charged with conspiracy to contravene the Immigration Act, 1971 by possessing forged travel documents.

With the suspects in custody, interviews under caution could now begin. More detailed investigations and new lines of enquiry would no doubt follow, not just in the UK, but also in a host of other countries where the tentacles of this international fraud had extended. Already it was becoming clear that this could well be one of the biggest international frauds ever. There were a number of senior officers at Scotland Yard who felt that due to the complexity of the case, presenting evidence to the Director of Public Prosecutions to put before a jury could well take some time. They were to be proven correct – many of those arrested on 13 August 1976 were to spend the best part of two years in custody on remand.

Every journey, though, begins with a first step, and to the Metropolitan Police and other agencies at home and abroad with an interest in the case, the initial focus rested on those who appeared to be at the centre of the web – Billy Ambrose and Henry Oberlander.

From the moment Billy Ambrose had first been placed under observation in May 1976, several archived files had been retrieved from the records office by C11 intelligence handlers, keen to get to work on some back reading. By 1976, not too many old hands were left in CID who could remember much further back than the previous decade. As we shall discover later in this book, the appointment of Sir Robert Mark as Commissioner of the Metropolitan Police in 1972 resulted in a seismic upheaval. Appointed as a new broom by the Home Secretary, Reginald Maudling, Mark set himself the task of ridding the force of what he called the 'institutionalised corruption' in the CID. His new broom was to sweep out a total of 478 detectives, who resigned or were given early retirement. This was a departure rate that was six times higher than under his predecessor. Fifty other officers, including the then Head of the Flying Squad, Kenneth Drury, were ultimately charged with corruption.

The pen picture of Billy Ambrose provided by the files was nothing if not illuminating. Within days of the mail train robbery in August 1963, Detective Chief Superintendent Tommy Butler was receiving names from informants of those suspected of taking part. On 16 August 1963, he wrote out a composite list of eighteen names. The sixteenth name on that list was Billy Ambrose.[7] For reasons not alluded to in the files, his name was removed from the active suspect list around October 1963. Had Butler good reason to remove his name? We cannot be sure, due to the lack of paperwork. Perhaps it was the case, as Ambrose loudly protested when arrested on 13 August 1976, that his wealth came not from crime but from the engineering and bookmaking businesses he ran? Had Butler been right to eliminate Ambrose from the train robbery investigation at such an early stage, or was there more to Billy Ambrose than met the eye?

Whatever else might be subject to speculation at this point, one thing was blindingly obvious: Billy Ambrose was a man of exceptional ability and fortitude, as the pages in his file make abundantly clear:

Criminal Intelligence Section,
New Scotland Yard
WHI 1212. Ext.
886/887

NAME	William David AMBROSE
ALIASES	William David Barnham
DESCRIPTIONS	Born 21.9.29 Stepney, E1. Height 5'10".
	Cleanshaven, light brown, receding hair.

DRESS	Wears double breasted suits		
CRO No:	21598/52		
PHOTOGRAPH	A good likeness, taken in 1960		
CONVICTIONS	Has convictions for larceny, assault, assault on police, receiving, causing grievous bodily harm.		
ADDRESS	Evenshade, 15 Sandown Road, Esher, Surrey, formerly 496 Barking Road, E13, and 14, Brock Place, Glaucus Street, E3		
ASSOCIATES	AMBROSE	Elizabeth	N/T
	CAHILL	Richard	360/45
	CAHILL	William	N/T
	CALLAGHAN	Jeremiah	9303/40
	EDWARDS	Ronald	33535/61
	OLIFFE	Edwin	N/T
	OLIFFE	Henry	N/T
	REYNOLDS	Bruce	41212/48
	SPINKS	James	1132/46
	STILL	William	11815/38
	VOSS	William	N/T[8]

The son of a professional boxer, Billy Ambrose Senior, Billy Junior followed in his father's footsteps in 1948, boxing professionally, first as a welterweight, and then at middleweight. In thirty-six fights he won thirty-one times, fourteen by knockout. According to the press cuttings of the day, that found their way into his file, he was well on the way to a title shot against British Middleweight Champion Randolph Turpin, when his boxing prospects came to an unexpected halt. His boxing licence was suspended in 1952 as the result of him being fined £50 for receiving stolen ham and cigarettes. On 3 March 1953, he was found guilty of robbery with violence at the Conway Stewart Pen Company in Stepney, and received a five-year jail sentence. This was effectively the end of his boxing career. On 16 February 1954, it was recorded that Ambrose had escaped from the hospital wing of Wormwood Scrubs Prison but had been recaptured soon after. He served out the rest of his sentence behind the high granite walls of the desolate and somewhat more foreboding Dartmoor Prison in Devon.

When he was released, he returned to London and opened a drinking club, which operated from two floors of a property in Duval Street, off the Commercial Road in Spitalfields.[9] According to C11, 'the Pen Club was owned by Ambrose and Jeremiah Callaghan', although 'Mrs Frances Sadler held the license and fronted the club'.[10] Not long after it had opened, the club hit the national headlines when, around 1.30 a.m. on Sunday, 7 February 1960, a fight started in the club bar area that ended in a fatal shooting.

According to the investigation file:

Three men, John Alexander Read, aged 28, unemployed, and Joseph Henry Pyle, aged 25, a street trader, both of St Agatha's Road, Carshalton, Surrey, and James Lawrence Nash, aged 28, steeplejack, of Sandringham Flats, Charing Cross Road, WC, went to the Pen Club with Mrs Doreen Masters aged 33, of Parkhill Road, Haverstock Hill, Hampstead, NW, looking for Selwyn Keith Cooney, alias Jimmy Neill and 'Little Jimmy'.

According to several witness statements, Cooney was struck on the back of the head with a bottle, and then attacked, resulting in a broken nose and the loss of two teeth. According to witness Joan Benning, who was with Cooney, Ambrose came to Cooney's aid, throwing punches at his assailants, before being shot. As Ambrose doubled up, Cooney shouted out, 'Don't let him get away.'

Billy Ambrose, whose occupation is referred to as a car salesman in his statement, had, before the fight started, been standing next to Cooney at the bar (who he refers to as 'Neill'):

I was standing to the left of Neill, who was having a drink at the bar. There were about 20 people in the bar and the juke box was playing. I was talking to my wife when someone pulled Neill round. There seemed to be a bit of a scuffle. When I turned round, I saw blood on Neill's nose and he was staggering. Someone cried out, 'He's got a gun.' I turned round and tried to get the gun from a man. I asked the man to give me the gun and I got pushed at that time. I heard a bang, and felt a burning pain in my stomach. I then got a blow on the head and it seemed to be a free-for-all. Five or six were fighting. A man I know as Jerry Callaghan pulled me round to go out. As I was going out, I saw Neill on the floor.[11]

Within seconds of Cooney shouting out, 'Don't let him get away,' a second shot rang out that hit Cooney in the head, killing him instantly. A general melee then broke out, during which the attackers left the club and drove away. According to other sources, Ambrose, in spite of being seriously wounded, helped Callaghan and John Simons carry Cooney's body down a flight of stairs and into the street.

Once outside, Ambrose managed to get to his car, parked a short distance away, and drove himself home to nearby Glaucus Street, Poplar. On arrival he stated that:

'I found I had an injury on the head and a bullet wound in the stomach. I tried to patch myself up and went to the London Hospital.'[12]

The London Hospital (known since 1990 as the Royal London Hospital), in Whitechapel Road, later issued a statement saying that Ambrose had been admitted during the early hours of the morning, was in critical condition, had undergone an emergency operation and was as well as could be expected. On arrival at the hospital, he had apparently told the nurse in A&E that he had been shot outside a club in Paddington that he would not name. After the operation he remained in hospital for a month.

Not long after Ambrose was released from the London Hospital, Parliament passed the Betting and Gaming Act 1960, which legalised off-course betting and allowed the opening of high street betting shops for those who were granted a gaming licence. In the first twelve months following legalisation, 130,000 gaming licences were granted. Billy Ambrose and Jerry Callaghan were among a host of individuals who successfully sought licences. In March 1961, Ambrose acquired the Barley Mow pub, off Whitechapel Road, not far from the Blind Beggar. However, on 17 April 1961 he was refused a drinks licence by local magistrates. His wife Elizabeth therefore became the publican and licence holder. As the 1960s progressed, Billy Ambrose prospered.

A decade later, Scotland Yard and Leconfield House pondered on his good fortune. There had been a few rumours in the East End that his business success had been founded on the proceeds from the Great Train Robbery, or if not, perhaps on other criminal enterprises dating back to the previous decade. It might equally be the case that he was simply a self-made man who had worked hard but had unwittingly, of late, been rubbing shoulders with the wrong type of people while going about his legitimate international engineering business.

Only a year before his arrest, in 1975, he and his family had moved from London's East End to a large luxury home in Esher, in the heart of the Surrey stockbroker belt, valued in today's money at around £2.5 million. The home they had left behind, at 496 Barking Road, E13, was looked up on the London Borough of Newham electoral register to see how long the Ambroses had lived there – it showed that they had moved in during 1969. The previous occupiers, who had been there since 1964, were a Mr Henry T. Smith and his wife, Mrs Margaret L. Smith. Almost as an afterthought, the following year's register was examined to see who had moved in after the Ambrose family had moved to Esher. Strangely enough, it showed that Henry and Margaret Smith had moved back in to 496 Barking Road.

How peculiar was that, and who were Mr and Mrs Smith?

DOING A DEAL

ONE OF THE CENTRAL questions asked repeatedly over the years has been why 'Joe, Bert, Sid and Fred' managed to evade arrest and prosecution, while the other twelve men present on the trackside at Sears Crossing were not so fortunate. While there are several answers to this, Joe, Bert and Sid do have one very important factor in common, as Ronald Biggs mentions in his 1969 manuscript:

> We had all arrived at the farm wearing gloves and it was Bruce's idea to dispense with them whilst we were inside the house. 'We won't wear gloves for two weeks,' he had said, 'and we can scour the place down when we leave – or even burn it down for that matter.' Only three members of the gang insisted on keeping their gloves on at all times – three of the four who were never wanted in connection with the train robbery, Sid, Joe and Bert.[1]

'Fred', the old train driver, as we shall learn later on in this book, did almost certainly leave his prints at the farm, but let's wait until we reach that point in the story.

While the fingerprints found at the farm were the only evidence the Crown eventually offered when the case came before the Assize Court in Aylesbury on 20 January 1964, the police actually had a wider body of evidence that they were either, for legal reasons, unable to publicly disclose, or which had been discounted or ruled inadmissible by the Director of Public Prosecutions.

At the trial, Arthur James QC, speaking for the prosecution, told the court that 'no witnesses would be able to testify that they had seen X or Y at the scene of the crime or in the preparation or planning of the crime'. Even by the legal standards of the day, the case, in terms of hard evidence, was not a strong as it seemed on the surface. There was not a shred of evidence that could or would be produced in court to connect any of those in the dock with the scene of the crime, i.e. at Sears Crossing and Bridego Bridge. Most of the fingerprints found at Leatherslade Farm were on movable objects. Even the two sets of prints that were found on non-movable objects (Wilson's prints on a windowsill and Wisbey's on a bath rail) could have been made just before or just after the date of the crime.

While Arthur James's well-crafted words seemed to imply that there were no eyewitnesses whatsoever, at any time or location, on closer examination of DPP files another interpretation is evident. The key part of his well-crafted statement to the court lies at the very beginning of his first sentence, when he accentuates the word 'would', as opposed to 'witness', as in: 'no witness *would* be able to testify'. Contained within the pages of the DPP files are a variety of witnesses who gave statements to the police relating to a number of men they saw: purchasing or obtaining equipment that would later be used in the robbery; at, and in close vicinity of, Leatherslade Farm and the villages of Brill and Oakley; at, and unmasked, on the railway track at Sears Crossing.

A number of these witnesses were only a matter of feet away from those they saw, and were able to give good observational descriptions that were retained by the police, even though they were unable to produce these in court due to the reluctance of the respective witnesses to give evidence under oath. In a number of cases, the police believed that this was due to fear of the consequences of going on the record. While we will return to the contents of these DPP files later in this book, one particular eyewitness account is of immediate relevance.

Brian Currington, a 28-year-old tractor driver employed at Little London Farm, whose fields surround Leatherslade Farm, had stood only a few yards away from three members of the gang as their Land Rover arrived and stopped at the farm gate:

> On Wednesday, 7 August, I first saw a Land Rover at the gate of Leatherslade Farm. The driver squeezed through between my tractor and the gate. I stood nearby when one of the three men in the Land Rover got out to open the gate. There were two other men in the Land Rover. I can only give brief details of the driver. He was about 25–30 years of age and about medium build. He had dark hair, brushed back. A tanned or weather-beaten complexion. I only had a side view of him and I noticed his ears were small and close to his head. I think he had a dark sports coat on, but I cannot be sure. They drove up to the farmhouse and as they went by, I noticed the Land Rover was loaded right up to the roof – it was bulging – but it was fully covered and I could not see what was in it. There were 2 suitcases on the back – on the tail board which was down – they were light grey in colour and very large. I remember the fair-haired man addressing the driver of the Land Rover as 'Barry' or 'Gary'.[2]

This last comment was of particular interest to the police, who already had knowledge of an individual they suspected was the Land Rover driver. According to Butler, very shortly after the robbery, 'several names of men physically involved in the offence were given to another officer and myself'. One of these was Henry Thomas Smith, CRO No. 1551/1947, who was living at 262 Fieldgate Mansions, Stepney.

Butler was quick to speculate that what Currington had actually heard was not 'Gary' or 'Barry', but 'Harry'.

Later that same day, Butler started flipping through the Criminal Record Office file he had requested from the Registry that morning. It had the usual rubber stamp and CRO number 1551/1947 written in large flomaster lettering on the front cover. Typewritten on thin, off-white paper, it was a narrative of the criminal career of one Henry Thomas Smith, born in the County Borough of Croydon on 20 October1930, to Henry Thomas Smith, a builder's labourer, and Mary Cahill, no occupation.

Two names that immediately caught Butler's eye as he came to the end of the first page of the file were 'Charles William Richardson, aged 23, scrap metal merchant, of Holderness House, Champion Hill, Camberwell SE, and Edward George Richardson, aged 21, metal sorter of Sidcup Road, Mottingham'. The two men had come a long way in the London underworld since the case outlined in Smith's CRO had been tried at the Old Bailey in December 1957. By 1963, the Richardson brothers were leaders of one of the two biggest and strongest criminal gangs in London; their firm ruled the roost south of the river – their rivals, Ronald and Reginald Kray, likewise held sway north of the Thames.

According to the file:

> While a gang of thieves was engaged in unloading a lorry laden with stolen lead at a garden in Brockley, south London, one of their number was crushed when the rear of the vehicle backed into a wall. They completed their task and some three hours later took their dying colleague to a hospital on the other side of the river, several miles away. There they told the hospital authorities they had found the man lying injured on the pavement 600 yards away from the hospital.
>
> Henry Thomas Smith, aged 26, car dealer, of Falkirk Street, Shoreditch, was sentenced to four years' imprisonment and Robert George Semaine, aged 29, window cleaner, of Hill Dene Avenue, Harold Hill, Essex, was sentenced to three years' imprisonment. Both had been found Guilty of stealing a lorry loaded with GPO scrap lead cable casings, valued together at £2,925.
>
> On the direction of Mr. Justice Glyn-Jones they were found Not Guilty of the manslaughter of George Benjamin Day. Charles Edward Candler, aged 34, the driver of the lorry, of Malpas Road, Brockley, SE, was sentenced to 18 months' imprisonment. He was also found Guilty of being an accessory after the stealing by Smith and Semaine and Guilty of receiving the stolen lead. Charles William Richardson and Edward George Richardson were also found Not Guilty of receiving the lead knowing it to have been stolen and they were discharged.[3]

NO CASE TO ANSWER

In addition to the CRO file, Butler also had the advantage of Smith's C11 file, which provided information about his activities since being released from prison. It appeared that Smith had used the proceeds of a previous robbery to purchase a driving school. This had been bought for the sum of £400 (£7,132 in today's money), from John Muskett and Charles Poulton of 1 Chatham Avenue, London N1. As part of the transaction, Smith had apparently agreed to take over the outstanding hire purchase on the cars. While he owned the business, it was, in fact, being run and fronted by his father, Henry Thomas Smith Senior.[4]

The file also listed Smith's known associates:

BENNINGTON	David J.	CRO No. 34924/51
BRIGGS	James R.	CRO No. 28136/51
CAHILL	Richard G.	CRO No. 360/45
CANDLER	Charles E.	CRO No. 41657/42
DAY	Derrick	CRO No. 19378/46
HOGARTH	Terence	CRO No. 766/42
LEYBOURNE	Charles W.	CRO No. 22346/44
REGAN	Daniel P.	CRO No. 217/47
SENAINE	Robert G.	CRO No. 29929/53
SMITH	Charles G.	CRO No. 46087/57
THOMAS	Eric G.	CRO No. 38286/45
WHITE	James E.	CRO No. 26113/55

As a result of information received about Smith's alleged participation in the train robbery and Keith Currington's statement on 14 August 1963, potentially identifying Smith arriving at Leatherslade Farm, Butler immediately took out a warrant to search Smith's flat and bring him in for questioning.

DS Jack Slipper was the officer who led the search of the flat:

On the 14 August, 1963 at 2.45 p.m., with Detective Sergeants Moore and Caple, I went to 262 Fieldgate Mansions, Stepney, a first floor flat. Margaret Wade, who was alone in the flat, opened the door. I told her we were police officers and that I had a warrant authorising us to search the premises for stolen bank notes. We entered and searched the premises but with negative result. Mrs Wade indicated that Smith was due home at any time. We remained on the premises and at 3.45 p.m. the telephone rang, Mrs Wade picked up the phone and said, 'Steam Company? No, you must have the wrong number.' She then replaced the receiver. It was obvious that the caller did not have the wrong number and no doubt it was

Smith himself. At 4.45 p.m. the telephone again rang. I picked up the receiver and said, 'Bishopsgate 5235.' There was a short pause and the caller said, 'Who's that?' 'I'm a police officer. Are you Harry Smith, the occupier of this flat?' The caller said, 'Yes, why?' I said, 'I would like to see you about a certain matter.' The caller said, 'What's it all about? Is it about my brother's bother?' I said, 'I don't intend to discuss it over the phone. Are you coming home?' The caller said, 'Yes, I'll be there in half an hour'. He then rang off.

At 5.00 p.m. the telephone rang again. I picked up the receiver and said, 'Bishopsgate 7235.' The caller said, 'Harry here. Look I know it's nothing to do with my brother – you've had your card marked. You want me for the train job. If you give me your name, I'll get a mate of mine to see you.' I said, 'I want to see you.' The caller said, 'You know I can't afford to see you.' I said, 'You've got three young children here, you can't stay away forever.' The caller said, 'I know that but I'm still not coming and I'll take some finding.' The caller then rang off. We then left the premises. Observations were kept on the premises for the following two weeks and Margaret Wade was followed away on two occasions but Smith was not seen.[6]

Smith certainly would 'take some finding'. After a few days it was clear that he had vanished from his usual haunts and had gone to ground. The police therefore concentrated on his family, friends and associates in the hope that one of them might lead to progress in the hunt.

DCS Butler refers to the enquiries centred around Smith's relations and with others known to be associated with him in a memorandum written for Commander Hatherill:

It is well known that Daniel Patrick Regan is a close friend of Henry Thomas Smith, and that their degree of friendship, which goes back to at least 1946, has increased considerably since the Mail Train Robbery. Regan is one of several brothers who, between them, operate several betting shops in the Metropolis under the name 'M. and M. Regan' and 'Michael Regan'. One of the shops owned by the brothers is at No. 38, Aldersgate Street, City, EC, next door to a café owned by James Edward White, CRO No.26113/1955, one of the three men who, so far, has eluded arrest for the robbery, and who is another associate of Smith and Regan.

When the association between Regan, White, Smith and probably others of those dealt with became known to us, Regan was brought to this office on 27 September and closely interrogated concerning the offence. He strenuously denied all knowledge of it. During the interrogation he admitted knowing Smith, White and several of the persons in custody for the offence, but asserted he had not seen any of them for weeks.

DCS Butler, later on in his report, concluded that: 'It was by now very strongly suspected that Regan was "looking after" Smith (and possibly White), and arranging for the safe custody and disposal of the large sums of cash.'

In this regard, attention very soon turned to Mrs Patricia Smith, Daniel Regan's sister, and her husband, Walter Albert Smith, who worked as a bookmaker's marker at the M. & M. Regan betting shop. Information received indicated that Mr and Mrs Smith were involved in laundering the stolen money by purchasing £5 postal orders at a number of sub-post offices and then, at a later date, en-cashing them. This led to DCS Butler contacting Royal Mail and requesting that a special notice be sent to all post office counter officers in the London Postal Region, drawing their attention to persons purchasing or en-cashing an abnormal number of £5 postal orders. Butler then obtained a search warrant for the Smiths' flat:

On the morning of Thursday, 10 October, Flying Squad officers led by DS Nevill and DS Slipper went to 14 Linel House, Murray Grove, Shoreditch, N1. During the search of the flat, which was occupied by bookmaker's marker Walter Albert Smith and his wife Patricia, DS Slipper became suspicious of Mrs Smith's stocky appearance, which he was not convinced was the result of her weight. When he challenged her on this, she became abusive and he informed her that he would have to summon a WPC to search her.

At this point Mrs Smith pulled up her skirt to reveal that her knickers were stuffed with money. When the WPC arrived, it was discovered that the money concealed in her knickers totalled £470 in rolled-up £1 notes. When Mrs Smith was asked why the pound notes had been individually rolled up, it was revealed that the couple had received a sack of £2,000 in £1 notes, and had hidden it on the roof. However, it had rained and the money had been soaked.

Mrs Smith had subsequently been rolling up the notes (to try and get rid of the crinkles caused by the rain) and drying them in her airing cupboard. In the airing cupboard a further £363 was found. Elsewhere in the flat, £325 was found in £5 postal orders. They were both arrested and charged with receiving £2,000 in stolen money.[7]

Flying Squad officers were also carrying out observations on a number of properties where they thought Harry Smith might be, or might appear. Further information on this front came from C11, to the effect that three days before the search of Patricia and Walter Smith's flat, Daniel Regan had completed the purchase of 496 Barking Road, Plaistow, from one Richard Cahill.

According to Butler's closed-file notes on the transaction:

> It was established that the house was purchased through R.J. Twyford & Co, Solicitors, of 287 Grays Inn Road, WC1, on 7 October 1963, from Richard Cahill, who is identical with George Cahill, CRO No. 360/1945, who has convictions for maliciously causing grievous bodily harm, attempted larceny, greyhound doping, etc. The house was bought for £2,000 by Daniel Patrick Regan, CRO No. 217/1947, who until about twelve months or so ago, was living at No. 590, Green Lane, Ilford. This latter address is said to be worth about £4,500 to £5,000. As far as can be ascertained, to date, this house is now occupied by a man named Timothy Regan, thought to be a nephew or cousin of the former occupant.[8]

DCS Butler therefore immediately assigned DS Jack Slipper to organise a round-the-clock observation team on the property. His report is contained in the same file:

> Numerous observations were kept on the house, even to the extent of borrowing a GPO hut and van which were placed opposite the premises for two days, but Smith was not seen, although Mrs Wade and the children were seen on many occasions. It was then considered that Smith might be in the premises and afraid to go out. As a result, a search warrant was applied for and executed on 4 November, 1963 but again proved fruitless.
>
> Mrs Wade, who was at home, was very abusive and stated that she had no money and that Smith was living rough, but in her purse was found ninety-three £1 Bank of England notes. When questioned about this money she claimed to have won it at a local Bingo Hall, which she refused to name. This money was taken possession of and the numbers checked against the stolen notes, but none was found to be identical. In a pram was found the Deeds of the house. These confirmed that on 7 October, 1963 it was sold to Daniel Patrick Regan, CRO No. 217/47, an associate of Smith.[9]

The observation operation in Barking Road was therefore called off, at least for the time being. The pursuit of Harry Smith had, thus far, proven entirely fruitless. There seemed little or no prospect of locating him any time soon. While the first two months of Butler's train robbery investigation had met with a flush of early success (nineteen quick-result arrests for robbery and receiving), the momentum was now visibly slowing down, if not juddering to a halt. While Butler's reports during this period indicate that he was, not without reason, banking on one or two of the wanted men being betrayed by their money minders, he must also have sensed, perhaps against his better judgement, that a change in tactics might now at least be worth considering.

The lack of progress in the Smith hunt was not an isolated frustration. The same dead end had also been reached in the pursuit of Bruce Reynolds, Ronald 'Buster' Edwards, Jimmy White, John Daly and Roy James. While Daly and James would ultimately be located and arrested in December 1963, as the result of 'information received' from the very people shielding them, the other men on the run seemed to be well bedded down.

From the very start of the investigation, it seems clear that Butler was being urged by his deputy, DCI Frank Williams, to put out feelers to some of those on the run and, where possible, negotiate terms with them in exchange for the return of stolen money. While the investigation had done reasonably well thus far in terms of arrests, with the exception of Cordrey and Field's share, it had singularly failed to retrieve anything but a tiny percentage of the stolen money.

Butler's view of Williams and his record as a senior Flying Squad officer seem to be somewhat of a contradiction. By the standards of the time, Butler was essentially an honest copper, give or take his alleged partiality for 'verballing'. While he saw Williams as a vital member of his hand-picked train robbery team, he was also wary, if not downright suspicious on occasions, that Williams was personally too close for comfort to a number of his high-profile criminal informants. After he retired from the Metropolitan Police, Williams described his outlook as follows:

> Every good CID officer needs to have as extensive a knowledge as possible of criminals, their habitats, their haunts and associates … information is vital, and the type of information needed cannot be gleaned from Sunday School teachers. It has to come from within the fraternity itself.[10]

While Butler would be dead by the time those words were written, he would not, in all likelihood, have disputed the reality of Williams's statement. His fear, however, was that eventually, in order to obtain information, some officers might be tempted to offer unofficial immunity to certain criminal contacts, in exchange for high-grade information or even monetary gain. As enquiries in the mid-1970s, carried out under the auspices of a new Commissioner, Sir Robert Mark, would eventually prove, this is exactly what had been going on in some quarters of the CID for a prolonged period of time.

It may have been this split personality view of Williams that led Butler to pursue a somewhat risky strategy in the later part of 1963, in terms of 'semi-sanctioning' Williams's unofficial activities, while at the same time keeping his two immediate CID superiors, Commander George Hatherill and Deputy Commander Ernie Millen, entirely in the dark about them.

According to Williams, he had received overtures during October 1963 from several already established contacts of his in South London, as to what deals might be possible, should one or more of those currently on the run give themselves up and return some of the stolen money. Williams claimed that:

> The suggestion of surrenders was an important development and I discussed it at length with Tom Butler on several occasions. He agreed that I should do everything possible to encourage the robbers to surrender through my contact, and he gave me to understand that George Hatherill and Ernie Millen, our senior officers, had been put fully in the picture and had agreed to this.[11]

In November 1963, Butler agreed to accompany Williams to Simpson's restaurant, at the Savoy Hotel, where they met, over dinner, a contact of Williams's, Frederick Foreman. Butler also apparently accompanied Williams to another meal, with another of Williams's contacts, although the name of the contact and the location of the restaurant are unknown. While there is nothing specific, on or off the record, as to what such a deal might entail, Williams was certainly of the view that Butler was, in principle, in favour of moving forward. According to Williams, his message to those considering a deal was that in return for giving themselves up with a significant sum of stolen money, he would guarantee strict fairness according to the evidence the police had.

After a period of weeks with no word or response from his contacts, Williams was told that £50,000 would be handed over to him at Nunhead railway station, on Gibbon Road, SE15. While Williams would later claim that Butler was fully aware of this, and had cleared it with Ernie Millen, on arrival at the rendezvous he told Frederick Foreman, who had brought the £50,000 with him, that Butler had backed out of the deal, and that he was unable to take the money.

Much mystery still surrounds these negotiations. Seven years later, awkward questions were beginning to be asked in senior circles at Scotland Yard about Williams's role in this episode, as well as the later deal he had struck with Ronald 'Buster' Edwards in 1966. As a result of the spot of bother Williams now found himself in, he apparently spoke to the then retired Ernie Millen in 1970. Millen told him that he and Hatherill knew absolutely nothing about the negotiations and denied point blank that Butler had ever mentioned a word about them. Who, then, was covering up the truth? Was Butler misleading Williams into thinking that his actions had official sanction, when in fact they didn't and he'd said nothing at all to the top brass? This is a possibility. If Williams's endeavour had backfired, or become public knowledge, Butler could always claim complete ignorance of the whole thing. The fact that Millen and Hatherill were equally in the dark would only strengthen Butler's claim that he knew nothing. Or, was Williams retrospectively covering himself in the early 1970s by claiming that he had acted only with Butler's approval (who, by this time, was conveniently dead)? Equally, Millen and Hatherill may have been the ones trying to exonerate themselves in this murky affair by denying all knowledge. Of the three possibilities, this, it has to be said, is the least likely.

What we do know, in terms of Harry Smith, is that a second attempt to hand over the sum of £50,000 was made a few weeks after the aborted affair at Nunhead station. This time, it was to be handled in a very different way in order to camouflage Williams's involvement in the affair. This time, a phone call was to be made to Scotland Yard at a pre-agreed time, 6.30 p.m. on Tuesday, 10 December 1963, saying that £50,000 of train robbery money was to be found in a telephone box at the junction of Black Horse Court and Great Dover Street, Camberwell, SE1, and that the police had five minutes to come and collect it.

Things very nearly went pear-shaped for a second time, as on that very same afternoon, by complete coincidence, Butler received a hot tip that Roy James was to be found in hiding at 14 Ryder's Terrace, in St John's Wood. When the call about the £50,000 came through to DCI Sid Bradbury at 6.30 p.m., Butler was fully engrossed in planning a raid on Ryder's Terrace and was completely unmoved by it, dismissing it as 'another hoax'. It was vitally important to the plan that Butler was with Williams when the money was found in order to validate the story. It was as much as Williams could do to persuade Butler to accompany him to the phone box, 'just to be sure that it really was a hoax'.

After some coaxing, Butler reluctantly agreed to go, and the two men headed for Great Dover Street in Butler's Mini. Sure enough, two large, tied sacks were waiting for them in the phone box. These were taken back to the Yard to be opened. When the sacks were emptied onto the floor of the Squad office it was clear that the money had recently been dug up, as it was damp and musty, and many of the notes were stuck together. The next day the money was driven under escort to Aylesbury and handed over to DS Malcolm Fewtrell. Bank inspectors were brought in to peel them apart, and when the money was finally counted the grand total was only £47,245 (i.e. £2,755 less than £50,000). This was put down to the fact that while the money appeared to be wads of £500, the robbers had not known that some of the wads were in fact less than this amount. The money handed back with the lesser-value wads matched the bank lists pertaining to the money on the train. This equally showed that this money at least had been taken straight from Leatherslade Farm and buried without any attempt to count it.

While the money promised had now been handed over to the police, another five months would elapse before Harry Smith was content to reveal his whereabouts to the police and surrender himself for questioning. During that period, DCI Frank Williams met Smith's close friend, Daniel Regan, on several occasions to talk terms.

Finally, on the afternoon of Tuesday, 5 May 1964, a telephone call was made to DCI Frank Williams at Scotland Yard, by Daniel Regan, to the effect that Harry Smith would be at the Peckford Scrap Metal Company, 50 New Church Road, Peckham. This was the yard run by Charlie and Eddie Richardson. Williams reported the call to Butler, who again declared that this must be a hoax. In spite of this, Butler agreed to accompany Williams to the rendezvous:

At 6 p.m. on Tuesday, 5 May, 1964 in consequence of a telephone call received at this office, I went with Detective Chief Inspector Williams to New Church Road, Camberwell SE5, and there saw Henry Thomas Smith in the company of Daniel Regan, who left forthwith in a motor car.

I told him we were police officers and added, 'Are you Henry Thomas Smith who at one time lived at 262 Fieldgate Mansions, Stepney?' He replied, 'Yes that's right.' I said, 'We are engaged on enquiries into the robbery of the mail train at Cheddington, Bucks in August last year and want to ask you some questions about your whereabouts at that time.' He replied, 'Yes all right but I can tell you straight away I am making no statement.'

He was taken to Southwark police station. On arrival I said to him, 'My information is that you lived at 262 Fieldgate Mansions, Stepney until the 14 August, 1963 and then disappeared.' Smith made no reply so I added, 'Do you recall a police officer answering the telephone that day in your flat and asking you to come home?' Smith replied, 'No, I don't. I said, 'Do you say you did not ring later on after first promising to come to the flat and telling the officer you had no idea why he wanted to see you.' Smith replied, 'I've had advice and told to make no statement even if you charge me with something.'

I said, 'Perhaps at least you will tell us why you did not go to live with your wife and child at the address at Barking Road that was bought on your behalf.' He replied, 'No I'm saying nothing except I am innocent of any robbery.'

He was asked whether he had any objection to his finger and palm prints being taken by police. He replied, 'No, have as many as you want.' Palm prints were taken by Detective Chief Inspector Williams. He (Henry Smith) was later detained at Cannon Row police station where he gave his name as John Smith of no fixed address. His palm prints were compared with those left at Leatherslade Farm but no identification was made. On Wednesday, 6 May, 1964 Smith was taken to Aylesbury police station and detained whilst arrangements were made for witnesses to attend an Identification Parade.

On Thursday, 7 May, 1964 Smith was placed with a number of other men on an Identification Parade. Ten witnesses who either saw or had dealings with the strangers in Oakley or Brill districts of Buckinghamshire at the material time were introduced to the parade. However, none made an identification. Smith was accordingly released on his personal undertaking to present himself at New Scotland Yard in fourteen days' time. Smith carried out his undertaking but no further evidence being available he was allowed to leave.[12]

Where had Harry Smith been since he vanished on 14 August 1963, and what were his plans now that he appeared to be off the hook? But was he really 'off the hook', or did Williams and Butler have two very different interpretations of what had occurred on 10 December, and the subsequent understanding arrived at? Most crucially of all, whatever the understanding amounted to, did Butler have any intention of abiding by it?

SAFE AS HOUSES

PORTLAND CHAMBERS WAS A local landmark. Its palatial-looking white stucco façade with nine Doric columns was not only the centrepiece of West Street, Fareham's main thoroughfare, it was also the home of some of the town's most prestigious law firms and chartered accountants.

Detective Inspector White and Detective Sergeant Suter of the Hampshire and Isle of Wight Constabulary were not used to being kept waiting. They'd already been seated in the plush outer lobby of Warner & Son solicitors for some time when they were at last ushered into the office of Mr Sturgess, one of three partners in the firm. The sale and purchase of 91 Privett Road, Gosport, was clearly not a topic the solicitor was overly keen to discuss. However, as DS Suter relates in his written statement of 17 June 1964: 'Sturgess told us that a cash deposit of £475 had been made on 91 Privett Road, and the balance of £4,275 was paid by Regan in £5 notes on 23 December 1963. This was paid into Lloyds Bank Limited, Fareham Branch the same day.'[1]

While not mentioned to Sturgess, the two police officers were already aware, having interviewed the vendors' solicitor, Mr Rogers of Blake, Lapthorne, Rea and Williams of 1 Bath Lane, Fareham, that Regan had initially offered the owners of 91 Privett Road, a Mr and Mrs Osgood, the sum of £3,000 with the balance of £1,750 to be paid privately in cash to Mr Osgood. Rogers had also confirmed that the Osgoods had rejected this offer on his advice, and that the payment had been made by a bankers' draft from Warner & Son.

Frustratingly for the police, they were later to discover that despite the large cash payment made into Lloyds Bank, 'a check against the Police lists (of stolen banknotes) was not made of the notes paid in by the bank'.[2]

Sturgess also volunteered to Suter and White that he had informed Daniel Regan of his appointment with them. Sutor noted in his report that this was 'unfortunate but of little consequence'.[3]

While at Portland Chambers that afternoon, White and Suter paid a visit to Mr Miller of A.J. Palmer & Co., Chartered Accountants, who acted as company secretary for Dales Properties (Fareham) Ltd. Portsmouth Police had already received a report from Companies House in London in response to their request for information on limited companies that Daniel Regan had any association with. This revealed details of two companies:

Dales Properties (Fareham) Ltd – incorporated 31 October 1963. Authorised capital £5,000. Registered office: Portland Chambers, West Street, Fareham. Directors Daniel Regan and Thomas George Pope. The list of principal shareholders include Richard George Cahill, Daniel Regan, Michael Regan, and Mr. and Mrs. J. Hill. Barclays Bank is quoted as security for the mortgages and debentures held by the company.

Gaye Flatlets (Portsmouth) Ltd – incorporated 23 March 1964. Authorised capital £50,000. Registered office: 10, Western Parade, Southsea, Hampshire. Directors Daniel Regan, Thomas George Pope.

A third company, **Dales Property (Developments) Ltd** is awaiting incorporation.[4]

According to DS Suter, Mr Miller confided to him that:

> he knew that about £10,000 in cash had been spent by Daniel Regan in the purchase of property and mentioned in passing that one large wad of £1 notes he remembered handling were somewhat damp and that many of the notes were stuck together. He said that due to his position, he could not divulge details the transactions made by Dales Properties (Fareham) Ltd, but by the end of July, he would be sending in a return to the Inspector, HM Taxes, No. 4 District, Portsmouth.[5]

DI White, no doubt trying hard to suppress his growing sense of irritation, pointed out to Miller than the mere fact that such a sizable wad of notes was damp should immediately have alerted him to the fact that the money might well have come from an illicit source, and very possibly the recent mail train robbery in Cheddington. Miller apparently made no further comment, and the two officers left without further ado to file their reports.

Later that same day, DI White also filed in his report that:

> Mr Sturgess telephoned to say that he hoped we did not think him too guarded, but he had a duty to his client. On reflection however, he thought he could tell me that Regan had made two other cash purchases of property to his knowledge: on the 9 January, 1964, £1,980, being purchase money of 14, Campbell Road, Southsea, Portsmouth. On the 11 February, 1964, £4,097.9.0d., being part payment purchase money of Havant Road properties, Cosham, Portsmouth. All monies paid in £5 notes and banked.[6]

Since receiving a request from Detective Chief Superintendent Tommy Butler, some four months earlier in February 1964, asking the Hampshire & Isle of Wight Constabulary to undertake enquiries into a number of property transactions of interest to Scotland Yard, White and Suter had been almost permanently engaged on this task, along with three detective constables.

In a later telephone conversation with Detective Superintendent Sid Bradbury of the Flying Squad, they were given to understand that the investigation was centred around the belief that the cash share of train robbery suspect Harry Smith was being used to purchase residential properties in the Portsmouth and Gosport area. They were therefore to approach estate agents and others in the property business in an endeavour to trace persons buying houses and other property for cash in the area, where information suggested Daniel Regan was actively seeking to buy real estate through a number of individuals of 'dubious character' acting as 'fronts' on his behalf.

It didn't take long for their efforts to bear fruit, as a report from DC Ronald Thomas shows:

> Information has been received in this City that Mr M.W. Pople has recently come into a very large amount of money which it is alleged is part of the proceeds of the mail train robbery at Buckinghamshire. Pople is well known locally as a property dealer and because he is an undischarged bankrupt, operates through his wife at 98 Hartley Road, North End, Portsmouth.[7]

Thomas further noted that:

> The informant alleges that Pople has used part of this money to buy ten race horses. It is alleged that the horses were bought at the Ascot Horse Sales at the beginning of February, 1964, and the auctioneers in respect of these sales were Bottrells of The Lodge, Flaxon, Yorkshire. The horses are said to be in training with Basil Foster, trainer, formerly of Newmarket, but now at Delamere, Baydon Road, Lambourn, Berkshire. Enquiries were made of the auctioneers, Messrs Botterills, of The Lodge, Flaxton, Yorkshire. Mr Botteril was himself the auctioneer at the sales, and he confirms that Mrs Pople purchased the horses. The horses were apparently paid for by two cheques.[8]

Enquiries made by Gosport police confirmed that Regan was associated with 'several persons of dubious character in the Gosport and Portsmouth districts'.

It was discovered that Pople was well known to local estate agents as a 'front' for Pope, who was regarded as an unscrupulous property dealer. Being an undischarged bankrupt, he employed other individuals to act as agents on his behalf, while his wife signed cheques, held bank accounts, and generally acted as the principal in the business.

Also included in DC Thomas's report is information about Thomas George Pope, a man whose backstory and connections provided a few more missing parts of the jigsaw:

Thomas George Pope is the proprietor of a wholesale and retail grocer's business, styled Dales Stores at 95, Highlands Road, Fareham, which was incorporated in April, 1961. The registered address of this company is shown as Portland Chambers, West Street, Fareham. It will thus be seen that Regan and Pope are directors of two companies dealing in house property. In addition, through his associates, Regan has the services of three other companies available to his if required.

At our request, a close observation was kept upon 32 Palmerston Way and 91 Privett Road, and in consequence of this, Pope's close association with Regan was established. As has already been said, Pope is well known to officers in Gosport as an astute and very unscrupulous property dealer, whose past activities make it necessary for him to employ others as a 'front' in any transaction involving persons in that area.[9]

Detective Sergeant Suter also made enquiries into Pope's background and history. According to his report of 4 February 1964, Pope:

originated from London and came to Portsmouth several years ago where he has carried on business as a street trader in Charlotte Street, Portsmouth, from a stall where he sold buttons. During the past six years he has become noticeably financially solvent and subsequently opened several businesses in this area, but he since sold them as going concerns and kept just one shop.

Pope is the man who stood surety for Walter Smith and his wife, in a substantial sum, when they were admitted to bail after being charged with receiving part of the proceeds from the Mail Train Robbery in Buckinghamshire, and has attended the Aylesbury Magistrates' Court on occasions when these persons have appeared for further remand. When the Recognisance Notice was served on Pope, he remarked that he was not a friend of Mr and Mrs Smith but that they were relations of his bookmaker friends in London. It was further learned that

Mr and Mrs Walter Smith are relatives of Daniel Patrick Regan, in as much as it was understood that Mrs Smith is his sister.

At this time, Pope also maintained that he was negotiating to purchase the Nelson Club, Nelson Road, Southsea. Pope's car has been seen outside of 32, Palmerstone Way on several occasions. Another vehicle observed was a Ford Zodiac, colour grey, registration number 483 FLB. The registered owner of this vehicle is Daniel Patrick of 590 Green Lane, Goodmayes, Essex. Regan, mainly during the evenings, and remaining there for long periods.

All the information concerning Regan then in our possession was passed to Gosport Police, and it was asked that intensive enquiries be made to establish all his connections and activities in that district. Our suspicions regarding the 'minding' of Smith and the furtive disposal of his share of the Train robbery cash was also made known.

I recommend that copies of this report be forwarded to the Chief Constable, Buckinghamshire Constabulary, for his Information, and copies of this report to forwarded to the Criminal Intelligence Department, C11, also Detective Superintendent Butler, Flying Squad, C8, New Scotland Yard, London, SW1.[10]

During March, information was obtained concerning the Nelson Club, which, it was ascertained, had been purchased on 7 December 1963 for the sum of £7,000. The purchasers were believed to be Pope and Pople. However, a local builder by the name of Williams, who carried out a number of alterations to the building, was questioned by police. He told officers that when he enquired who his invoice should be made out to, he was told that it should be Daniel Regan. Police therefore concluded that Pope and Pople were, in all likelihood, a front for Regan in terms of this purchase.

While a whole host of property purchase investigations were being carried out confidentially by the Hampshire and Isle of Wight Constabulary, with the aim of not alerting those involved, a national newspaper was about to make another investigation. They were soon involved in front page news.

Yard Men Foil New Rail Raid Plan – by Percy Hoskins

Plans of another Great Train Robbery have fallen into the hands of Scotland Yard. The target this time: a West Country express carrying £5 million to £6 million in notes. Again, everything was planned with military precision – for somebody had once more given a gang accurate information about the cargo and the train movements. Now the big question disturbing the authorities is: Who is the tip-off man in the Post Office? The information shows he is not a low-ranking official.

The Yard learned of the new plot from underworld informants three weeks ago and elaborate precautions were taken by Commander George Hatherill. The Chief Constables of every county the train passes through were called to a secret conference at the Yard. A defence scheme involving road blocks and the abandonment of county 'frontiers' for pursuit purposes was drawn up. Ever since, on the nights the train has carried valuable loads there has been a general standby at selected 'danger spots.' Although no raid has been attempted, Commander Hatherill does not believe the scheme has been abandoned, but that the thieves noting the precautions have changed the target.[11]

Hoskins immediately put his finger on the issue of inside information. It seems clear, as he concludes, that whoever the mysterious inside man was at the Post Office, he had to be a particularly high-ranking official. Most intriguing was the suggestion that some members of this gang 'were connected with the gang concerned in the Up Special TPO Robbery on 8 August, 1963'. As it turned out, the leak Hoskins had received, clearly from someone at the conference, was a very accurate reflection of what had been discussed:

Memorandum

A meeting took place this morning at Scotland Yard of Metropolitan Police and the Chief Constable on the route of the SWTPO. Mr Morgan Phillips, Chief of Police in the British railway Polices, was present and from the Post Office Messrs Wesil, Osmond, Yates (IB) and Shires (LPR) were present. The meeting was called by Commander Hatherill but in fact it was chaired by Mr Bacon Assistant Commissioner of the Metropolitan Police.

The object of the meeting was to discuss a threatened attack on the SWTPO. Commander Hatherill explained that information had been received which suggests very strongly that an attack on this TPO was being planned by criminals some of whom were connected with the gang concerned in the Up Special TPO robbery. The timing of the attack was not known but was likely to be in the early part of the year extending into spring and early summer.[12]

By the end of April, Commander Hatherill had decided that the threat level had reduced sufficiently to stand down many of the security measures on the South-West TPO route. Meanwhile, back on the property front, enquires were now being made with a view to establishing the details relating to the purchase of 91 Privett Road, Gosport, and 32 Palmerstone Way, Gosport. The suspicion reached was that Harry Smith was either living with Daniel Regan at 32 Palmerstone Way, or at another property in the Portsmouth area. When Smith gave himself up in Camberwell on 5 May 1964, as the result of Daniel Regan acting as go-between, train robbery investigation officers were sent down to Portsmouth to take part in a joint operation. According to DCS Tommy Butler:

> arrangements were made with officers of Hampshire and Isle of Wight Police to obtain Warrants to search 32 Palmerston Way and 91 Privett Road, Gosport. On the 6 May 1964, the day after Harry Smith's arrest in Camberwell, Detective Inspector Roberts and Detective Sergeant Slipper travelled to Gosport, met local officers, and thoroughly searched the two addresses.
>
> As far as is known here, Regan had no idea we knew of these two addresses. It was apparent that Regan was living permanently at 32, Palmerston Way. In a wardrobe in his bedroom was found two sheets of paper which show in some detail property transactions entered into by some person or firm. When asked to explain what the figures and addresses were intended to convey, Regan declined to answer unless his solicitor was present. Having some knowledge of the cunning type of individual Regan is, the officers asked him to sign and date the two documents, thus proving they were the ones taken possession of. After some reluctance, Regan did this, and the papers were seized. Regan was obviously annoyed that the officers had found the pieces of paper, and this fact tends to show he was hitherto unaware that we had knowledge of the address.
>
> Photostatic copies of the obverse and reverse of both papers were made and copies are attached. It will be seen there are a number of addresses upon which cash has been expended. On the reverse of the sheet a number of figures are written, together with a cryptic comment '£38,500 won't show'. The second sheet had two more addresses and a total figure of £17,350 was recorded, whilst underneath is written 'Harry in firm £56,421'.[13]

Butler concluded his report by noting that:

> It will, of course, be appreciated that the Regan brothers (some of whom are shown as shareholders in the firms already mentioned) normally handle sums of ready money in the course of daily business in their betting shops. To a certain extent, this fact affords coverage. Regan has himself informed other persons with whom he is connected or had business dealings with in Portsmouth, of his connection with the betting shops. The reason for this is not difficult to understand, bearing in mind the vast sums of money he was handling during this period.

It can, however, be said with certainty that the cash expended on all the property is the proceeds of Smith's share of the Train Robbery loot.

In DS Slipper's own report, he refers to searching 91 Palmerstone Way in Daniel Regan's presence, and in particular the bedroom: 'In the wardrobe in his bedroom, I found two sheets of paper bearing details of addresses and figures obviously appertaining to the purchase of property, etc., to the extent of £95,000.'[14]

The addresses included some thirty-two houses in all, including thirteen houses in one street – M'Tongue Avenue, Bosham, a drinking club and a hotel, in the Portsmouth and Gosport area. In addition, Slipper referenced 'the house at Barking Road in which Margaret Wade is living, and which has now been sumptuously furnished'.[15]

Butler noted, with some frustration, that, 'as far as can be established, not one identifiable note was passed, for the transactions have been conducted through various firms of solicitors and through banks'. The latter, certainly by late 1963, were very much aware of the possibility that large sums of cash would be expended in the purchase of houses and other types of property:

> One bank manager, a Mr Harris of the National Provincial Bank (one of those that was hardest hit by the robbery), High Street, Cosham, heeded the various sums being paid into account between September 1963, and February, 1964, and made enquiries of his Head Office. It will be observed that a total of £33,245 was paid in, the greater part being in £5 notes. His intuition was unquestionably correct, but on the facts presented, nothing was done.[16]

Further light was shed on the various property transactions that had taken place when, on 8 June 1964, Pople agreed to visit Portsmouth Police Headquarters for an interview. Detective Superintendent Griffiths and Detective Sergeant Robertson, who interviewed him, believed that he had only agreed to cooperate as they suspected there had recently been a rift between him and the Regans. While he declined to make any written statement, he did agree to the presence in the room of a shorthand writer who would take notes of the interview. Pople was reasonably frank with the officers, who conducted the interview with the aid of a schedule prepared from the pieces of paper found at Regan's address in Gosport.

According to Pople, he first met 'these people' in October or November 1963. He had received a telephone call from Thomas Pope, who he had met once or twice in the Dolphin Club. Apparently, Pope wanted some advice on property in Portsmouth, and asked if he could meet Pople to discuss this further.

They eventually met in a Portsmouth pub called Dilleys, in Hambrook Street. Pope told Pople that he was acting on behalf of someone in the bookmaking business, who wanted 'big stuff for flats or flatlets'. Within days, Pople had offered him '17 Kimberley Road and other properties in Britannia Road, Cottage Grove and Ivy Street'. However, word later came back from Pope that 'they said no, don't want these bits of rubbish, but they say they'd buy Kimberley Road. They're not mugs. They are shrewd business people.'

Pople told the police that, following this, Pope introduced him to Daniel Regan, who told him that 'they wanted good property, no mortgages, and they would pay cash'.

Whenever Pople found a property, he met Daniel Regan, who handed over the money in cash:

> I estimate that I paid into my bank in cash in the region of £60,000. I think I have sold them about £75,000's worth of property, and the properties I have been involved in are 14 Victoria Street, 2 Waverley Grove, the property at Cosham in the High Street, (the corner from Havant Road to the High Street), 12 or 13 houses in Bosham, M'Tongue Avenue, two next to the Police House at Bosham (near M'Tongue Avenue) – £12,500. 97 Westfield Road.[17]

Pople also spoke briefly about their parting of ways. 'I said, I don't want your money, and that was the sole reason for finishing.' He said that Regan had responded by saying, 'It has come to our knowledge that you think we are crooks … come and see our shops, M & M Regan Ltd, best shops in London – beautiful shops.'[18]

Griffiths and Suter showed Pople a photograph of Harry Smith and asked him if he had ever seen or met him. 'I am almost sure I have seen him in the Nelson Club. I don't know his name. The fellow who goes round with the girls.'[19]

When the interview was over and the shorthand notes typed up, Griffiths sent a copy to DCI Butler at Scotland Yard:

> Attached to this report is a copy of the shorthand notes taken in the room, and the officers' interpretation of certain passages, all of which have been numbered. There is no point in reiterating all the aspects covered, but some of his assertions are worthy of mention:
>
> (a) Pople's initiating move resulting in the introduction of Regan to Warland.
> (b) Pople's insistence that Regan is the only man to pay cash to him.
> (c) that Regan and his associates 'bought other land but not from me'.

(d) his description of Regan as a 'shrewd mean man' is entirely accurate.

(e) that transactions in which he has figured involve about £90,000 cash.

(f) that, since he ceased association with them, the Regan group are represented by the man Warland.

(g) that Sturgess (a solicitor) is the man behind the scenes.

Officers are certain that Pople, despite his insistence to the contrary, has a fairly good idea where the money originated. He has, he says, been threatened by Regan after the severance of their business association, and the officers feel that he fears the London man and his group.[20]

With something in the order of £100,000 of Harry Smith's share now accounted for in property dealings in the Portsmouth and Gosport area, and his role in the robbery established, C11 was content that he was the man Biggs would later call 'Bert'. So who, then, was the man Biggs referred to as 'Sid'?

X MARKS THE SPOT

Set in a rural location with stunning views of the surrounding countryside, Beaford House is approximately five miles from Torrington. The front of the house overlooks lawns and fields which slope down to the River Torridge and hundreds of acres of woodland. This large, imposing, detached country house is the ideal place for a large family or group to come and stay whilst enjoying all that North Devon has to offer, and is ideal for celebrating a special occasion. Outside, there are opportunities for fishing and shooting. There is a large, well tended garden with plenty of space and sitting out areas for all to enjoy and a play area for small children. Located just outside the village of Beaford, there is also a local pub within walking distance.

North Devon has plenty to see and do, and is home to some of the best beaches in the country including Woolacombe and Saunton. The nearest beach is at Instow and is ideal for children. The town of Great Torrington is only a short drive away and has most amenities you may require.[1]

Beaford House in Devon was indeed an ideal place to be when 'celebrating a special occasion'. It was to play a key role in the hunt for those suspected of involvement in the train robbery in the months of September and October 1963. Moreover, it was to be the focus of a fruitless two-year-long operation to find a sum of approximately £200,000 of train robbery money, which the police were convinced had been buried close to Beaford House.

The Beaford saga began as the result of one of the earliest pieces of intelligence received after the robbery, on the morning of Saturday, 10 August 1963. According to DS Cummings and DCI Walker of C11, an informant had provided information that: 'Bobby Welch (identical with Robert Alfred Welch, CRO No. 61730/58), was one of the gang responsible for the robbery. They said that Welch was missing from home and that his wife had received a message that he would be back in two or three days' time.'[2]

Welch's name therefore found itself on Tommy Butler's first list of eighteen suspects, dated Tuesday, 13 August 1963. On 26 August 1963, Commander Hatherill produced his own list of fourteen names, based on several informant sources. His list contained a number of names not on Butler's list. One of those new names was referred to in one of DCI Butler's regular investigation reports:

Information has been received to the effect that one of the men involved in the robbery was named 'DANNY'. He is thought to be identical with Dennis PEMBROKE, CRO No. 27206/1956. As a result, a warrant was obtained on the morning of 6 September, 1963, to search the home of Pembroke. Flying Squad officers, led by DCI Williams and DS Slipper, searched No. 22, Hood House, Elmington Estate, Camberwell, SE5. Nothing incriminating was found. Pembroke was brought to this office on 6 September, 1963, and closely interrogated. He strenuously denied complicity in the in the matter. Certain tests of a physical nature were made, and as these failed to confirm our suspicions, he was allowed to leave.[3]

Apart from having his finger and palm prints taken, details of the 'tests of a physical nature' referred by Butler are to be found in a report written by Dr Ian Holden, the Principal Scientific Officer at the Metropolitan Police Laboratory (C7), on 18 September 1963. In the report, Holden refers to the fact that on 16 August 1963 he visited Buckinghamshire Police Headquarters in Aylesbury, where he 'made a preliminary search of a large number of items taken from Leatherslade Farm. On 17 August, 1963, at Buckinghamshire Headquarters, Aylesbury, I removed hairs, fibres, etc. from a large number of sheets, blankets, pillows, rubber beds, clothing, etc. These hairs and fibres were retained for further examination.'[4]

Further on in the report, in a section that was initially closed until 2045, he refers to 'hairs (head and pubic)' in respect to D. Pembroke being brought to the laboratory.[5]

Butler also commented briefly on the Pembroke interview: 'Pembroke is one of those close-mouthed individuals who counteract interrogatory subtleties by monosyllabic replies. He would admit nothing that could not be proved to the hilt, and was quick to ask for the attendance of a legal representative.'[6]

This observation of Butler's is borne out by the partial record of Pembroke's interview. For reasons that are not entirely clear, only the first page of the interview appears to have survived:

Statement taken and answers to questions recorded by Thomas Butler, Detective Chief Superintendent, Flying Squad, in the presence of Chief Inspector Frank Williams. Initials and signature of Dennis Pembroke were witnessed by both officers.

– Is your name Dennis Pembroke?

–Yes.

– Would you care to tell me where you were on the night of 7/8 August, 1963, which was a Wednesday night, Thursday morning?

– I was at home.

– I have told you the district in which this offence was committed. Do you know the Cheddington district at all?

– No.

–When were you last anywhere near it?

– Never.

– Do you know Oakley or Brill, which are villages in Buckinghamshire?

– No.

– Do you know Leatherslade Farm, which is on the Thame Road, Oakley, Bucks?

– No.

– Do you know or are you acquainted with any of the persons who have been charged in connection with this matter? Mr and Mrs Pilgrim, Mr and Mrs Boal, Roger John Cordrey, Mary Manson, Charles Frederick Wilson, Roger William Pelham, and Ronald Arthur Biggs?

– I don't want to talk about that.[7]

Despite Pembroke's strenuous denials and the absence of any forensic evidence that might place him at Leatherslade Farm, Butler was convinced beyond doubt that Pembroke had been at the farm and had played a part in the assault on the train. His certainty seems to have flowed from information received, as well as telephone taps on the lines of a number of those suspected of involvement in the robbery. Just as he knew in his guts that Harry Smith had also been involved, he reasoned to himself that time and persistence would eventually lead to convictions against Pembroke and Smith.

After the Scotland Yard interview, Butler contacted the War Office for Pembroke's service file and read and re-read his C11 file for anything at all that might give him even the smallest of clues. If his suspicions were correct, Pembroke would have something in the region of £150,000 in cash stashed away somewhere. If he could directly connect him to any of the stolen money, he wagered that, at minimum, he could charge Pembroke with receiving stolen money. As would later prove to be the case, this offence alone would be deemed worthy of a fourteen-year jail sentence by the time the train robbery case reached the ultimate stage of the judicial process.

Keeping close tabs on Pembroke would therefore be vital if Butler was to stand any chance whatsoever of linking him with a substantial amount of the stolen money. While Butler was, by nature, an excessively cautious man who rarely confided anything to even the closest of colleagues until he was good and ready, there is reason to believe that he may well have had other motives for keeping the intelligence on Pembroke close to his chest. Known to regularly work long into the night well after the rest of the train robbery squad had gone off duty, Butler would often sit alone at his desk sifting through files and reports, line by line.

From the War Office file and C11 intelligence, he gradually began to build up a picture of Pembroke and his character. From his army 'Record of Service' (W5258), it was clear that this was a highly exceptional man who, according to his commanding officer, had shown courage and resilience while under enemy fire. Unlike many men of his generation who had served in the armed forces in the 1950s, Pembroke had not spent the majority of his time square bashing on a parade ground. He had not only seen active combat, but had been in the front line of one of the bloodiest and most challenging guerrilla wars that the British Army had ever fought: the so-called Malayan Emergency. This was a guerrilla war fought between the Chinese-backed Communist Malayan National Liberation Army, known as the MNLA, and British Commonwealth forces, who called the guerrillas CTs (Communist Terrorists).

After establishing a network of camps in the most inhospitable and inaccessible tropical jungle, the MNLA began a campaign of raids against police stations and military installations. Tin mines and rubber plantations were also attacked and sabotaged in an attempt to cause maximum economic as well as military damage. The irony of the conflict was that many of the MNLA fighters had been trained in guerrilla war tactics, and supplied with weapons and resources, by British military advisors during the Second World War to fight the Japanese army then occupying Malaya.

British and Commonwealth forces responded to the MNLA campaign by attempting to starve out the guerrillas and at the same time cut them off from their supporters in the general population. This involved the forced relocation of some 400,000 Malayans to newly constructed camps within the jungle called 'new villages'. The British campaign got off to a bad start with troops making little or no headway against the guerrillas. By early 1950, the guerrillas were murdering more than 100 civilians a month. By the end of the year, 504 British soldiers had also been killed. The following year, 1951, was no better. On 6 October that year the situation took a decisive turn for the worst when the MNLA assassinated the British High Commissioner, Sir Henry Gurney. Three weeks later, on 25 October, the British general election resulted in the return to office of Sir Winston Churchill. He soon got to grips with the escalation in Malaya by appointing General Gerald Templar to replace Gurney.

Templar, who was credited with a change of approach, introduced a 'hearts and minds campaign' to win over the population, and the insurgents, by giving them medical supplies and food aid. Leaflets were also dropped urging insurgents to give themselves up along with their rifle, and collect a $1,000 reward. Rewards were also given for information on CTs. This about-turn resulted in two-thirds of the guerrillas being captured, killed or recruited to fight against the MNLA, and incident rates fell from 500 a month to less than 100 per month. The British military experience in Malaya influenced many future anti-guerrilla operations around the world, most notably in Vietnam, where American forces unsuccessfully endeavoured to mirror British tactics used against the MNLA.

It was clear that since his discharge from the army, Pembroke had put his military experience and survival skills to effective use in his new career in crime. According to South London sources, he was an excessively cautious and methodical man who, unlike many loose-tongued contemporaries, never spoke about or discussed his 'work' with anyone. He treated civilian life like an ongoing military operation and knew that 'loose tongues cost lives'. His C11 file noted that he had been convicted for the first time in 1956 and that his declared occupations on civvy street were as a plumber and later as a 'general trader'. While there had never been a shred of evidence against him, C11 sources indicated that he was strongly suspected of being a key player among a gang of men who had, from the summer of 1960, pulled off a successful string of hold-ups on British Railways' Southern Region.[8] Trains were halted by a mixture of trickery and signal manipulation, and although the amounts of money stolen were not substantial, they were achieved with precision and planning and without a single arrest. Likewise, his name was also cross-referenced with an international Swiss watch smuggling operation. While a number of the men involved in the operation were eventually arrested and jailed, no evidence of Pembroke's involvement was ever established, although it was clear that at least two of the convicted men, John Murphy and Patrick O'Nions, were close associates of Pembroke. As related in Chapter 4 of this book, Pembroke was later arrested and charged with assault and criminal damage in October 1962 after a confrontation with a press photographer outside Lewes court, prior to one of the smuggling case hearings.

Within eleven days of Danny Pembroke's 6 September interview at Scotland Yard, he had left his London home, and together with fellow train robber Robert Welch and several others, had journeyed to the North Devon village of Beaford.

While Butler was immediately aware of this, it is noteworthy that while he alerted the Devon Constabulary, they were effectively cautioned to keep a watching brief only, and under no circumstances to intervene in any way, unless at Butler's specific behest. Furthermore, they were specifically instructed not to go near the Beaford House hotel, where the men were staying, for fear of alerting them to the fact that the authorities knew they were there. Neither did Butler send any Scotland Yard officers to Devon. Instead, he confidentially contacted Clifford Osmond, the director of the Post Office Investigation Branch, and to all intents and purposes mandated them to send men to North Devon to mount an around-the-clock observation operation.

We know retrospectively that Butler's number two, Detective Chief Inspector Frank Williams, expressed surprise and frustration that he and his squad were kept in the dark by Butler about Beaford, and that no Scotland Yard officers were allowed anywhere near it for some months afterwards.

From the regular reports Butler received back from Clifford Osmond regarding the IB's North Devon operation, it seems clear that he may well have feared that one of the men at Beaford had a contact in the Flying Squad, and was possibly maintaining communications with him even while in Devon. Butler's paranoia about corrupt officers at Scotland Yard compromising his investigation may well have stemmed from an incident that had occurred a few days earlier, on 12 September. It was on that day that a resident in Old Forge Crescent, Shepperton, called the police and told them that their new neighbours, Mr and Mrs Green, bore a striking resemblance to a wanted poster they had seen at the local post office of Ronald 'Buster' Edwards and his wife June. Within minutes Butler and a team of Flying Squad officers tore out of Scotland Yard and drove at full speed in the direction of Shepperton. To Butler's anger and frustration, when they burst open the front door, the house was empty and the Greens were gone. It was clear that they had left within the last thirty minutes … the teapot in the kitchen was still warm, strongly suggesting that the occupants had left in a great hurry. How else, Butler reasoned, would they have known that police were on their way to the house, unless they had been tipped off by someone at the Yard itself?

Light is shed on the Post Office IB operation in North Devon by Clifford Osmond's deputy, Richard Yates:

I was told that some of the suspects in this case were staying at an isolated farm near Beaford, Devon and that over £200,000 of the stolen money was being held there or at a bank in the area. In discussions with Chief Superintendent Butler, I undertook the task of trying to establish directly who were at Beaford, the vehicles used and habits of the suspects and I sent an IB team to Devon, together with IB radio sets. Patient and continual observation from remote points, coupled with efficient radio communications, enabled the suspects to be followed to important spots including Exeter and Barnstaple, and they were identified as:

Charles Lilley	CRO	27967/42
John Sturm	'	19274/54
Ronald Harvey	'	1196/51
Bobby Welch	'	61730/58
Danny Pembroke	'	27206/56[9]

By examining records at the local telephone exchange, the IB fixed the group's arrival at Beaford House as being approximately 17 September. From that date, regular calls were made by the suspects from telephone number Beaford 305 and a tap was placed on the line. According to the IB's log of calls, the majority were made to their home addresses back in London and to South London bookmakers, where bets were placed. However, looking at the list of calls, two in particular stand out.

In the afternoon, at 4.38 p.m., a call was placed to Whitehall 1212, lasting for two minutes and one second. Just over an hour later, at 5.58 p.m., a further call was made to the same number that lasted for six minutes and two seconds. Unlike the other calls logged in the report, no destination, name or address appears opposite Whitehall 1212. The number is, in fact, the telephone number for Scotland Yard. Why would one of the five men make two calls to the Yard shortly after arrival? According to Welch, he had fled to Devon as the result of a tip-off from a police officer that the net was closing in. Was the call placed to this officer at the Yard, or is there an alternative explanation?

Yates also reports further details about the farm:

The suspects at Beaford Farm were frequent visitors of the Globe Inn in Beaford where Messrs Boniface and Petrie are the joint landlords. It has been learnt that the suspects drank lavishly at the Globe and that the landlords were frequently embarrassed by having to change £5 Bank of England notes.[10]

Reviewing the Beaford case in a report for Commander Ernie Millen, Butler would later state:

From reports received from Devon Police and from other sources, it became evident that the five men were in no hurry to leave Beaford House, although Lilley flew from Exeter Airport to London on several occasions and returned after only a short stay in the Metropolis. They spent money in Beaford village (and doubtless elsewhere) in an extravagant manner, but the suspicions of the local residents were apparently lulled by their belief that the men were bookmakers from London visiting Devon for a quiet holiday. Nobody seemed to entertain any suspicion that they might be spending money stolen from the Mail Train at Cheddington, Buckinghamshire, a few weeks earlier, despite the widespread publicity then in existence, calling attention to anybody who appeared to have ample monetary resources, especially in five-pound denominations.[11]

On one particular evening, Wednesday, 9 October, local tongues were set wagging by the almost comical charade that was played out at the village pub, the Globe Inn, when Charles Lilley, Robert Welch and Danny Pembroke arrived for a drink. As a number of those present later told police, it was customary on the day of the Harvest Festival at Beaford Church for the gifts donated to be auctioned to raise funds for the church. The produce included traditional harvest fare such as sherry, fruit, vegetables and tinned groceries. That evening the pub was apparently packed to the rafters – it was certainly to be a night to remember. According to Walter Lake, a 40-year-old farmer, he spent the entire evening drinking at the bar without having to buy one drink himself. According to him, the three men were 'throwing their money about' from the minute they arrived. At 7.15 p.m., the big moment arrived when publican George Petrie began the auction. From the off, Pembroke, Lilley and Welch were bidding 'very high prices' for items that in previous years were lucky to go for a few shillings at tops. They did not, however, keep the articles they had won, but handed them back to Petrie for re-auction. By the end, the total proceeds had broken all previous records, and the Reverend Challen, who was in the lounge bar, was looking as pleased as Punch.

It was at this point, according to later statements, that Pembroke, Lilley and Welch approached Challen, sat down at his table, and asked him if he would like to play a game of 'Cardinal Puff' with them and raise even more money for the church. Challen, slightly taken aback, thanked them, but politely pointed out that he did not gamble and, besides, he could not afford to play. Before he could protest further, Pembroke had put a five-pound note into his hand, 'to start playing with'. Not to be outdone, Lilley wrote the vicar a cheque for two guineas (£2 2s) as a harvest dona-tion. As word spread, a small crowd gathered around the table to watch the game, as it became increasing obvious that the three men were conspiring to lose each and every hand of cards to the vicar. By the end of the game, a beaming Challen sat counting out his winnings, which amounted to a bounty of £26 7s. With the addition of Lilley's cheque for two guineas, the grand total came to £28 9s (£508.15 in today's money). The vicar's prayers for a bountiful harvest had indeed been answered. Ironically, when later questioned by police, Challen confessed that 'he had given the matter a good deal of thought, and had decided that the men were not honest'. However, to the surprise of the police, he had decided that 'the church should keep the money'.[12]

In mid-October 1963, they began to leave Beaford House separately, Lilley and Welch being the last to leave on 20 October 1963. Lilley apparently paid the bill for all the guests, in five-pound notes.

Unsure as to when and whether any of the men might return, Butler waited a further two months before finally requesting, on 21 January 1964, that the Devon Constabulary 'discreetly approach the owners of Beaford House' and 'question them about their guests'. He promptly received a report from Superintendent Bond of the Okehampton Division. As a result:

It was quickly discovered that our fears concerning the owners of Beaford House were entirely without foundation. They proved most helpful and are still doing all in their power to assist this enquiry, having retained a very close liaison with the local detective officer. The owners are Mr and Mrs Wickett, who when seen, readily offered every assistance to the police, who took the opportunity to thoroughly search that part of the house, including the cellars. In a written statement, Mrs Wickett explained how she was introduced to Charles Lilley by the licensee of a Public House known as 'The Fellowshp Inn', Randlesdown Road, Catford, SE6, quite near Lilley's home address. In June 1962, the Wicketts moved to Beaford House, which they converted into a guest house. In July of that year, Lilley stayed there with his family and another family for a fortnight. Another visit to Beaford House was made by some of Lilley's family and friends in May, 1963. On 15 September, 1963, Charles Lilley telephoned the house and asked if he and four male friends could visit the house for a few days. Lilley and the men mentioned arrived two days later.

Mrs Wickett gained the impression that Lilley was a textile merchant, and she mentions his frequent flights to London, allegedly in connection with his business. The others also left the house for days on end, but always returned. Instead of staying for 'a few days', the men remained at Beaford House until late October, Lilley and Welch being the last to leave.[13]

It is notable that when Robert Welch arrived back in London by train on 25 October 1963, the police were fully aware of the train he was on and were waiting for him at the station. A report by Chief Inspector Frank Williams is very clear that:

We heard from an informant that Welch was to travel to London to meet his brother. I briefed my team and we set ourselves up, out of sight. I saw Welch come out of the station, meet his brother and they both walked towards a waiting car. We had a team of five men in the area, two waiting in nondescript cars and others strolling casually in the street. As Welch opened the door of the car, we pounced. He stood absolutely still with a look of blank astonishment on his face. He was dumbfounded and had difficulty in speaking when I told him who I was.[14]

Welch had every good reason to be astonished. How on earth had the police known he was due to arrive at 8.45 p.m.? Who could possibly have told them? This again adds weight to the view that there was a two-way line of communication through an unknown person in Devon and an officer at Scotland Yard. Thanks to the IB's telephone tapping reports, we know for a fact that someone at Beaford House had made calls to Scotland Yard shortly after arriving there on 18 September. We also know from Butler's reports about the communications he was receiving from the POIB, that, 'Whilst staying at Beaford House, the men spent a lot of their time fishing in the River Torridge nearby, or in the extensive woodlands, allegedly shooting pigeons. Whilst they were in the woods, firing was certainly heard, but there is no record of successful marksmanship.'[15]

Two months later, Butler reported that:

On the 30 January, 1964, Pembroke, Harvey, and Sturm arrived at Beaford House and stayed there until the 17 February, 1964. There was a great deal of movement, but by the 17 instant all had departed. On the 23 February, 1964, Sturm and Harvey returned to the house, leaving again on the 27 February. On that occasion Mrs Wickett received payment from Harvey. Amongst the notes he handed to her were twenty £5 notes, the numbers of which were duly supplied to Police. One note is within 129 of one of the stolen notes, and unquestionably came from one of the series stolen.[16]

Butler referred to a further visit to Beaford four months later:

On Friday 19 June, 1964, between 6 p.m. and 7.00 p.m., Pembroke and Sturm again visited Beaford House, arriving in an Estate Cortina, Index No. 173 HLX. Pembroke's wife Margaret and three children (twin girls age 7 and a boy aged 4), and Sturm's wife and two children arrived by train on Saturday 30 June, and were met at the station by their husbands. They stayed until the 27 June, 1964. On this occasion Sturm settled the bill and paid Mrs Wickett £70 in £1 notes, all of which she describes 'mouldy', indicating storage somewhere in a damp place.[17]

Finally, on 4 June 1965:

Lilley, Pembroke and four other men whose identities are not yet established, arrived at Beaford House, having made arrangements to do so earlier. They remained for one week, departing on the 11 June, 1965. Mrs Wickett was paid a total of £125 in £5 notes, but these prove of no assistance, none of the serial numbers being near those of the stolen notes. As on their previous visit, one man stayed in the house whilst others went into the woods nearby with shotguns. Although one of the men was somewhat despondent on arrival at the house, he perceptibly brightened in his attitude after a visit to the woods. One is forced to the conclusion that the men have a cache of stolen money somewhere in the woods.

Devon Constabulary reports seem to share this view, although Superintendent Bond of the Okehampton Division despondently noted that:

We are doing all humanly possible to locate it. The task is rendered well-nigh impossible by virtue of the size and character of the terrain and the fact that there is no mechanical or chemical device known to science capable of indicating the spot in which paper, wrapped in leathercloth, plastic material, rubberized cloth or cellophane, is buried under soil.[19]

Butler also tells us that:

Efforts made to locate the hiding place with a Police dog also proved unsuccessful. Continuous observation was put on the woods while the men were there. The latter is a particularly difficult enterprise, for the house commands an extensive view of the woods. This may be one of the main reasons for one man always remaining in the house. With a pair of binoculars, he could, from an upstairs window, see strange persons in the vicinity of the woods, warn his confederates. Each time any of the men visit the house, a prearranged plan is put into operation. Despite the lapse of time and the obviously diminishing store of stolen money, it still offers one of the most promising possibilities of effecting the arrest of Lilley and Pembroke. Both men have interests in a betting shop or shops. A few hundred pounds traced to their possession would be easily explained away to the satisfaction of any Court, irrespective of what Police might think about it. It is for this, as well as other reasons, that no further interrogations of these men have taken place. To secure their conviction we must have iron-clad evidence of the kind of which the most sympathetic jury must take note.[20]

No evidence, iron-clad or otherwise, was ever to come Butler's way. While Charles Lilley would stay on Butler's radar for two more years in the hope of nailing him for money laundering, Danny Pembroke was to miraculously disappear shortly after his last visit to Beaford in 1965. Where had he gone? It would be a long time before Butler had even the smallest of clues.

A SOUND INVESTMENT

DURING THE SPRING AND early summer of 1964, the political landscape was changing fast. At the turn of the year, the opinion polls were forecasting a landslide victory for Labour. When Prime Minister Harold Macmillan had resigned the previous October, the Conservative Party had been flat on its back after a string of scandals. To cap it all, the man chosen to succeed him as Prime Minister, Sir Alec Douglas-Home, was immediately lampooned by the TV satirists and the clever set, who said that the 58-year-old outsider was an aristocratic caricature and a man out of touch with the mid-twentieth century, not to mention the ordinary working-class voter. However, as the months passed by, Home seemed to be winning over the voters with his straightforward, no-nonsense personality. What was more, the economic tide was beginning to turn too. Unemployment was dropping steadily, and a consumer boom was starting to take hold.

For the entrepreneur, everywhere you looked investment opportunities seemed to beckon. At the Peckford Scrap Metal Company at 50 New Church Road, Camberwell, SE5, business was booming to such an extent that the managing director, one Charlie Richardson, was looking to diversify and turn his hand to new opportunities. The scrap metal business he had started in 1951 with a bounced cheque had ridden the crest of the 1950s construction boom. Admittedly, he had deployed a number of equally profitable sidelines over the years, particularly in the consumer retail trade. Those in the know were calling it 'long-firming'. The forces of law and order were calling it fraud. Essentially, in Richardson's own words, it worked this way:

> You gathered large quantities of goods from manufacturers and importers or even other wholesalers and you sold them for less than the purchase price you negotiated with the supplier. So if you negotiated a thousand radios at £10 apiece in street markets and shops, the profit was £7 apiece because you did not pay the supplier. I liked the audacious simplicity of it. The key to the formula was getting the suppliers to believe you were going to pay in order to part with the goods. That was easy as I soon learned that people believe what they want to believe and any supplier of goods wants to believe they have found a new lucrative outlet for their goods. So, you start off by ordering a fairly small amount of goods and paying cash on the button. These are then sold to retailers for the wholesale price

and everybody is happy. This goes on for a few months and they suggest you open an account to be invoiced each month or whatever. If they don't suggest it then you do, and in any case, references are taken up. You've got a few thousand in your bank account for the company and the referees you give them are other companies you own that have nothing more to their name than headed note-paper. The references come in, you get your account and for a few months you are the best customer they've ever had, always paying within a day of receiving an invoice. Of course, he is not the only supplier you are buying from with this bogus company; you have a whole string of happy suppliers. Then one day you run around them all with a good excuse for a really big order. By then you're on first name terms and they are dying to help you. They pull all the stops out to meet your order, excited by their good fortune. It is several weeks before they wonder where their money is. It might be several months before they start chasing you for the cheque and even longer before they realize they are never going to get paid. They run round to your premises to find an empty flea pit which had been rented under a false name. In the meantime, you have flooded the market with their goods at less than wholesale and lots of ordinary innocent punters go home delighted at the bargain price they have paid for a radio or toaster. It's sort of Robin Hood; the rich get robbed.[1]

For some time, the government had been telling British industry that the key to future prosperity lay in finding new markets abroad. Charlie Richardson had found just the place – South Africa. He had not long met a small-time screenplay writer named Richard Aubrey (*Dicky, Old Mac, One Eyed Soldiers*), who had recently returned from a trip to Namaqualand. This barren and arid region of the Northern Cape stretches from the Atlantic Ocean on the west coast to Pofadder in the east, and to the Orange River in the north. According to Aubrey, it was the promised land. According to Richardson, Aubrey told him: 'It's not like over here, miners working a mile underground risking their lives for coal. You walk along and pick up opals off the ground. Charlie, they're sitting on the biggest pot of gold in the world. It's the end of the rainbow.'[2]

Aubrey had mentioned a man by the name of Thomas Waldeck, who already had some concession rights there. As a result, Richardson began doing some homework on South African mineral rights and then looked around for a firm of lawyers who specialised in South African law, and had some representation out there. He quickly found such a firm in Victoria Street, SW1. They examined the information Aubrey had given him and undertook to have it checked with their office in South Africa. Within a week they reported back that Waldeck had been granted mineral concessions in Namaqualand by the South African Mining Commission on 9 August 1963. The reference numbers to the concessions were 5659 to 5773. Waldeck had apparently formed a joint venture operation on 5 September 1963 with three other men to exploit the prospecting rights, which covered a multiplicity of semi-precious and base minerals.

On the strength of this highly encouraging news, Charlie Richardson then made contact with Waldeck and arranged to fly over to South Africa to meet him. On 24 August 1964, he flew out to Johannesburg from London Airport by BOAC, accompanied by Jean Goodman, Richard Aubrey, Ken Nicholson and his brother Eddie Richardson. According to the police investigation file on Waldeck, he was a very well-connected businessman who was also a member of The Broederbond, or 'Band of Brothers',[3] which was a politically powerful and highly influential South African secret society. According to a report in the file, Waldeck had 'acquired extensive mineral rights in Namaqualand, as a result of his close friendship with an unnamed official, also a Broederbond member, working in the South African Mining Commission'.[4]

Furthermore, and somewhat more intriguing, was the fact that the area within Namaqualand in which the concessions existed had been closed to prospecting since 1928. In order to obtain the concession through the unnamed South African Mining Commission official, Waldeck had agreed to pay the official a percentage, ranging between 20 and 30 per cent, of any future profits he might make from the development rights.

While on the August 1964 trip to South Africa, Richard Aubrey introduced Richardson to a journalist he knew, who worked on the South African *Sunday Express* newspaper – a man by the name of Gordon Winter. As Richardson would only later discover, Winter was an agent of the South African counter-intelligence agency call Republican Intelligence. This had been set up after South Africa left the Commonwealth in 1961, and could therefore no longer officially depend on the assistance of MI5 in matters of counter-intelligence. At the behest of the South African government, the RI was therefore founded by Hendrik van den Bergh, and was closely modelled on MI5, with whom it was to maintain some unofficial lines of communication. In 1969, RI became BOSS, the Bureau of State Security.

Aubrey had disclosed to Winter that he was accompanying Richardson on his visit to South Africa, and that he hoped that a deal could be brokered whereby Richardson might provide much-needed capital to the under-funded Waldeck. Winter was keen to meet Richardson, and Aubrey therefore arranged for them to meet, which they did:

on the afternoon of 26 August, at the Ambassador Hotel, in Pretoria Street, Hillbrow. Three days later, Charles Richardson met with Thomas Waldeck, who explained that he and three partners had set up a company, Concordia Developments (Propriety) Ltd, to exploit the concessions. However, there had been some discord of late between the partners, due to the inability to raise sufficient capital for the venture.[5]

The net result of the meeting between Richardson and Waldeck was an undertaking on Waldeck's part to provide further documentation about the concessions and Concordia Developments. Not long after the first meeting with Waldeck, Gordon Winter invited the Richardson party to his home for tea. It was here that he introduced his wife, Jean La Grange, to Charlie Richardson. Unlike Winter, who was British born, La Grange was an Afrikaner. Her father was a prominent member of the ruling National Party and a personal friend of the Minister of Justice, John Vorster. Vorster would, in 1966, become Prime Minister of South Africa, following the assassination of Hendrik Verwoerd by Dimitri Tsafendas, a Greek Communist. She too was involved in RI and worked through the same RI handler as her husband, Jack Kemp.

Gordon Winter's usefulness to RI was in the fact that to the outside world he was a journalist who, by South African standards, was on the liberal end of the political spectrum. The paper he worked for, the *Sunday Express*, was likewise seen as a liberal paper. This gave him unfettered access to a host of individuals seen as being hostile to the National Party's apartheid regime. While showing Richardson around during his brief stay, Winter took him to the shantytown of Soweto and introduced him to Winnie Mandela, wife of the recently imprisoned Nelson Mandela. He introduced him as a fellow journalist from England, and the two chatted politely about her husband's recent trial.

Another brief contact, introduced by Richard Aubrey, was a man, unnamed in the records, who apparently sought Richardson's involvement in a planned diamond smuggling operation. He proposed concealing the diamonds in fish before they were frozen for export. He asked Richardson if he could assist with fishing vessels that could take the frozen fish to the UK. Richardson agreed to follow this up on his return to London.

At the end of that week, the Richardson party, with the exception of Kenneth Nicholson, flew back to London. Shortly after his return to London, Richardson received a telephone call from Waldeck.

To sweeten a potential deal with Richardson, Waldeck informed him that in addition to the concessions they had discussed at their earlier meeting, he also had the rights to prospect a 48,000-acre parcel of land in Meir, on the border of the Kalahari Desert and Bechuanaland. This concession included the right to prospect for diamonds. As a result, the pair were soon agreed on a partnership deal whereby Waldeck's current partners would bow out, leaving Waldeck and Richardson each with 50 per cent of the shares in Concordia. The initial terms of the agreement would be as follows: Richardson would make an initial down payment of £10,000 and pay a further £10,000 on completion of the agreement; Richardson would finance all exploration operations undertaken by Concordia, and provide all the necessary equipment and machinery; Richardson would receive a 50 per cent ownership in the mineral rights currently owned by Waldeck, and was guaranteed the right to 50 per cent of any further rights Waldeck acquired within the period of the agreement between them; all profits arising from their joint venture would be split 50/50 between themselves; the agreement between them would last for five years, expiring on 1 January 1970.

It would seem that some of the new investment was to be used to pay off the mining commission official who had paved the way for the concession in the first place. As a result of the agreement, a new company, Concordia Developments (Namaqualand) Ltd, was set up in place of Concordia Developments (Propriety) Ltd. The agreement and relevant paperwork flowing from the new partnership agreement with Waldeck was dealt with by Richardson's South Africa legal representatives, Cliffe Dekker and Todd, of 94 Main Street, Johannesburg, who had been recommended to him by a Bedford business associate, Major Herbert Nicholson.

During the discussions prior to the signing of the agreement, Richardson had talked loosely with Waldeck about a sum of £100,000 being available to finance the project. However, the records suggest that at this time, nothing like that sum of money was at Richardson's disposal.

On 24 October 1964, Kenneth Nicholson, who had remained in South Africa, sent a telegram to Charlie Richardson in which he confirmed 'Reward Served' in reference to the mining official's pay-off. A letter dated 26 October 1964, name redacted, from a shipbuilder in Milford Haven who had two trawlers for sale, could well be to do with the diamond smuggling proposal that had been made back in August. However, there is no indication in the files that this scheme led anywhere other than interim enquiries among a few UK trawler firms.

The big question now, however, was having secured a partnership deal with Waldeck, on the basis that something in the region of £100,000 was available for the investment, where actually was the £100,000 to be sourced? The records indicate that several different possibilities were explored simultaneously. For example, on 10 October 1964, Richardson had made an application for a £50,000 loan from the Iranian Bank of Saderat, via the head office in London's Fenchurch Street. In the letter of application, Richardson set out his proposals for:

> the development of the whole area of the Coloured Areas in South Africa, in respect of minerals and rare earths. As I have intimated, I have complete faith and confidence in the project supported as it is by the South African government, the White Paper being deposited and perused by you, including further documents, and agreements that are confirmed by Attorneys of the Supreme Court of South Africa, covering both South African and British law.[6]

While waiting for a decision from the bank, he set about organising a new company, the Anglo–American Engineering Corporation Ltd, to deal with overseeing the heavy plant and machinery that needed to be exported to South Africa. Originally registered at Peckford Scrap Metal Company, at 50 New Church Road, the directors were: Sir Noel Dryden,[7] Ken Nicholson and Michael Leaworthy. The company soon moved its operations to 231 Rotherhithe Road, Bermondsey, which had the benefit of larger yards and bigger office space. The yards under the railway arches came in particularly useful for concealing the company's ever-growing collection of plant, mainly stolen from building sites and motorway construction sites. John Bradbury, who had been one of Richardson's most successful long-firm operators, was brought in to service and repair the machinery. His Bradbury Trading Company, a dealer in 'bankrupt stock', had also been registered at 50 New Church Road, until it disappeared off the face of the earth in the summer of 1964.

When the Saderat Bank eventually responded to the loan application, it was a no. This meant that an alternative source of funding was needed, and quickly. The answer was to be found a lot closer to home than a Middle Eastern bank. The Richardsons knew personally a number of those who had been involved in the train robbery, such as Ronald 'Buster' Edwards, Tommy Wisbey, Danny Pembroke, Jimmy Hussey, Bob Welch and Harry Smith. With Buster Edwards on the run, and Wisbey, Hussey and Welch in prison, Charlie Richardson set about negotiating an investment opportunity with those still at large and those representing the interests of some of the others, such as Charles Lilley. C11 were soon to hear whisperings about the 'opportunity of a lifetime'.

According to information received, Pembroke had invested something in the region of £25,000, and Wisbey a similar sum. With the contributions put in by several others, who had also bought a slice of the pie, the total investment was speculated to be around £100,000. The sums invested would, according to the agreement reached, be repaid with interest once the mining venture was up and running and making a profit. With the money now secured at last to make a start, Richardson sent John Bradbury to South Africa on 4 November 1964 to assist Ken Nicholson with the heavy plant and the exploration preparations.

Shortly after Bradbury arrived in South Africa, another familiar face from the not too distant past resurfaced – Buster Edwards's old friend, Jimmy Collins. According to C11, Collins had been an established member not only of Edwards's own firm, who had run into trouble during the Westminster Bank raid at the Corn Exchange, Mark Lane, EC3, on 18 July 1962,[8] but had initially been a member of the team put together for the BOAC wages snatch at Comet House, London Airport, in November 1962. However, if C11 sources are to be believed, Collins was voted out by the team for 'losing his bottle' and failing to turn up. Despite this, it would seem that he and Edwards remained on good terms.

While Collins's name was included on a train robbery suspects list compiled by Commander George Hatherill on 26 August 1963, it is clear that he was not considered a serious candidate, for his name is not mentioned again in the investigation files following that date.[9]

Collins was sent out to South Africa in November 1964 to run and be responsible for the perlite mining operations at Mkuse, a small town in Northern KwaZulu-Natal, overlooked by Ghost Mountain, some 350km from Durban. It is open to speculation whether his appearance, and the responsibility he was given, was purely down to Charlie Richardson considering him the best man for the job, or whether Collins's presence was a result of, or a condition of, a hypothetical Edwards investment in Richardson's scheme. John Bradbury's spell working for Charlie Richardson in South Africa was not to last long. Shortly before Christmas 1964, Thomas Waldeck's wife confessed to him that she had been having an affair with Bradbury. An enraged Waldeck not only threatened Bradbury, but contacted Richardson to demand that he be sacked. This Richardson did. Besides, Jimmy Collins seemed so much more reliable and much less prone to being distracted from the job in hand. His communication skills, however, Richardson found a little lacking:

1 March, 1965

Hello Chas,

This is at the hurry up because we are 20 miles from the nearest post box. I am at the perlite mine getting the perlite ready for Germany and Hungary. We hired 10 boys. They cost four shillings a day and their food which is nothing. You just buy a sack of meal. It's just like oats and a sack of sugar and that's all that they get, except on a Saturday they get a TOO POUND TIN OF JAM. THIS IS THE TRUTH.

Chas, you wouldn't believe it you have got to see this place to believe it. THE German KID and ME are here in the Mkuse. Its so big you carnt realise it. There is perlite all over the place and all kinds of coloured stone's some of them opals, I am running around like a lunatic with A PICK & SHOVEL DIGGING FOR DIAMONDS. HONEST. DON'T FORGET TO COME. THERE IS A HOTEL WITH A SWIMMING POOL 25 MILES away you could STAY THERE … I AM WALKING AROUND LIKE Buffalo Bill, I HAVE A SHOOTER A RIFEL A KNIFE TALK ABOUT BILLY THE KID. HE'S GOT NOTHING ON ME
Jimmy[10]

Three days later Collins was penning another one of his punctuation-free letters, peppered liberally with words and occasionally whole sentences written in capital letters:

Hello Chas,

JUST A LINE hoping everything is OK. NOT much to say. they have found more perlite than you can dig up in a life time. They havent sent the samples to Germany or Hungary yet. you know about about the opals and diamonds. I will be there to morrow when I will Be able to Tell you more more. CHAS, TW Waldeck is a NICE chap. But I don't think he has too much of an idea. Honest, he lives in a different world from us, ITS hard to explain, if you was here just for a couple of days you no what you want done and you go all out to do IT. But they seem to waite for everything to come to them, or you carnt do it that way in SA. There is nothing wrong in its just that they move slow nobody can do anything but Tom. he is the only one who no's anyone. So just come over for a couple of days don't stay LONG. Then you can get things going. or send someone who will be able to do so. Herbert held a board meeting YESTERDAY. I don't know too much about IT. ONLY that Herbert TRIED TO get things cracking. I couldnt be there Because I am NOT A MEMBER OF THE BOARD. I am going with Herbert, Brian to Toms tonight to a BARBACUE.
Jimmy[11]

While having no formal role in his brother's operations in South Africa, Eddie Richardson did undertake a number of visits to South Africa on his brother's behalf during the period 1964–66. However, his trip there in the summer of 1965 had nothing to do with mineral prospecting.

After his major success producing and starring in the 1963 hit movie *Zulu*, actor Stanley Baker was contracted to do a second South Africa-shot film, *Sands of*

Kalahari, starring Susannah York and Michael Davenport in the spring and summer of 1965. A Boeing 707 was chartered to fly over the crew, technicians and equipment, and Baker invited Eddie Richardson and his friend Harry Rawlings to come over with them.

Eddie Richardson had known Baker socially for a number of years. In 1964, Baker was involved in organising a football match between a team put up by Richardson and a Fleet Street Sports Writers' team. Richardson's team lined up as follows: Danny Pembroke in goal, Billy Rawlings, Reg Saunders, George Wisbey, Albert Dimes, Frank Fraser, Bert McCarthy, Eddie Richardson, Peter Warner, Ron Jeffries and Ronnie Oliver. Baker had, for some years, rubbed shoulders with members of the criminal fraternity, and was quite open about the fact that: 'I admit that I'm fascinated with men who live outside the law – men who rebel against the social structure, who take such terrible risks with the lives of themselves and their families.'[12]

Information in the hands of C11 led to speculation that other names of interest had possibly gone out to South Africa with or to visit Baker on the *Kalahari* set. Danny Pembroke, who had not been seen in his usual haunts for some time, was a speculated name. Several months later, Detective Chief Superintendent Tommy Butler went on record in an investigation report, expressing the view that Ronald Biggs, and one of the men who escaped from Wandsworth with him, Eric Flower, were together in South Africa.[13] This, of course, later proved not to be the case, but South Africa at this time was certainly welcoming a good number of faces that were of interest to the Yard.

It was also during this period that Charlie Richardson was in communication with an American company who had approached him. They were keen to either buy into his South African venture or purchase the shareholdings of himself and Thomas Waldeck. Waldeck and Richardson had therefore flown out to Miami to meet one of the directors. Talks seemed to be making good progress and they flew to Nassau for further meetings with others involved. Interestingly, the American authorities, who kept a strict eye on visitors of interest, noted that another Englishman, already resident in the Miami area, was present at the Miami meeting – a man by the name of Danny Gavin. Sometime later, when Scotland Yard began a 'belt and braces' investigation into the Richardsons, speculation was entered into as to who, in reality, Danny Gavin was. By this time, the Americans had lost trace of him and the view was that Danny Gavin, in all probability, was an alias. C11 believed there were reasonable grounds for thinking that Danny Pembroke and Danny Gavin might be one and the same.[14]

Following the Miami/Nassau meetings, further talks took place over the next month or two, which resulted in an offer of £1 million from the Americans.

This offer was rejected by Richardson and Waldeck, who were of the view that more money could eventually be made by staying in than by selling up.

They were also pursuing further capital investment from the Pretoria Portland Cement Company, one of the biggest mining concerns in South Africa. A meeting had taken place with the PPCC Managing Director, who was presented with a detailed plan of their exploration proposals. They offered the PPCC a 49 per cent share of the perlite at Mkuse for 1 million Rand (£500,000). PPCC expressed strong interest and proposed to send their own geologist to the site in order to further discussions.

Just as Richardson's operation was potentially on the cusp of success, news came in on 30 June 1965 that would eventually scupper his well-laid South African plans, and ultimately lead to his arrest and imprisonment in the UK. On the front page of the *Rand Daily Mail*, and in the Johannesburg morning papers, were headline stories about the murder the previous evening of Thomas Waldeck by an unknown assassin.

According to the investigation report into Waldeck's murder, he was:

at his home in Melrose, Johannesburg, eating dinner with his wife Corris and their two sons. The dinner was interrupted by a continuous ring on the front door bell. Waldeck rose from the table, put on the entrance hall light and half opened the front door. He was there confronted by a man in a kneeling position, wearing a black nylon stocking over his face, proceeded to fire four shots at close range, before rising to his feet and running away.[15]

For some months the South African police were baffled by the case. There were no apparent leads, no eyewitness accounts, and no forensic evidence of any kind. It soon emerged that Waldeck's life was insured for a substantial sum. The insurance company, far from happy with the police investigation, had appointed a private investigator, Gideon van Gass, to undertake an independent probe. It was he who eventually unearthed the fact that Corris Waldeck had been having an affair with John Bradbury, Richardson's former associate. It was not long before the Johannesburg CID issued warrants for the arrest of Bradbury and a man by the name of Harry Prince. Bradbury was arrested on 4 January 1966, but Prince disappeared and as a consequence was not to stand trial. Bradbury therefore stood trial alone for the murder of Waldeck, arguing that it was Harry Prince who was the assassin.[16]

While the truth will never be known for sure, the judge found Bradbury guilty of murder on the basis that even if Prince was the gunman, Bradbury was a willing accessory and aided the assassin's escape from the scene of the crime. Bradbury was sentenced to death for the murder, but managed to escape the hangman by getting his lawyers to contact Scotland Yard in London. As a result, two detectives flew over to Johannesburg. By the time they arrived, Bradbury had already put together an extensive and detailed resume of handwritten notes on the Richardsons and their activities in the UK. This he was willing to impart to Scotland Yard, in exchange for their assistance in having his death sentence commuted. After a series of interviews, a thirty-eight-page statement by Bradbury was drawn up, signed and taken back to London. Bradbury's death sentence was eventually commuted to life imprisonment. He was finally released on parole after only eleven years, in October 1977.

At 10.30 a.m. on 30 June, Charlie Richardson had received a telegram from Corris Waldeck, informing him of her husband's murder. He had immediately replied: 'Dear Corris, Deeply shocked and sorry to hear tragic news. Making arrangements to fly out to you first available flight. Our heartfelt sympathy to you and your family. Chas, Jean and family.'

In fact, he was unable to fly out immediately and instead sent his father and brother Eddie. On 2 July, he wrote to his South African lawyers Cliffe Dekker & Todd:

Dear Mr Borgwardt
By now you have heard the tragic news concerning the death of Waldeck. My wife and I are stunned by this terrible news, it seems unbelievable. By next week I shall be in Johannesburg with the Hungarian people. In my absence, my father Mr C.F. Richardson, my brother Mr E. Richardson together with Mr Collins and Mr Kruger are in Johannesburg and will be in contact with you.
The good work you have maintained all along I know will be continued by your good self.
Chas. Richardson[18]

On 9 August, he appointed former airline executive Victor Doel to sort out the multiplicity of legal and business problems created by Waldeck's death. This he managed to do in double-quick time. As a result, an agreement between Richardson and Corris Waldeck, for the entirety of her late husband's shares, was signed on 23 September 1965. For £50,000, to be paid in stages, he purchased all the various interests he had shared with Waldeck before his death. As a result of the deal, he received all the rights to the perlite that Waldeck had acquired on 11 February 1965.

Now, as the exclusive owner of the perlite rights in Mkuse, he hoped to sell a 50 per cent share to Pretoria Portland Cement Company. This money would then be used for the development of the mine.

During October 1965, Victor Doel had been negotiating with the company, and as a result they had sent drilling teams down to the mine. Although they were making only slow progress, they seemed to be increasingly interested.

According to the files, Pretoria Portland Cement were not only drilling at the mine, they were drilling into the back history of Charlie Richardson, and were more than a little concerned at what they found. On 18 February 1966, they sent him a letter in which they set out the conclusions of their assessment of the Mkuse mine.[19]

In their view, the perlite occurred only spasmodically in the seams that had been examined, and its recovery would prove costly. The reserves approached only a fraction of the claimed 26,000,000 tons. They also doubted that the perlite could command anything like the price Richardson and Doel had claimed. Furthermore, there was no reliable information in their proposal about demand for perlite, and little chance of recovering the outlay:

> Our assessment of the whole proposed venture is that neither the exploitation of crude perlite nor the production of an expanded perlite from pilot plant stage to full commercial production is an economic proposition. We record that we shall not negotiate further and that we now withdraw completely from the proposed venture.[20]

Just when it seemed like things couldn't get any worse for Charlie Richardson, they did. In the early hours of the morning of 30 July 1966, as the England football team were preparing to meet West Germany that afternoon at Wembley in the World Cup Final, police arrested him at his home.

It was around this time that actor/producer Stanley Baker began putting together plans for a new movie based on the story of the Great Train Robbery. Having secured the backing of American movie mogul Joseph E. Levine, who would be the executive producer, a deal was done through Paramount Pictures for Oakhurst Productions Ltd[21] to produce the project, with Peter Yates hired to direct the film.

On 1 February 1967, a budget of £357,143 (£6,367,859 in today's money) was given approval.[22] Oakhurst Productions also took steps to avoid potential legal problems that had hampered previous efforts by consulting two QCs and three American lawyers for advice.[23] It is believed that Oakhurst also liaised with the lawyers of the convicted robbers in order to avoid any potential legal issues, and equally to seek their input in terms of the film's authenticity. The producers were careful to ensure that all the robbers in the film were given fictionalised names and personalities. They were also fortunate to be able to film the Scotland Yard scenes in the recently vacated Norman Shaw building, and base the railway location filming near Market Harborough, on a recently closed railway line. While Oakhurst had bought the rights to Peta Fordham's book *The Train Robbers*, Stanley Baker used his connections with members of the South London criminal fraternity to contribute to the authenticity of the story.

Gerald Wilson, who wrote the screenplay, recalls that:

> Peta Fordham had written a book based on the robbery. Her agent was Jonathan Clues, anyway, Jonathan was my agent and they interviewed me and gave me the commission to write the screenplay. I interviewed some of the people involved who had not already been arrested.
>
> I set about to write the script, largely using her book as the basic material, plus things that I had been told and information I had been given. [24]

One of the key people Wilson was introduced to by Stanley Baker was Danny Pembroke, whom he had associations with through the Soho Rangers football team referred to earlier in this chapter. While not confirmed, it is believed that Harry Smith was also introduced to Gerald Wilson.

As a result of the first-hand input, the movie, particularly the robbery scenes, was considered to be particularly authentic. For many members of the public, it was also the first time they were aware of the gang bringing with them their own driver, although he failed to move the train. The movie also provided the opportunity for a number of Baker's associates to avail themselves of stunt work, particularly on location at Market Harborough. Again, Danny Pembroke was one of those who participated.

Some months after the release of the film *Robbery*, C11 heard that Danny Pembroke, now a 'Turf Accountants General Manager', living in Bromley, had an interest in Pyes Farm, in Crowhurst, Sussex, through a newly created company called Farmgate Investments Ltd. Little was to be learnt about Farmgate, whose registered office was at 70 Finsbury Pavement, London EC2. Nothing more was noted until 1970, when Pembroke made a number of planning applications in respect to a parcel of land on the Pyes Farm property. [25] By this time, of course, C11 had no real interest in Pembroke, but were perennially keeping an eye open in terms of information such as this. In 1971, Farmgate were eventually to sell parcels of the property. A local Sussex newspaper article, from the *Argus*, was also added to the file when the comedian Ronnie Corbett later bought Pyes Farm. Farmgate Investments Ltd was, according to the file, wound up shortly afterwards. Interestingly, when Corbett wrote his autobiography in 2000, he recalled working at Winston's Club in the late 1950s, early 1960s:

I used to enjoy socializing in the room after the show and got to know quite a lot of villains, who I thought were rather attractive in a Runyonesque sort of way ... I knew some of the Great Train Robbers before they robbed the train. I used to see Bruce Reynolds in the club ...[26]

Corbett also frequented the Star Tavern in Belgravia, where a similar clientele of 'actors, villains, bohemians and burglars went to drink',[27] as well as being a regular at Freddie Foreman's betting shop in Nunhead Lane.[28]

Whatever else was landing in Danny Pembroke's file from time to time, there was absolutely nothing to suggest that he was doing anything other than leading a hard-working, enterprising life; to all intents and purposes his criminal activities were now a thing of the past. How, though, were C11's other persons of interest faring?

THERE FOR THE TAKING

Tuesday, 20 July 1971

PORTSMOUTH HARBOUR RAILWAY STATION sat on a vast wooden pier, situated between Gunwharf Quays and the city's historic naval dockyard. Six days a week, Monday to Saturday, a passenger ferry from Ryde, Isle of Wight, docked at the Harbour Station. In addition to the passengers and other cargo, it carried a locked and sealed post canister containing sacks of high-value packets of cash and other valuables. On arrival at Portsmouth, the red security canister was unloaded onto a secure platform, unlocked by waiting security postmen, and the HVP sacks loaded into a Post Office mail van. The van was then driven to Portsmouth head post office, where the sacks were stored. Later in the day they were taken to Portsmouth and Southsea Railway Station and put onto a Post Office control train to Southampton via Eastleigh. From there they joined the South Western Travelling Post Office train from Southampton to Waterloo.

Like the Glasgow–Euston TPO that was robbed on 8 August 1963, the South Western TPO took on further HVP sacks at each additional stop between Portsmouth and Waterloo, often arriving at its final destination with a total cash cargo of around £1 million plus, according to the time of year.

Since the Great Train Robbery of 1963, HVP security had been greatly ramped up, and no further attempts had been made to rob a mail train. Even prior to 1963, at each stop where HVP sacks were loaded onto the TPO train, security was tight with a police escort to oversee the transfer. However, so far as the Isle of Wight was concerned, as with so many other aspects of life, things went on unchanged. The HVP sacks from the island, on the first stage of their journey to London via Portsmouth, were the subject of minimal security – no police escort, no radios, and only two postmen in a van with a handheld alarm between them. Although only a fraction of the sum taken in 1963, the money ferried across the Solent each day was certainly a risk worth taking for a substantial return.

On Tuesday, 20 July 1971, with a holiday season and a heatwave in full swing, the consignment of banknotes, totalling £81,996.50 (£1,031,560 in today's money), came from the following Isle of Wight branches of the Midland Bank:

£25,095 from Newport Branch
£6,599 from Freshwater
£4,050 from Cowes
£8,652 from Ventnor
£10,000 from Shanklin
£13,500 from Sandown
£14,100.50 from Ryde[1]

Just before 3 p.m., railman Douglas Honey drove the Lister truck down to meet the incoming ferry:

> The security box was unloaded off the boat and put down behind my truck. The truck was hitched to the trailer and I started to drive up No. 1 Platform. By this time a number of passengers had got off the ferry and I drove up between them towards the Gosport Gate. I pulled up close to the gate with the doors of the security box facing the gate. The two postmen were there but I cannot remember if the gates were open at this time or not. I got down and unhooked the box, got back on the truck and turned around and drove back towards the concourse.[2]

Kenneth Dukes and his family had been on the Isle of Wight ferry and were walking towards the main exit of Portsmouth Harbour Station just before 3 p.m. He and his wife had their four children with them and were walking slowly along the platform because of the young ones. At one point they had to stand to one side to let the GPO trolly pass them on the way to the loading bay. When they were about level with the trolly, Dukes noticed a man standing in the door of the waiting room:

> I describe this man as about 30 to 35 years, 5ft 8ins tall, slim build, wearing an unusual type of peak cap, in a denim material, which I believe was coloured grey and black. His shirt was a pink coloured, bearing a pattern of other pink colours within it, and I think it could have been a paisley pattern. He was not wearing a jacket. His trousers were tight fitting, a grey fawn colour and I believe they were of a terylene type material. I would know this man again. A second man then came out of the waiting room, following behind the first man. He about 40 years of age 5ft. 11ins, and was average build.[3]

Dukes also recalled that the first man had a smooth complexion with a 'very nice tan'. The second man wore a three-quarter length fawn showerproof coat (despite the heatwave), and had an identical cap to the first man. He had a full brown/grey moustache that completely covered his top lip. Within moments of emerging from the waiting room, the two men ran past the Dukes family, along the platform towards the loading bay. As they ran, both men opened the holdalls they were carrying. Dukes, now to their rear, saw the first man pull out what appeared to be a grey revolver. He was unable to see clearly what it was the second man pulled out from his bag, but described it as about 18in to 2ft long and had the same metallic appearance as the first man's revolver.

At the loading bay, driver Albert Gibbs was standing by the Post Office van as his colleague Eric Hills started to throw the sacks from the canister into his mail bag. Gibbs recalled:

> I was facing Mr Hills and a person came rushing at me with a gun. The weight of this person overbalanced me as I was taken by surprise. He managed eventually to shove me into the back of the van. He pushed me in sideways. He said, 'Get in that van or I'll kill you.' I finished up in the back of the van half on my side and half on my back. While this was happening, I was trying to press the button of the alarm. The person was on top of me but he grabbed a mail bag and then he got up and went round the side of the van. I got up quickly in order to have a look, but I could not see much because my glasses had been knocked off, but I saw him put the mail bag in the back of the waiting van. I still had the alarm in my right hand, but I had got the button going, and the alarm was going. I thought that the man who pushed me was wearing a light-coloured suit. There had been two men on the platform. The other man had a gun. He was tall and the gun seemed to be a shot gun. Overall length about two feet long.[4]

Eric Hills, the other postman at the scene, heard a noise to his left and the sound of the gate rattling, quickly followed by a voice, which said:

> 'Get into that van or I'll kill you.' I looked over my right shoulder and saw a man with a shotgun and then I stepped into the van. While this was going on Mr Gibbs, who had been knocked into the van, was struggling on the floor with a man with a revolver. I stepped into the van, and the door closed. The man with the gun picked up the bags one by one and threw them out of the van. He did not get them all – there was one bag upon which I had my foot, and he tugged at it and then hurriedly left the van, leaving this bag behind. When the chap with the gun left the vehicle, a shot was fired. As far as I could judge this was by the revolver, although I am not certain about that.[5]

As Douglas Honey drove his Lister truck back down towards the concourse, he heard a bang behind him, which he mistook for the sound of a train, 'cos they do bang sometimes'.

Charles Keely, a sailor on shore leave from HMS *Plymouth*, who had just bought a ticket to Gosport, also heard a bang, but knew a gunshot when he heard one:

I turned back and I saw a man with a gun, and then I realised that there was something wrong, and then I started running back up. As I turned around, I saw a man with a gun above his head in his left hand. I saw a mail bag flung down behind a little blue van and the mail bag half hit another man who was bending down. There was a mail van and the blue van was alongside it, with the back towards the platform. As I started to run up, the van started to pull away. When I got near the top, I saw a white car and I was shouting as I was running. I shouted to the white car to block the road, but the white car continued to go slow and the blue van went beside it. The two men I mentioned earlier scrambled into the van. I saw the number of the van and I went to the entrance of the railway station, where I saw the driver of the mail van. I wrote down the number of the van within a minute or so of this happening – CLM 169H.[6]

At 3.05 p.m., several minutes after the robbers had made their escape from Portsmouth Harbour Station, PC David Lucas was on foot patrol in Queen Street, Portsea:

I was standing outside the Anchor Public House. I was engaged in a conversation with a member of the public when I noticed a Ford Escort van, colour light blue, travelling at an excessive speed and my attention was drawn to a loud squealing of tyres as it turned left into the street by the side of the Royal Naval Arms. In the space of approximately 30 seconds, I noticed a Ford Escort or Cortina Estate emerge from the side street and turn left into Queen Street and drive off at fast speed.[7]

PC Lucas then walked to the rear of the Royal Naval Arms where he saw the light blue Ford Escort van, registration number CLM 169H. The front passenger door was wide open and the rear doors were slightly open. He then radioed in a description of the Cortina Estate and remained with the light blue van until fingerprint and photographic officers arrived.

The van was examined at 3.40 p.m. by DC Cedric Shiner, who found a black PVC holdall containing two navy blue balaclavas, two live 4-shot 16-bore cartridges, and two live 6-shot 12-bore cartridges. Under the number plates were found the impressions of the original plates, VYO 319G.

Two days later, the Cortina Estate, registration number OYV 751F, was found in the car park of the Queens Hotel, alongside an Austin 1100, registration number FUL 728C, which had also been used in the robbery. On the rear seat of the Cortina were three white bags, one of which was empty. Behind the back seat was found a fourth bag. The bags were taken to the Scenes of Crime Search Room at Police Headquarters, where they were opened to reveal a quantity of torn packets and unregistered mail, general debris, a tintack, a piece of Sellotape, sealing wax, a pair of sunglasses, a pink shirt, and the vehicle's original licence plates XDA 664. It was also noted that a number of these items had orange-coloured fibres on them.

Hampshire Police were quickly able to establish that all three vehicles involved in the robbery had been stolen in North London; the Escort and Cortina on the same day, 15 July, and the Austin on 17 July. Bearing in mind the origin of the vehicles, CID officers pondered on the possibility that a London team might be involved in the mail robbery. However, with so little tangible evidence to go on at that time, it was really much too early to speculate.

Early on Tuesday, 27 July, not too far from where the Ford Escort and Austin 1100 had been stolen, a high-value cash robbery in North London hit the headlines.

The traffic that morning had been unusually busy and the news on Stanley Norman's car radio wasn't any better than it had been for the last few months, certainly down on Earth, that was. Up on the moon, *Apollo 15* had just touched down and astronauts David Scott and James Irwin were apparently preparing for a ride in the Lunar Roving Vehicle. No traffic congestion for them to put up with. Down on Earth, according to the BBC News, things were going from bad to worse. The British Army was busy carrying out early morning raids in Northern Ireland, rounding up terrorist suspects, while another rail strike was being threatened by the Nation Union of Railwaymen and the drivers' union, ASLEF.

Despite the traffic, Stanley Norman reported for duty at the Freightliner Depot, in York Way, N7, with just minutes to spare. After having the operation of his vehicle and its alarm system explained to him, his escort, Joseph Hallett, set out the route they'd be taking from York Way to the Headquarters of the Midland Bank at 27 Poultry, EC2, a short distance from the Bank of England.

It was around 9.40 a.m. and they'd only driven a short distance from the depot, having turned left off York Way into Wharfdale Road, when a blue van stopped in front of them. Within seconds of stopping, a man had jumped into the Freightliner's cab on the driver's side, gun in his hand and wearing a blue balaclava, which only showed the eyes. A second man entered on the passenger side. According to Norman:

Someone suddenly opened the door and there were two men there on the driver's side, and they each held a gun. I think it was a pistol. One of them said, 'Don't move.' One of the men leapt into the cab and said, 'Turn off the alarm.' I did so. I was then ordered to move over to the nearside of the cab, which I did. Mr Hallett then opened the nearside door of the cab and jumped out. The man leapt across the cab and held Mr Hallett by the collar, and told him to get back in. We were then told to keep our heads down and take our glasses off. I then heard the sound of the engine trying to start. Then I lay down and I was tied up.[8]

When it eventually stopped again, Hallett and Norman were taken off the Freightliner to a waiting van. Meanwhile, the 300 linen bags of mixed silver coins were unloaded from the Freightliner by the hijackers. As the van headed off towards Hackney, where it would, on arrival, be abandoned, Stanley Norman recalled the journey:

I heard a person, other than Mr Hallett, cough. I can also remember background noises while we were stopped, the most distinct being a wireless playing in the distance. I also heard traffic in the distance, like heavy lorries moving. I heard the noise also of people walking by. On two or three occasions the door opened and a person said to us, 'You'll be alright soon, you'll be having a nice cup of tea.'[9]

At 11.52 a.m., Acting Inspector Trevor Jones, in charge of the situations room at New Scotland Yard, received a radioed message that a lorry driver and his mate had been found, bound and gagged, and that their Freightliner had been stolen. Detectives were quickly in touch with Midland Bank officials, who had also reported the non-arrival of a large consignment of silver coins.

Neil Marshall, of the Church Street, Sheffield Branch of the Midland Bank, had the previous day prepared a consignment of mixed silver coins, that were placed in a Freightliner, which was then padlocked by branch staff and sealed. John Black, the Deputy Chief Cashier of the Midland Bank at their Head Office in Poultry, EC2, later made a statement for the police that he was expecting to receive £30,000 (£377,400 in today's money) in silver coins from the Sheffield branch, but the delivery failed to turn up and he immediately informed Scotland Yard.

Back in Hampshire, July and August 1971 were turning out to be among the busiest on record, particularly in terms of robberies and warehouse break-ins. In early August, Hampshire CID were contacted by J. Sainsbury's Limited, who reported the disappearance of 290 cases of cooked ham from their warehouse in Basingstoke.

According to Saitro Ataid, a Sainsbury's stock clerk:

Each commodity is given a code number and in respect of cartons of cooked ham this is 23/203. I have checked my records and I am able to say that 1,500 cartons of 1lb tins of Holland House brand ham were received at the Basingstoke Depot on the 12 and 13 May, 1971. A further 1,500 cartons of this same ham (Holland House Brand) were received into the Basingstoke warehouse on 1 August 1971. A second brand of ham is also recorded under the code 24/023. This is Vianda Skinless and is purchased from Foodwell Limited in cartons of 24 x 1lb tins. From the computerised stock results, the following deficiencies have shown up at the Basingstoke Depot since the first purchase on the 12 May 1971. The figures are as result of a physical check on the dates shown:

Week ending	5.6.71	Shortage	158 cases
Week ending	3.7.71	Shortage	13 cases
Week ending	31.7.71	Shortage	119 cases

These two brands of tinned ham are only sold through the retail shops of J. Sainsbury Limited. The value of each carton of Holland House Ham is £8.20p, and the value of each carton of Vianda Ham is £8.07½p.[10]

The mystery facing Sainsbury's, and indeed Hampshire CID, was how such significant quantities of ham were managing to exit the Basingstoke warehouse in working hours without anyone there apparently noticing. Neither was there any sign of forced entry under cover of darkness.

Up in London, another series of robberies was taking place involving Green Shield Stamps. Today, Green Shield Stamps are as obsolete as the dinosaurs, but back in the 1960s and '70s they were almost an alternative to cash. Created by entrepreneur Richard Tompkins in 1958, the stamps were essentially a sales promotion scheme that rewarded shoppers with stamps they could exchange for gifts and household goods at Green Shield stores. For every 6d (six pence) a shopper spent, they'd get one Green Shield Stamp. For the best part of a decade the scheme was huge and even referenced in rock songs. Petrol stations and supermarkets in particular dished out hundreds of thousands of stamps a year, along with many other high street retailers. However, the bubble burst in 1977 when Tesco decided to opt out. Sky-high 1970s inflation also had a hand in killing off Green Shield. As inflation climbed, the purchasing power of the stamps declined. Eventually, the Green Shield catalogue became cash only, and the operation was rebranded as Argos.

So far as the Green Shield Stamp robberies were concerned, there was no mystery as to how the stamps were being stolen; by whom was the question that thus far had no answer.

Herbert Thatcher, a Green Shield Stamp Company representative from Edgware, told police about a typical incident in August 1971:

I am based at our East Ham office and work the North West London area. I was issued with a total of 1,750 pads and coils of Green Shields stamps from stock at the East Ham office by Mr Wingate. Later that day, about 10 a.m., I left my car parked and locked with the alarm switched on, in the High Street near Forest Gate. I reported the theft of the car to Forest Gate Police Station. I later went to Greenhill Grove, Forest Gate, where I saw my car. I checked it and found all the Green Shield Stamps missing.[11]

Another representative from the East Ham office, John Malin, tells a similar story:

I was working from our branch office at East Ham and was issued with stocks of Green Shield Stamps as follows:
   HBGP 200-249
   HBCE 550-599
   HBCB 150-199
   1AAB 200-729
   HM5X 680-699
These stamps were issued by Mr Wingate. This stock of Green Shield Stamps I then carried in my firm's motor car. On Friday, 8 May, about 12 noon, I parked my firm's car, a Ford Cortina registered number TJJ 661F in Cornwall Avenue, Finchley. I left the vehicle to go to shop premises in Ballards Lane, Finchley, having first ensured that all the doors and windows were secure, and the alarm system switched on. I returned to the vehicle within three or four minutes to collect some savings books for the customer, but found the vehicle missing. I made enquiries at the houses nearby but found nobody who had seen the vehicle driven off. I then reported to the Police at Finchley Police Station the theft of the vehicle. I was informed about four hours later that day that my vehicle had been recovered. I attended Finchley Police Station and examined my car and found that my entire stock of Green Shield stamps was missing, that is 280 pads/coils as per receipt D.7832. The total value of these being £910 [£11,447 in todays' money].[12]

Meanwhile, back in Portsmouth, the forensic team were hard at work studying the items found in the Cortina Estate, the Ford Escort van and the Austin 1100. On the basis of the already established connection between North London and the vehicles involved in the Portsmouth Harbour mail robbery, and early forensic analysis of a fingerprint identified as belonging to Michael Regan, Hampshire CID decided that the time had arrived to widen the investigation. Detective Inspector Roland Jacob from Hampshire CID therefore took out search warrants for a number of locations, which were all to be searched at the same time on the morning of 1 September 1971. Jacob himself, together with eight other officers, drove to Gosport to search the home of Daniel Regan:

At 10.05 a.m. on Wednesday, 1 September 1971, together with Detective Constable Mosley, and other officers, I went to 74, The Avenue, Gosport, where we were admitted to the house by Mrs Regan. Daniel Regan was in bed. At 10.15 a.m. Daniel Regan came into the room. I introduced myself and showed him a search warrant for his house.

Regan said, 'What exactly is it you are looking for?' I said, 'We are investigating the Mail Robbery at Portsmouth Harbour Station and, as you probably know, there was £82,000 stolen.' Regan said, 'That was a long time ago. I know I was at home on my own that day. I've got a bit of money about. There is about four to five grand in the little garage. All silver which I need for change in the shops. I have got some more notes upstairs which I can show you.' A search was then made of the house. DC Mosely then went to the small garage at the side of the house. In the far corner, concealed by boxes and furniture were twenty-five pillow cases containing coins. I said, 'How many bags are there?' Regan replied, 'I don't know.' I said, 'Where did all this money come from?' Regan replied, 'I bring it home from the shops.' I said, 'Why keep all this money here?' Regan said, 'If any creeper comes round here, he's going to have to work for it. You don't think they're going to hump that lot about.' I said, 'You haven't lived here very long though, did you bring it here with you?' Regan said, 'Most of it, yes. I have added to it since I moved in.'[13]

Jacob then informed Regan that he would be removing the money to Portsmouth Central Police Station, pending further enquiries. At around 11.30 a.m., Detective Sergeant Bennett and DC Mackett arrived at the house, having completed a search of the licenced betting office of Timothy Regan, at 341 Forton Road, Gosport. He immediately showed Jacob a .22 pistol and ammunition that had been found at the betting office.

In a separate statement, Mackett related the details of the search he had undertaken that morning:

During a search I opened a cupboard in the rear office of the premises. In the cupboard I saw a small box which was tied with string. Miss Angela Puddick, who works at the office, untied the string and opened the box and inside I saw a pistol and some rounds of .22 ammunition.[14]

The visit to the betting office also resulted in the police coming across another old and familiar name from the 1964/65 train robbery enquiry – Thomas William Pope, the son of Thomas George Pope. He too made a statement about the .22 pistol:

I live at 341a Forton Road, Gosport. There is a betting shop underneath me. I am a bookmaker myself at 142 Clayhill Road, Alverstoke. At one time I used to run the shop underneath where I live for my father. He gave this up approximately June or July 1970. I did not go on working at 341 after my father sold out. Mr Daniel Regan also had an interest in my father's business. I have seen a box similar before. I would not swear it is the exact box. I saw this in June 1970, on a Saturday morning.[15]

When DC Jacob asked Regan about the gun found at the betting shop, he said, 'Well, it's no good me saying I didn't know it was there. I did. I have handled it some months ago.' Jacob then reminded him that because of his previous convictions he was prohibited from holding a firearm. Regan replied that he was aware of this but the shop was his brother's shop not his. Jacob asked him if he could say why he had the gun and where it came from, to which Regan replied, 'You will have to give me a chance to think. There is an answer but I can't think of it at the moment.' Following this exchange, Jacob stated that Regan would be placed under arrest and cautioned him. He was then taken into custody at Portsmouth Central Police Station.

One further discovery of significance found at Regan's home that day were three books wrapped in brown paper: *Railway Signalling and Communications*, *Remote Control of Railway Interlocking Equipment*, and a BR 1114/1 manual.

Jacob then went to Regan and asked, 'What have you got these books for?' Regan replied that, 'One of the chaps gave them to me to see if I could sell them as they are old.' Jacob then asked him about the name 'G. Tunbridge' on the inside cover of the second book. Regan replied, 'I don't know the man. George Pinching gave me the books.'

At the same time as DI Roland Jacob was at the avenue in Gosport, and DC Mackett was at the betting office, DI Kenneth Crossland was knocking on the door of Gaye Flatlets Ltd:

I am a Detective Inspector in the Scenes of Crime Section of Hampshire Constabulary. On Wednesday, 1 September, 1971, I went with other police officers to the premises of Gaye Flatlets, Western Parade, Southsea. I supervised a search of Flat 8 in the premises at 12 Western Parade, carried out by Scenes of Crime Officers.[16]

Among the items found here was a carpet, whose fibres matched the fibres found in the van, and two balaclavas.

It was also decided to place Regan's associates, both in Hampshire and London, under close observation. This included Harry Smith, who had, since May 1970, established A1 Self Service at 73 Kingsland High Street, London, E8. He also expanded the operation in late 1970 by opening a warehouse called A1 Cash & Carry at 2a John Campbell Road, N16. Another shop at 96/98 Weymouth Terrace, E2, was opened in June 1971.

While Harry Smith and John Regan were apparently the owners, an associate, James Thomas Spinks, fronted up the business in Kingsland High Street. His brother-in-law, Bennett Clark, initially ran the other shop in Weymouth Terrace. Harry Smith was often observed by plainclothes police officers at the Kingsland premises supervising operations and working in the office above the shop, reinforcing the view that he was actually running the entire operation. Spinks was someone else already known to C11: 'James Thomas Spinks, born 24/11/31 in Shoreditch – CRO 1132/46. Convictions for larceny, handling stolen goods, and gaming. Suspected person, wage robberies.'[17]

Police also interviewed a number of suppliers to A1 Self Service and A1 Cash & Carry. One in particular was Alan Hawkins, the representative of United Biscuits Limited. He met with Harry Smith in the office on several occasions and Smith told him that the business was taking £900 per week, and that he was also running a scrap metal business too.

On 21 September 1971, at nine in the morning, DC Clifford Ball went to A1 Self Service, with DI Bradley, DC Bennett and DC Moseley:

I commenced a search of the premises. I first went to the basement. I then went to the rear ground floor adjacent to the alleyway leading in from Gillett Street. At about quarter to ten I went into a small inner store room. There I found on the floor a £100 Midland Bank silver label, stamped on the back with 'Sheffield Transport, 23 July, 1971, Leadmill Garage Counting Office'. I drew the attention of DI Bradley to the presence and position of this label and as a result of finding it, the search was discontinued until further assistance was forthcoming. In the meantime, I went upstairs to the front of the building and after making a cursory search, I went to a room and in the fire place I found a carrier bag containing stockings and a navy-blue balaclava helmet. I went to the first-floor front room where I took possession of the main carpet. I went back the following day and at 5 p.m. I took possession of 3,960 Benson and Hedges Red cigarettes and 220 Benson and Hedges Blue cigarettes.[18]

When Ball's discoveries were added to the other items found at A1 Self Service by other officers, the tally was a significant one: 67,600 cigarettes of various brands (delivery labels had been removed from the cartons); thirteen cases of 24 x 1lb tins of Holland House Ham; six unopened boxes of Green Shield stamps (series HMK5 440-447); one opened box of Green Shield stamps (series HMK5 440-447).[19]

Harry Smith was arrested by Hampshire CID officers on 19 October 1971 and taken to Portsmouth, where he was charged with robbery and handling stolen property. He stood trial at Winchester Crown Court between 21 February and 24 March 1972, alongside Daniel Regan, Timothy Regan, Michael Regan and James Thomas Spinks. The centrepiece of the prosecution's case was a 20-page forensic report by Brian Rees, the Principal Scientific Officer at the Home Counties Forensic Science Laboratory in Aldermarston, Berkshire.

When the trial ended on 24 March 1972, all the defendants, apart from Harry Smith, were found guilty. Mr Justice Mais jailed Daniel and Michael Regan for fifteen years and ten years respectively. James Thomas Spinks was jailed for three years on three counts of handling stolen cigarettes, ham and Green Shield Stamps. When the convictions eventually went to the Appeal Court, Daniel and Michael Regan had their convictions for conspiracy to rob and robbery quashed. However, their convictions for receiving and handling stolen property were upheld, the sentences being seven and five years respectively.

The Winchester trial of 1972 appears to be the last time that the name of Harry Smith was to come before a court. As fortunate as Smith was, there were two other men who whose identities were almost certainly known to the police, but were never to set foot in a courtroom. One was the man whose inside information made the Great Train Robbery possible in the first place. The other man supposedly had the ability to drive a locomotive. His subsequent participation in the robbery was to make him a potential target for those who feared his loose tongue might endanger the liberty of the rest.

THE INSIDER

ACCORDING TO C11 INTELLIGENCE, it was solicitors' clerk Brian Field who first encountered the man who allegedly provided the inside information about the movement of vast sums of cash on the Glasgow–London mail train.

Field worked for solicitors T.W. James and Wheater, of 3 New Quebec Street, London W1. The firm's office was just around the corner from Baker Street, the fictional home of Sherlock Holmes. What Holmes would have made of the Great Train Robbery and the hunt for the insider is anybody's guess.

'Elementary, my dear Watson' is the quote most often associated with Sherlock Holmes. In fact, it frequently comes as a surprise to many to learn that in none of the fifty-eight short stories and four novels written by Sir Arthur Conan Doyle between 1886 and 1927 does Holmes ever say these words.

However, there is one phrase, more than any other, that Holmes utters in a host of stories, that perhaps defines his entire approach to detection: 'When you have eliminated the impossible, whatever remains, however improbable, must be the truth.' This very simple adage was employed by Post Office investigators in 1963, and enabled them to make a good deal more progress in identifying the source of the inside information than has ever previously been made public.

The mystery of who this insider was has become as intriguing as the Great Train Robbery itself. The long-accepted story goes that a corrupt solicitors' clerk, Brian Field, who had worked previously with two of the gang, introduced them to an Irishman with inside information on the Royal Mail train carrying millions of pounds from Glasgow to London. Gang member Gordon Goody claimed that he and Buster Edwards met the insider, known as the Ulsterman, on three occasions in London Parks in the spring and summer of 1963.

In 2014, in a book and film about his life,[1] Goody claimed that the insider's name was Patrick McKenna, and gave the filmmakers a number of details about his approximate age, circumstances and place of birth.

When the documentary makers went to great lengths to find the birth records of a man by this name, who was working for the Post Office in 1963, they finally found an individual who fitted the criteria. When they informed Goody of this on camera, the conversation between him and the interviewer was nothing if not illuminating:

INT: Would you recognize him?

GG: Would I recognize him now? I don't know, it's 50 years on.

INT: (handing Goody four photographs) Is it him?

GG: Do you know anything about him?

INT: Is it him?

GG: Do we know anything about him?

INT: We do, yeh.

GG: Tell me about him.

INT: He's not with us anymore, he died in 1995, he never lived in London when you met him, he married someone in Manchester, and he lived in Manchester, worked in the Post Office in Manchester, became a Postal Inspector in Manchester.

GG: Well, I've got to say …

INT: Is that him?

GG: (very long pause) … Have you spoken to the family?

INT: Not yet.[2]

After more prodding and prevaricating, Goody eventually stated that he was 99 per cent sure that he was the same man he met on four separate occasions between May and August 1963.

Many who watched the programme reacted to Goody's response and general demeanor with more than a little scepticism. Even when it was revealed that the man had died in 1995, Goody was still clearly uneasy. Unwilling to commit himself, he wanted to know more about the McKenna they had found, and in particular, whether his family had been contacted.

Some have suggested that having come up with the name Patrick McKenna, the last thing Goody was expecting was that the filmmakers would then research records to the extent they did and, against the odds, actually come up with a birth certificate and photographs of a man who fitted the information he had provided.

It is also worth bearing in mind at this point how much Goody's story had evolved over the years before he named 'Patrick McKenna'. We shall examine, in a moment, the story he originally told the rest of the gang back in the spring of 1963. By the time that he first spoke about the insider to author Piers Paul Read in 1976, in a taped interview, he was very clear about three things: a) that when he and Buster Edwards met the Ulsterman for the second time at a cafe by the Serpentine in Hyde Park, he had searched the man's jacket, which was hung over the back of a chair when he went to the toilet; b) that although all the pockets were empty, he found the man's name and address on a tailor's label sewn into the lining of the jacket; and c) that he deducted from the name that the Ulsterman was a Protestant, and from the address, that he came from a rural area. He and Buster did not let on to the Ulsterman that they now knew his name.[3]

How, one might ask, does any of this fit with the information he provided to the documentary makers in 2014? Now, he, Buster and the Ulsterman meet in Green Park, not Hyde Park, and there's no mention of a tailor's label in the lining of a jacket on the back of a chair. In this new version, the jacket has been left on the grass while the Ulsterman goes to buy an ice cream. Again, Goody searches the jacket, but this time finds a spectacles case, which he opens to find the name Patrick McKenna inside. This time, according to the new story, Goody tells a startled Ulsterman that he's opened his spectacles case and knows his name. The fact that the man he identifies in 2014 turns out to be a Roman Catholic, in total contradiction to his 1976 account, is now conveniently airbrushed out of the story.

Goody's claim about the late Patrick McKenna of Salford was understandably hotly denied by his surviving family. Mark McKenna, Patrick McKenna's grandson, spoke for the McKenna family when he said of Goody: 'He made out that the film was conclusive proof that my Grandad was the Ulsterman and it could not be anyone else. It is just a load of rubbish to be honest, my Grandad wasn't the Ulsterman.'[4]

Patrick McKenna, it has to be said, was an ordinary postman in Salford at the time of the Great Train Robbery, doing door-to-door deliveries on foot like hundreds of thousands of other postmen. Mark McKenna told Channel 4 in a 2019 interview that his grandfather's working life revolved around 'leaving home, going down to the end of the road to the sorting office, getting his post, delivering the post and going back home'. Quite simply, he would not have known or been aware of any information about Travelling Post Office trains, and did not have access to the type of information, and indeed the type of documents, that were supplied to the robbers by the Ulsterman. So, if Patrick McKenna wasn't the Ulsterman, who was?

In 2019, a taped interview between Roger Cordrey and author Piers Paul Read came to light, through Cordrey's son Christopher. On the tape, Roger Cordrey talked about his initial reaction to being told by Buster Edwards that they had an inside source of information about the Glasgow–London mail train:

I had asked them actually to find out a couple of things which they came back with. They told me that their information was coming from a very good source. They showed me something, a list I had asked for, a list of the HVP movements and the number of bags. The official bit of paper I got with it was pretty good proof to me that they were in contact with someone that knew what they were doing.[5]

Satisfied that his fellow villains had credible and reliable information about the movement of High Value Packages (HVPs), Cordrey agreed to take part in the robbery. We also know from Cordrey's taped account that among the documents he was given was a Travelling Post Office Schedule document. This is not something that any postal worker at a local sorting office is either going to come across in his everyday work, or, more to the point, going to be able to get access to. There is no way in the world that Patrick McKenna, or indeed any ordinary postman, could have obtained the grade of documents that were given to Roger Cordrey.

Significantly, the robbers were also told by the Ulsterman that this could just be the beginning; he had access to information from all over the country in terms of money movements by both road and rail, and again this is a major clue in itself. It is not just something that someone in a sorting office may, by chance, come across or overhear.

Probably the most important surviving and currently available official document written by an investigation officer about the identity of the insider was written by Richard Yates, the Deputy Controller of the Post Office Investigation Branch. In his report and observations about the initial phase of the Branch's hunt for the insider, he notes that 'information regarding the general treatment of HVPs and their transit on the Up Special Travelling Post Office, is known to a wide section of Post Office staff, and to some extent professional criminals'.

However, he goes on to observe that:

while such general information would be sufficient to stimulate interest among criminals to plan a robbery, it would be totally inadequate for a gang to be able to launch a successful attack of the nature of that under review. I hold the view that meticulous planning would be undertaken by criminals of this calibre, that the arrangements would be precise and that, consequently, detailed information would be essential before embarking on such a venture. Furthermore, I think that provision would be made for any changes in procedure to be notified to the gang. Post Office employees in general, would not, of course, be in a position to keep abreast of daily changes in TPO working.

This report is without doubt the most critical and incisive summary ever written about the insider and where his information might have come from.

Yates then names what he believes to be the only four possible sources of a leak:

1 – from among staff at GPO Headquarters in London.
2 – GPO officers employed in special security postal work.

3 – from postal workers on board the TPO.

4 – GPO officers attached to the HQ of the TPO section.[6]

As one might expect, based upon Yates's logical analysis of where a leak might have occurred, 'discreet but general enquiries were made without success concerning the supervising and administrative staff at GPO HQ and in LPR but this was cut short when information mentioned [by Commander Hatherill] came to hand, although all of the facts have been passed on to the police'.[7]

On Thursday, 29 August 1963, Clifford Osmond and Richard Yates of the Post Office Investigation Branch had attended a meeting at Scotland Yard. During the meeting, Commander Hatherill had said that 'the previous Tuesday, he had seen an informant who had given him a list of 14 names of the bandits who had formed the robbery team; that he (Hatherill), was satisfied that those 14 criminals were "certain" offenders and that the money had already been divided into 18 lots.'[8]

Most interesting, for Osmond and Yates:

Mr Hatherill said that, according to the informant, this team met at Leatherslade Farm on 7 August at 11.00 p.m ... only one man – Goody - was late (said to have been half an hour late, which would make it 11.30 p.m.) and that Goody's explanation of his late arrival was that he had been waiting for 'the message'. The informant apparently said that 'the message' contained information about the number of men to be found in the HVP coach at the time of attack, and that there were 'a hundred bags on the train'.

Osmond and Yates put it to Hatherill that the times mentioned would be important, and he agreed that the information in the message must have been available to Goody around 11.30 p.m., and certainly not later than midnight. Hatherill added that the informant had said that this information came from a Post Office man on the train. It was assumed by Hatherill, and Millen (who said he had been with Hatherill when he met the informant), that the information from the man on the train had been passed on by telephone.

However, Yates then interjected that he had, on 9 August, taken steps to trace and check every ticketed call made to the London area from stations and towns at which the Up Special TPO had stopped, and that nothing suspicious had been found. Furthermore, the build-up of HVP sacks on board the TPO did not reach a total of 100 until the train reached Tamworth at 1.23 a.m., and that if any information about loads were given out by a member of the train crew in time for it to reach Goody by 11.30 p.m., then it must have been at Preston where the TPO stopped at 10.50 p.m., or given some time latitude, at the next stop, i.e. Warrington at 11.36 p.m. Even at Warrington, however, there were only forty-six HVP sacks on board. The train reached Crewe well after midnight, by which time Goody had apparently arrived at the farm. There were, at this point, only ninety-one sacks at Crewe.

Yates says very clearly in his report, following the Scotland Yard meeting on 29 August 1963, that 'Mr Osmond and I felt very sceptical about the accuracy of this information, but I pushed ahead with IB inquiries on the basis that some latitude might, perhaps, have to be allowed'.[9]

Bearing in mind that Hatherill's information about the informant on the train came to light on 29 August 1963, this means that the Post Office investigation branch spent fewer than twenty days investigating Post Office HQ staff. We know from now opened Post Office IB files that they spent the best part of four years exhaustively investigating and carrying out observations and phone taps on the postal staff who were on the TPO on the night of the robbery. Conversely, there is no mention in any Post Office IB files known to exist of why the Post Office IB did not return to the matter of HQ staff, having found nothing whatsoever on the TPO staff. Neither is there any trace or further references relating to 'all the facts' that were 'passed on to the police' in relation to the albeit very brief HQ staff investigations.

If this story was flawed in terms of its accuracy, was it the informant who was at fault, or the information itself? Interestingly, we can be reasonably well assured that the story about the 100 bags, told by the informant, was exactly the one that the men at Leatherslade Farm were told. Ronald Biggs, who wrote an account of the robbery in a small bungalow in Melrose, Melbourne, in late 1969, had never seen or heard the informant's story before. Indeed, the document was not released to the public until the year before he died in 2013, yet his version is literally identical to the informant's story, albeit more detailed:

> At eleven thirty, or there abouts, Goody was dropped off at the bottom of the lane by Brian Field. Gordon greeted us with the news that we wouldn't be doing anything until the following night as he had been informed that there were only a very small number of registered sacks on the train.

Twenty-four hours later, Biggs recalls that:

> About 11 o'clock that night we started preparing to leave the farm. We got our army uniforms and moved the land rovers and truck out of the sheds. Gordon had

gone to a phone box in the nearby village and had received the glad tidings that the big load was on the way. This information came from Brian Field who had earlier been in contact with our man up North. 'At least a hundred bags!' Goody had announced elatedly.[10]

The 100 bags claim by Goody can therefore be seen as a statistical nonsense. Of course, it could have been deliberate bravado on Goody's part to raise the men's spirits as they were about to leave the farm. Equally, the 100 bags figure could have been an estimation on the part of the informant, based upon the number of bags on the train by the time it reached Preston. Someone with a very detailed overview of the TPO operation could, possibly, have calculated that based on statistics from previous months and years, that the likely total would be at least 100 bags by the time the train made its final stop at Rugby at 2.12 a.m. However, this theory raises an even more profound question: who could possibly have had such a wide overview of operations, and indeed access and knowledge relating to previous HVP bag statistics on the Glasgow–London route? Certainly not an everyday postal employee.

Could someone on the train have made a call to Brian Field from one of the stations en route, or given information to someone else en route who could have phoned it on to Field?

If there had been a phone call to Brian Field's home in Pangbourne, or to a public phone box near to Leatherslade Farm in the late hours of 7 August 1963, which there clearly must have been, the call had not come from Glasgow, or indeed any of the towns where the Travelling Post Office Train had stopped. According to Richard Yates:

> despite the risk of staffing difficulties in Telephone Manager's offices, early arrangements were made to obtain and list particulars of every ticketed call made from telephones situated within (a) 5 miles and (b) 30 miles of Leatherslade Farm. These (many thousands) have since been systematically examined by IB staff and information passed to the police. Telephone managers throughout the country have been put to much trouble over IB requests for this and other telephone information, but assistance has always been willingly and readily given.[11]

A similar exercise was conducted in relation to the towns that the TPO stopped at on its journey from Glasgow. Nothing was found. However, no one was checking for calls made from London to Pangbourne or to phone boxes within a circumference of Leatherslade Farm. A call from London would not have attracted the least bit of attention from Post Office staff, who, as Osmond states in his report, were sifting records of telephone calls made from a variety of locations between Glasgow and Rugby.

We have good reason to believe that one of the last things 'the insider' had told Goody and Edwards before the train robbery was that 'when you've done this, there's another one you can do in Leeds. It involves a van with a driver, his mate and a security guy. You're looking at three million.'[12] If this is true, we can conclude that in addition to his involvement in TPO security matters, 'the insider' also had knowledge and access regarding information on Post Office van security.

From the very earliest days of the investigation, Butler had, so far as his public statements were concerned, nailed his colours to the mast in terms of an insider. Simply put, there was no insider so far as he was concerned. It therefore came as a complete surprise to Clifford Osmond when his deputy, Richard Yates, reported that:

> Information has been received from Chief Superintendent Butler, New Scotland Yard, that a Mr Albert William Bish, who resides at 3 Swanwick Close, SW15, is employed on the Up Special TPO and that he may be a contact of Mr Douglas Goody, one of the offenders sentenced to thirty years imprisonment for the Mail Train robbery (Up Special TPO) on 8 August, 1963.[13]

While the Post Office Investigation Branch thoroughly probed every aspect of Bish, along with thirty-five other Post Office employees, and established to their satisfaction that he was in no way connected to Goody or indeed to anyone else associated with the robbery, Yates's report again brings into question exactly what Butler thought privately, as opposed to what he said publicly. If he genuinely believed there was no insider, why did he flag up Bish's name, and on several other non-public occasions speculate on who the insider was? One can only conclude that he knew, or had strong suspicions, that there was indeed an insider, but in the same way that he flatly denied publicly that any of the robbers had evaded arrest or detection, he had little choice but to continue the mantra that there was no insider. To say otherwise would have gone against the grain for 'one day Tommy'. Even to speculate publicly of such a man's possible existence would immediately provoke questions from the media and other quarters as to why Butler and his team had no clue whatsoever as to who or where this individual was.

When, to return to Sherlock Holmes's observation, we eliminate the possibility that the insider was a) working on the Glasgow–London mail train, b) was based up north counting mail bags on a railway station platform, or c) his name was Patrick McKenna, we are left effectively with one possibility. Looking again at Richard

Yates's list of the four groups of Post Office employees from whom the leak or leaks might have emanated, we are left with only one real possibility: the insider was living in London, occupying a senior post at Post Office Headquarters.

Bearing in mind that it was supposedly Brian Field who had been in direct contact with the insider, the police and IB had hoped that either he or John Wheater, who they saw as the weakest links, might eventually reveal further details in prison. However, once Field's sentence had been cut on appeal from twenty-five years to five years in 1964, any chance of him saying anything vanished. Wheater, however, was a different kettle of fish. In 1966 he divulged that:

> I did get the impression that there were some other people involved who were not brought to trial and have not been named by the Police. One thing I learned pointed back to well before the raid – to a link between the gang and somebody in Post Office security. This somebody made contact through an intermediary with one of the men who stood trial, and it was this man – one of my fellows in the dock – who gave me the information when I was discussing with him how he became involved. The intermediary – a relation, I think, of the Post Office security man – put up the proposition that large sums of money were being moved by train at various times and that it was there for the taking so to speak. This made my fellow prisoner a lynch pin in the whole thing. I was never able to discover who the intermediary was. I was told that after the robbery money was passed to the intermediary for himself and for the Post Office man.[14]

Looking at the minutes, correspondence and memos originating from the records of Post Office Security during the early 1960s, we can see a number of officers whose responsibilities cover both TPO security and Post Office van security, i.e. the movement of cash by road. Only one man who worked in this section appears to be a Protestant Ulsterman.

Percy Hoskins, the crime editor of the *Daily Express*, later recalled that a certain senior Scotland Yard officer had called at his Park Lane apartment and over a drink divulged off the record that a senior Royal Mail officer was strongly suspected of being the man mentioned in Hoskins's 20 April 1964 story speculating about the 'inside man'. According to the information given to Hoskins, 'The man had joined Royal Mail in Belfast twenty or so years before, had worked his way up through the ranks and eventually moved to England after the war where he settled into a quiet middle class suburb in South London.'[15]

Hoskins's informant had added that the man now held a key post in Royal Mail security, and had written down his name and address on the strict understanding that the brief background information he had given Hoskins would only ever be used in a story if the man in question were to be arrested. Hoskins knew that he had no legal grounds for a story of any kind, but his curiosity, if nothing else, had to be satisfied.

One Wednesday a few weeks after his conversation with the Scotland Yard officer, Hoskins took the train to Beckenham Junction and walked a short distance to the 'pleasant tree lined road of spacious semi-detached houses' where the man lived with his wife and mother. It was the middle of the day and Hoskins (rightly) sensed that the man would be at work. When he knocked at the smart bay-windowed house, the wife opened the front door and Hoskins spoke to her for a few minutes on a pretext.

With no documents or information available in terms of what the police source told Percy Hoskins about why and on what grounds the Beckenham man was interviewed, he is one of the three individuals I have mentioned earlier in this book that I have resolved not to identify.

From what can be gathered from Post Office records, the Beckenham man was transferred from Post Office HQ to an equally senior post in another part of the UK, albeit one that had no connection with security work. Coincidentally, this move took place not too long after Hoskins's April 1964 article in the *Daily Express*.

Talking of coincidences, when Gordon Goody's 2014 film tie-in book *How to Rob a Train* was published, a researcher examining the information about Patrick McKenna in the book noticed a reference to McKenna once having 'lived at Southall Road, Beckenham'. Not only is there no such street in Beckenham, or indeed in Greater London, but so far as we know, McKenna never in his life lived at any time in Beckenham. Whether this was an intentional or an unintentional error on Goody's part, we'll never know. He died on 29 January 2016, just over two years after the book was published.

CANNES

Danny Pembroke's Criminal Record Offi[...] file photograph, taken on 27 October 1962. (Metropolitan Police)

The village of Beafor[...] in Devon where Danny Pembroke and four others hid out during September and October 1963. (Royal Mail Archives)

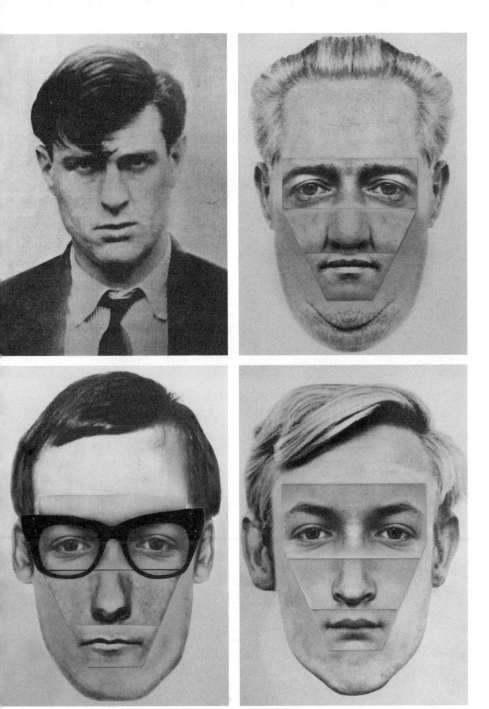

Clockwise from top left: Harry Smith's Criminal Record Office file photograph. (Metropolitan Police); An Identikit picture of 'Old Alf' the train driver, based on a description given by Ronald Wyatt, who saw the old man close to on 7 August 1963 at Leatherslade Farm. (Thames Valley Police); An Identikit of the man seen by Frank Alderman and Denis Walton at the Buck & Ryan tool shop in Euston Road shortly before the London Airport robbery. (Thames Valley Police); The second of the two men seen at close quarters by Ronald Wyatt on 7 August 1963. This one is an excellent likeness of Bruce Reynolds, which suggests Wyatt's description of 'Old Alf' was really accurate. (Thames Valley Police)

A scene of crime photograph taken in the lobby of Comet House, where the London Airport wage snatch took place on 27 November 1962. (The National Archives)

A scene of crime photograph taken from the top-floor toilet window at Comet House, looking at the Barclays Bank branch on the far side of the management car park. (The National Archives)

Identikit of an unidentified
[ro]bber seen in Faggs Road,
[Fel]tham, some five minutes
[afte]r the London Airport
[ro]bbery on 27 November 1962.
[(M]etropolitan Police)

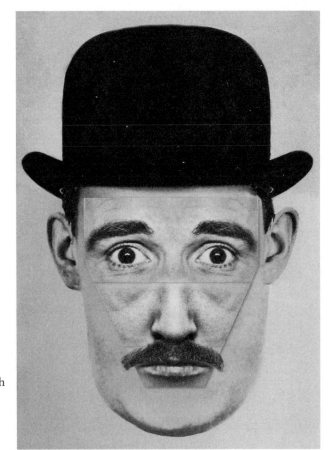

[Th]e Richardsons' Peckford Scrap
[Me]tal Company at 50 New Church
[Ro]ad, Camberwell, where Harry
[Sm]ith surrendered himself for
[pol]ice questioning on 5 May 1964.
[(Th]e National Archives)

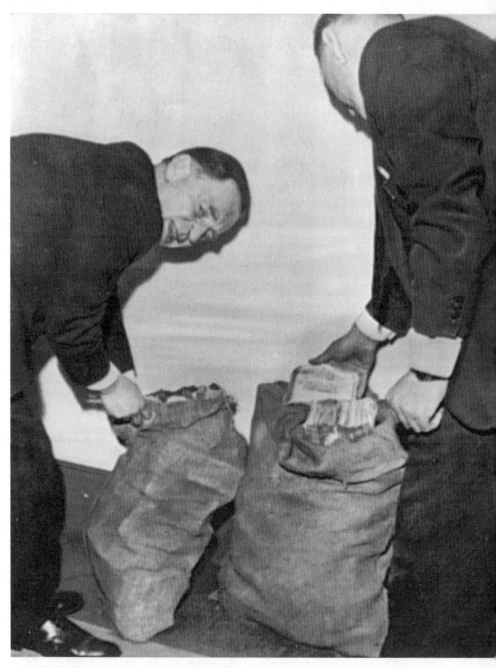

The two sacks of cash totalling £47,245 left in the telephone box at Black Horse Court, Great Dover Street, SE1, at 6.30 p.m. on 10 December 1963. (The National Archives)

The tapping of telephone lines was a key part of the Great Train Robbery investigation and brought about early leads and arrests. (Royal Mail Archives)

The Registry housed the records of hundreds of thousands of suspects, previous offenders and intelligence sources. (Metropolitan Police)

Leconfield House, in Curzon Street, Mayfair, the headquarters of the Security Service (MI5 between 1948 and 1977. (Author's collection)

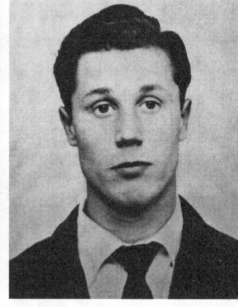

Sir Richard Jackson, the nominal founder in 1960 of C11, Scotland Yard's Criminal Intelligence Section. (Author's collection)

Ronald Harvey's Criminal Record Office file photograph taken on 14 October 1952. A file note written in 1963 observed that, while bein over ten years old, it was still a good likeness o Harvey. (Metropolitan Police)

The Wolles Store at 19 Boulevard Croisette, Cannes, where £217,000 'jewellery was stolen by a 'gang of British crooks' thought to include Roy James and Micky Ball on August 1961. (Police & Gendarmerie Records, High Court of Grasse, France)

A photograph of Roy James and Micky Ball found in French police files, taken while they were staying at the Hotel Martinez in Cannes, 1961. (Police & Gendarmerie Records, High Court of Grasse, France)

The Identikit system was one of a number of pioneering ideas introduced to the UK by Sir Richard Jackson. (Metropolitan Police)

Danny Pembroke (centre, standing) among a group of fellow servicemen in the Malayan jungle. (Danny Pembroke Jnr)

Danny Pembroke's experience in the British Army was to be an invaluable asset in avoiding arrest and conviction. (Danny Pembroke Jnr)

796 Barking Road E13, seen by C11 as a common denominator linking George Cahill, Danny Regan, Harry Smith and Billy Ambrose. (Author's collection)

The producers of *Robbery*, the 1967 movie based on the Great Train Robbery, sought out the help of the unconvicted robbers as script consultants. (Embassy Films Ltd)

Portsmouth Harbour Railway Station, scene of the 20 July 1971 Travelling Post Office robbery. (Author's collection)

THE OUTSIDER

Monday, 20 January 1964

THE BUILDING HAD ONLY been completed the year before to house the brand-new headquarters of the Aylesbury Rural District Council. It was the only place in Aylesbury that could possibly accommodate such a vast number of police, barristers, solicitors, court officials, prisoners and journalists, who would be attending the trial of the train robbers, scheduled to begin on 20 January 1964.

The Council Chamber would be the makeshift courtroom. It had none of the austere atmosphere of the Old Bailey. By contrast, it was light, airy and spacious, being some 40ft wide, and 30ft long, with a 20ft-high ceiling. It had five large high windows in each wall as well as twelve clusters of lights.

The Lord Chancellor's Department in Whitehall had been quite specific about how the members' chamber should be transformed into an Assize Court. The dock, for example, had to be constructed exactly to the supplied dimensions to hold twenty defendants seated in two rows of green upholstered leather chairs. It was finished off with 4in-high metal spikes around the entire perimeter.

The accused were the centrepiece in the courtroom – one could hardly miss them surrounded by a posse of police officers and sitting collectively in the pen-like dock, which some Fleet Street scribes compared to the one at Nuremberg. The accused sat in order of indictment: in the front row Boal, Wilson, Biggs, Wisbey, Welch and Hussey. In the back row sat Daly, James, Goody, Brian Field, Lenny Field and John Wheater.

Mr Arthur James QC, the prosecuting counsel, summed up the situation pretty well in his opening remarks to the jury:

> None of the men who were in the train will be able to pick out any individual as being one of the participants in the raid. Mills the driver will tell you there were fifteen people involved and that is the way we put the case before you – that there were fifteen people on the track.[1]

The reality was that the Crown had not one shred of evidence to connect any of those in the dock with the scene of the crime. Indeed, the Director of Public Prosecutions was not entirely convinced that it was possible to prove in court the amount of money stolen, either. That was why the decision was made not to charge the accused with stealing a certain sum of money, but charging them with 'robbing Frank Dewhurst[2] of 120 mail bags'.

The Crown did have fingerprint evidence, forensic evidence and documentational evidence connecting those in the dock with Leatherslade Farm. In essence, the case put to the jury was that the farm was the centre of the robbers' operations. This had been proven by the vast amount of material from the train that had been found there, such as mail sacks, money wrappers, and a small quantity of money that had been left behind. The prosecution's assertion, therefore, was that if an individual could be proven to have been at Leatherslade Farm, then they were, de facto, on the track at Sears Crossing, and thereby guilty of armed robbery and conspiracy to rob. Even in 1963, this was a very tenuous legal argument. Today, in light of the Police and Criminal Evidence Act of 1994, and a host of other precedents, such a contention would be a non-starter.

Arthur James's words to the jury implied there were no eyewitnesses, period. However, this was not quite the case. The prosecution had decided early on not to rely on them in court, partly due to the fact that several had indicated that they were not able to be 100 per cent sure in their identifications, or irrespective of this, were unwilling to testify to what they had seen. The other main obstacle was that several of the eyewitnesses had described individuals who had not, as yet, been arrested and charged. For example, Lillian Brooks, who believed the person who collected the key for Leatherslade Farm was Bruce Reynolds; and Norman Owen, who stated that he could identify Reynolds as the man to whom he sold two pairs of rock-climbing boots at Benjamin Edgington, 144/146 Shaftesbury Avenue, WC2. One of the best eyewitnesses was Ronald Wyatt, a 52-year-old farmer whose family had lived in the area for generations. Again, he did not want to testify specifically about the individuals he saw, as neither of them were in the dock. He did, however, make a detailed written statement to the police about Leatherslade Farm:

14 August 1963
First of all, I would like to clarify what Leatherslade Farm is; it is a home and buildings surrounded by about 4½ acres of land. About twenty-five years ago, my father owned the house and the land, and he sold it and it has subsequently come into the hands of Mr Rixon. I rent sixty acres of Crown property which immediately borders Leatherslade Farm. In July, 1958, I rented one field from Mr Rixon, one of the conditions being that I tidied it up. I finished renting this field about the end of the second week in July, 1963, when Mr Rixon went away. After Mr Rixon's father had gone, the house looked bare and all the curtains had

been taken down. Mr Rixon's father and mother stayed at the house for about a fortnight after their son had gone. Mr Rixon's brother and father had been gone only a few days, when I noticed that curtains were up at the windows. I didn't pay much attention as Mr Rixon told me before he went away that the farm property had already been sold. He didn't say to whom, but he did say that the new owners were going to keep pigs.[3]

To say that the police were somewhat sceptical of a Wyatt's account was an understatement. However, it would later prove to be to be among the most helpful pieces of evidence, in terms of shedding a glimmer of light on one of the recurring mysteries of the Great Train Robbery: the identity of the man named 'Fred' in Ronald Biggs's serialised story that would appear in *The Sun* newspaper seven years later.

Wyatt was one of the first to be formally interviewed on 14 August 1963, the day the police arrived at the farm. Not only was he the only person to have ventured up the narrow lane to the farm while the robbers were in occupation, he actually spoke face to face to one of them for several minutes, while getting a close view of a second man who was sitting in a deckchair sunning himself:

I didn't see anyone at the house until Wednesday, 7 August, 1963, at about 10 a.m., when I saw two men standing near a shed where Mr Rixon used to keep his lorry. This shed is just across the lane from the house and is about 10 yards from the house. I noticed that in the shed was an object covered by a green sheet, like a tent covering. From the size and shape, I would think it was a large car or a lorry under the green sheet. I went up to the two men and as I did so, one of them walked away. I asked the one still standing there if there were any dogs about because I'm not very keen on dogs. He told me that there weren't any. I said, 'Are you the new owner?' He said, 'No, I'm just one of the decorators.' I said, 'Well when do you think the new owners are going to come up here?' He said, 'He won't be up here for quite a long time.' I said, 'Who is the new owner?' He said, 'Mr Fielding of Aylesbury. If you want to get in touch with the firm who sold it to him, get in touch with Midland Marts, the auctioneers at Banbury. We then had a bit of conversation about the possibility of me renting a field in the future, as we walked up to the house, I didn't go in though. Sitting in a deck chair was a middle-aged man. He was sitting outside the door nearest the French window. I also saw two lilo-mattresses, with a book on each, lying on the ground, inflated, a few yards, from the deck chair. The man I was with told me that the inside of the house was in a bad condition. I thought this was strange because only just before Mr Rixon left, I had seen the inside of the house and it appeared to me to be in good condition. We said goodbye to each other and I left, and returned to my fields. Each morning up to and including Sunday, I saw smoke coming from the chimneys, but I don't remember seeing smoke after that. On several days I have heard the sounds of metal being hammered. I think I remember there being a fire outside the house but I'm not sure. I would describe the man to whom I spoke as being about 20–30 years of age, 6' tall, medium build, dark hair, very fresh face, wearing glasses. He was wearing white shorts, mauve shirt, red shoes. He spoke rather like a gentleman as opposed to a workman – the man who was with the man I have just described and who walked away as I said, I'm, afraid I didn't see him again, unless it was he who was sitting in the deck chair when I reached it. Now the man in the deck chair was aged about 50–60 years, very full in the body and face, ruddy complexion, fair grey hair. He was wearing white shorts and mauve shirt. As the man who walked away was also dressed in white shorts and a mauve shirt, it is very likely that it was the man who I later saw sitting in the deck chair. This statement has been read to me and it is true.[4]

Wyatt's assertion that he had seen an old man sitting in a deckchair at the farm was initially dismissed by officers, for at that early stage, an old man was not known to have participated in the robbery. In fact, some senior officers had remarked upon how odd it was that after train driver Jack Mills had been hit, he was dragged into the passageway behind the driver's cab and handcuffed, only to have his handcuffs removed several minutes later and brought back again to the cab to drive the train on for another half mile. It would be some weeks before they learnt that the robbers had brought their own driver with them, who had not been able to move the locomotive. The driver they had recruited was not a criminal; in fact, his participation in the robbery has been much debated over the past five decades. Was it purely for the money he was promised that he risked the danger of arrest and imprisonment, or were there perhaps other factors at play?

Bringing outsiders, or 'civilians', in on a big professional job such as the train robbery had its own dangers and risks for the rest of the robbers too. Buster Edwards's 'bowler hat gang' learnt this to their cost when they recruited a 22-year-old alarm engineer, Louis Jacobs, to help them break into the vaults at the Westminster Bank, Corn Exchange, Mark Lane, in the City of London on 22 July 1962. When the alarm was unknowingly triggered, two policemen and two bank security officers suddenly appeared, and a pitched battle broke out inside the bank, and then spilled out onto the pavement in the melee that followed.

Although the gang ultimately got away, they had not been wearing masks at the moment the police arrived, and feared that a number of them had possibly been recognised. The following day they had arranged to meet in a pub, but within minutes of them arriving, two police squad cars pulled up outside. Those inside were marched out and taken to Bishopsgate Police Station. Four of those arrested – Jimmy Collins, Leonard White, Kenneth Ali and the alarm engineer, Louie Jacobs – were later charged and appeared at the Old Bailey in August 1962.

While in custody, Jacobs apparently took little persuasion to sing like a bird, and not only gave Queen's evidence against the other three men in the dock, but gave police the names and nicknames of the others who had not been in the pub at the time of the raid. These included Buster Edwards, who had been late for the rendezvous, and drove straight past the pub when he saw the police cars outside. However, it was decided there was insufficient evidence to charge Edwards, despite the fact that Jacobs had given police his phone number. White, however, pleaded guilty and was sentenced to four years, while Collins and Ali denied the charges and were found not guilty by the jury.

The necessity of acquiring unique skills, this time someone who could drive an English Electric Deltic diesel locomotive, outweighed the risk of involving him, just as the recruitment of the alarm engineer, Louis Jacobs, was seen as key to pulling off the Westminster Bank raid. They only stopped to worry about the consequences of their driver being picked up by the police after the robbery. Information later picked up by C11 suggested there had been talk about finding him and silencing him.

Over a period of time, information that the gang had recruited their own driver began to filter through. Several cryptic comments had been picked up in phone taps that did not mean a great deal at the time. However, later, with the benefit of hindsight, the pieces began to fit together.

The most compelling evidence that someone else had been present at the farm who was not a known suspect, and was, more than likely, not even a criminal, came to light as a result of a mammoth fingerprint search by C3, the Yard's Fingerprint Department, who arrived in the late afternoon of 14 August.

Led by Detective Superintendent Maurice Ray, the team comprised five fingerprint experts, a police photographer and four laboratory staff from the Forensic Science Laboratory. The exercise was nothing if not thorough. According to Detective Chief Superintendent Ernie Millen, Ray's operation was 'the biggest fingerprint exercise on the scene of the crime ever known in the history of detection. They worked around the clock for three days.'[5]

All in all, 243 photographs had been taken of 311 fingerprints and 56 palm prints. Understandably, the first thing the police did, for reasons of elimination, was to take the fingerprints of the Rixon family, and indeed anyone else who the

Rixons named as having visited the farm during a defined period of time. This task was made a little easier by the fact that the Rixons kept themselves to themselves, and hardly anyone outside of the immediate family circle had been inside the farmhouse for a considerable period of time before the family moved out.

Details about this elimination operation were reported in DPP file 2/3718/1, which was originally closed until 2045. A redacted version of the file, i.e. one that has had sections, and indeed whole pages, removed and retained until 2045, was opened on 25 June 2010.

Mention of the fact C3 found a fresh set of unidentified fingerprints at the farm is to be found in an investigation file that is still, at the time of writing, officially closed until the year 2045. In the file, Tommy Butler refers to fingerprints 'left at Leatherslade Farm and not yet identified'.[6]

The existence of the unidentified prints has never been officially mentioned during the course of the past six decades. In spite of a mammoth effort, police were unable to identify these prints against those held on any individuals suspected of, or associated with, the crime. A likely theory voiced by the fingerprint department was that the prints either belonged to someone within the criminal fraternity who had never had the misfortune to submit to fingerprinting, or someone outside of the criminal fraternity who, like the vast majority of law-abiding citizens, would not have had their prints on file at the Yard.

In DPP file 2/3717 are to be found Detective Superintendent Gerald McArthur's reports on the conduct of the investigation. They contain several references to the matter of fingerprints and the steps taken to identify and eliminate prints already at the farm before the robbers arrived. The file was originally closed until 2045. A redacted version was opened on 25 June 2010. Two pages were redacted under FOI exemptions, and remain closed until 2045.

The prints referred to by Tommy Butler could belong to the man Biggs refers to as 'Joe', but much more likely to the train driver he originally called 'Fred', who was, as we shall see in due course, a law-abiding citizen with no criminal record.

On Wednesday, 4 September 1963, Ronald Biggs was arrested at his home in Redhill and charged with robbery and conspiracy to rob. This came as a major surprise to the other train robbers, as Biggs had no previous record of a working association with any of them. How, then, had police got onto him? Other gang members also feared that with Biggs now under arrest, attention would soon focus on his associates, and, perhaps sooner rather than later, on the old man he had recruited to drive the train. If that happened, and he was brought in for questioning by the police, he could easily crumble under interrogation and identify most of them by sight.

According to investigation reports,[7] 'during the first week of September' a revelatory new discovery came to light:

At this time information came to hand that Biggs had recruited an ex-Railway Engine Driver known as 'Old Alf' to drive the TPO after Driver Mills had been knocked out but that 'Old Alf' had failed to get the train to move because of the broken vacuum and that Driver Mills had to be brought back to the foot plate. 'Alf' has not so far been identified.[8]

Was the fact that the existence of the retired train driver came to light at approximately the same time as Biggs's arrest purely a coincidence? How did this information come into the hands of the police in the first place, and how did they respond to such a significant development?

It seems that from the off, the police suspected that the old train driver lived in Redhill or the general Redhill area. Surrey police therefore began an immediate investigation to identify 'Old Alf', led by Detective Inspector Basil West. The first and most obvious step for West and his team was to go through Biggs's contacts and associates in fine detail, in the hope that a train driver might turn up among them, or at least someone who knew of Biggs's possible association with a retired train driver.

West began, naturally enough, with Biggs's criminal contacts, which perhaps unsurprisingly failed to turn up any leads. He then progressed to the network of people Biggs had come into contact with, and worked with, since his release from Wandsworth Prison on 2 December 1959, when he moved to Redhill.

Armed with information about Biggs, passed on to him by Scotland Yard, he noted that Biggs had married Charmian Powell on 20 February 1960 at Reigate Register Office, moving into a flat in Elm Road, Redhill, and then proceeding to rent a semi-detached house at 37 Alpine Road, Redhill. Biggs had undertaken a carpentry course in prison and had found work with Reigate Borough Council on release, before seeking better paid work with a number of local builders. He was soon hired on a subcontract basis by Herbert Budgen, a builder, painter and decorator of 37 Garland Road, Redhill. West interviewed Budgen on 6 September, and asked him about any connections he might be aware of between Biggs and anyone who had worked on the railways. Budgen was unaware of any such individuals, although he did volunteer the fact that his firm had undertaken a number of maintenance jobs for British Industrial Sand Ltd, before, during and after the period of Biggs's employment with his firm. BIS, as they were often referred to, were a large and long-established firm who had a network of railway sidings at

Holmethorpe, which spurred off the Redhill mainline and was literally a short walking distance from Biggs's home in Alpine Road. Budgen also told West that he had last employed Biggs in early 1961, after which Biggs had set up on his own with a bricklayer, who had also worked for Budgen, by the name of Ray Stripp.

Police were already aware of Stripp, and had interviewed him the day after Biggs's arrest. The interviewer gleaned little of value and added no more than what was already known.

West's early enquiries threw up only one person by the name of Alf who had any link whatsoever with Biggs:

Alfred John Spooner
D.O.B: 18 July, 1911, Redhill, Surrey
Address: 12 Brambletye Park Road, Redhill, Surrey
Motor Vehicle: Maroon Ford Anglia, Index Number: 1610 R.K.[9]

Spooner was put under observation for a matter of days before it was established that he was, in fact, the father of 'Janet Mary Stripp, wife of Raymond Stripp, Biggs' business partner'. Besides which, it was also found that Spooner was a retired electrician, and had, so far as enquiries could ascertain, no previous connection with any type of railway employment.

It was possibly around this time that C11 reported some new information received from 'sources', which indicated that Alf may not actually be the driver's name. It was probable that, due to the apprehension about involving an outsider, and to avoid a scenario whereby his name might be leaked to someone outside their circle, it would be better to introduce him to the others by another name – hence 'Old Alf'.

By this stage in the investigation, DI West had decided to visit British Industrial Sand Ltd, and made an appointment to visit the Managing Director, Mr Haydn Taylor.

On 23 September, in his Redhill office, Taylor told West that the Holmethorpe operation, the boundary of which was at the eastern end of the curve from the mainline, was worked in accordance with a Private Sidings Agreement between the company and British Railways, which set out the legal terms of the operation and the contractual fees and obligations between the two parties.

He explained that when a British Railways loco arrived with empty wagons and departed with loaded wagons, the crew – a guard and shunter – were British Railways employees. However, the movement of the wagons between the exchange sidings and the loading point was undertaken by the BIS staff who drove the loco, set the points and coupled/uncoupled the wagons. When West asked how many men were employed on shunting work and where they were recruited from, he was told that there were two men shunting and that they were both former British Railways employees.

When he asked Taylor if either of the men had been away from work on 8 August, Taylor replied that one of them had taken a holiday from Tuesday, 6 August, and had returned to work on Monday, 12 August.

West gave Taylor a general description of the man he was interested in, which had been supplied by Buckinghamshire Constabulary, to which Taylor replied that it bore a striking similarity to the man who had been on holiday between 6 August and 12 August.

West was also given to understand that the man would be retiring from BIS very shortly due to reasons connected with his health, which had been declining over a period of time. He had apparently left the employ of British Railways early, some years before, in order to undertake lighter, less demanding work at Holmethorpe.

Whether Biggs met this man during one of his several visits to Holmethorpe to undertake maintenance work, and subsequently did some work on his home, is purely conjecture. What we do know is that no action was taken against this man. In fact, there is no evidence that he was either questioned or directly approached in any way. It is highly likely that further enquiries were later made about him and his state of health. Observations earlier in this book regarding comments made by Biggs relating to the old driver's general demeanour, comments and behaviour at the farm do suggest, at best, an extraordinarily naive and simple man. They may also suggest a man who, for whatever reason, at that stage in his life, was not fully able to cope with, understand or rationalise the reality of events going on around him. Discreet observations were certainly carried out that showed 'there is no indication that either he or his wife, is spending money freely. It has been confirmed that there is no record of either of them having deposited or invested any large sums of money.'[10]

The consensus view on the old man's payment was that he almost certainly never received it. Ronald Biggs was supposedly looking after it for him, but once he was arrested on 4 September, he effectively lost direct control over the money he had. There may, of course, be another explanation as to why the man did not receive his money, of which we are unaware. Biggs certainly refers to the money in his 1969 account, and others who were at the farm refer to his share being counted out in interviews with Piers Paul Read.[11]

A DPP document suggests that even if the old man was interviewed, any possible information that he might be persuaded to divulge about any persons or incidents he had allegedly witnessed would be deemed unreliable in court due to his diagnosed state of mind. It is primarily for this reason that I have not divulged his name in this book. He was arguably more of a victim than a perpetrator, so far as the train robbery was concerned. No doubt, at least so long as he had the ability of recollection, he would have sat at home in anticipation of what he feared would be the inevitable knock on the door one day, either from the police or someone connected with the robbers.

The DPP appears to have taken the view that he was a vulnerable old man who was taken advantage of, and, indeed, used by Biggs as a bargaining chip to gain admission to the gang, in exchange for introducing him as someone who could move the locomotive.

Indeed, fifteen years later, in 1978, the author Piers Paul Read, who had met Biggs in Rio de Janeiro and interviewed him about the robbery, asked him if he knew what had happened to the old man: 'he could not even remember his family name: he showed the same indifference to the fate of the man he had involved in the robbery, and whose whack he had taken, as he did towards his first wife Charmian who remained in Australia.'[12]

Read's rebuke of what he saw as the hidden side of Biggs's otherwise jovial and outgoing personality, in terms of how he used the old man for his own ends, appears to have been well received by those who read his manuscript at Scotland Yard. It was not, however, Read's opinion of Biggs, or even Biggs himself, that was of prime interest to the small group of C11 officers known as 'the bookworms' – they were looking for bigger fish.

PART 3

WILL THE REAL BILL JENNINGS PLEASE STAND UP

THE BOOKWORMS

Wednesday, 8 May 1957

THE CLOCK IN THE House of Commons Chamber was at two minutes to three o'clock. On the green upholstered leather benches, MPs were taking their seats. Outside, the rain lashed down and the wind blew – it hadn't stopped all day. Five minutes before, there were hardly any members in the Chamber; now the place was filling up fast. Anticipation was in the air. The Rt Hon. John Profumo MP, the minister at the dispatch box that afternoon, was acknowledged on both sides of the House as an able performer and an up-and-coming prospect; some were even tipping him for the top job one day.

As the Under-Secretary of State for Colonial Affairs, there were a whole host of possible questions that he might have expected to have been called upon to answer that afternoon. The gradual decolonisation of Africa was beginning at some pace, not to mention initiatives in the West Indies and the Far East. However, it was none of those pressing topics that galvanised several Labour members that afternoon, they had the bit between their teeth about something entirely different: an Ealing comedy film starring Alec Guinness, Stanley Holloway and Sid James. *The Lavender Hill Mob* was all about a daring plan to steal £3 million of gold bullion from the Bank of England. The caper is perpetrated by an insider, an apparently unambitious London bank clerk, Henry 'Dutch' Holland (played by Guinness), who was responsible for the bank's security arrangements.

Mr Anthony Wedgewood-Benn and Mrs Barbara Castle in particular were incensed that the film had been declared as unsuitable for African audiences in a number of colonies and had, as a result, been prohibited from being shown in theatres and cinemas there. Mr Wedgewood-Benn told the minister that the only other nations who had seen fit to ban the film were Eastern Bloc communist nations such as Hungary and Czechoslovakia. Profumo sensed from the start that he was on a sticky wicket. His reply only succeeded in winding up Wedgewood-Benn still further. The film was, Profumo told the House, 'considered unsuitable for African audiences because it contained scenes judged to encourage disrespect for law and order'.[1]

What Profumo couldn't tell the House, and what was not to be revealed to the British public for another thirty years, was that the British Board of Film Censors were not entirely convinced that the film was suitable for British audiences either.

The original story of the Lavender Hill Mob by T.E.B. Clarke, a former policeman, ended with Henry Holland living it up in Brazil on the proceeds of the robbery. This, so far as the censors were concerned, was absolutely unacceptable – there was no way in the world that the British Board of Film Censors would issue the film with a Certificate for 'Universal Exhibition' with an ending like that. The notion of a film that effectively told its audience that crime could pay, and that criminals could indeed 'get away with it', was not something they were willing to sanction. After a good deal of hand-wringing by Ealing Studios, it was reluctantly agreed that the ending would be changed and re-filmed. The film would still open with Holland sitting in a posh restaurant in Rio de Janeiro, explaining to a fellow ex-pat he is dining with how he came to be living a life of luxury in Brazil. However, at the end of the film, as Holland rises from the table to leave the restaurant, it can clearly be seen for the first time that the two men are in fact handcuffed together – his fellow diner is actually a plainclothes Scotland Yard officer who has come to Rio to arrest him and take him back to London. A delicious plot twist, and in the view of some critics, a masterful ending … but not the one originally intended by the writer.

An earlier Ealing film, also written by T.E.B. Clarke (based on a story by Ted Willis and Jan Read), *The Blue Lamp*, was much more to their liking. While this was an early example of a 'social realism' film, as opposed to a comedy, Clarke's story followed a traditional moral parable in which the police, as exemplified by the film's lead character, PC George Dixon, are the honest guardians of a decent society. They battle the post-war rise in violent, antisocial crime, perpetrated by and typified in the film by the ruthless loose cannon Tom Riley (played by Dirk Bogarte).

There had always been a similar parallel, and a long-standing genre in the book trade, whereby retired senior police officers wrote their memoirs, or at least a newspaper serialisation, about their most famous cases. This stretched back to the very early days of Scotland Yard and the Jack the Ripper murders, which also coincided with the birth of the tabloid press. It was almost a rite of passage, akin to the footballer's testimonial match.

There was also, in truth, a ready market for insider 'true crime' police stories, and these were just the type that were acceptable to the mood of the times – the police always catch their man and the crooks are almost always brought to justice.

The notion of criminals telling their story, either directly or by proxy, before the 1960s was rare, if not unheard of. The notion that crime must not be seen to pay, and that criminals should not be paid or seen to profit from for their story being told, was the mantra handed down by the government to the publishers of the day. Things were about to change, though. In May 1964, Brian Field's German-born wife, and former nightclub dancer and hostess, Karin, struck a deal with the German magazine *Stern*. She told the story of the train robbery, from her own perspective, to *Stern* journalist Henry Kolarz. It was his job to ghost-write the story for her, which would appear in *Stern* as 'Das Super Ding' (or in English, 'The Super Crime').

This was to be the first partial telling of the story from someone on the robbers' side of the fence. The *Stern* account was in total contradiction to the story she had told the police, and which she told under oath in the witness box, only three months earlier. In that account, for example, she and her husband were at home alone on the evening of Friday, 9 August, and had received no visitors between 7 and 11 August. In the *Stern* version, she not only described how she helped Roy James get back to London, but also stated that eight of the gang slept overnight at the Fields' detached home at Whitchurch Hill, near Reading, on 9 August. While she seeks to minimise the role of her husband in these events, she names the eight men as Goody, Wilson, Welch, Hussey, Wisbey and two other men she refers to as George and John (who seem to correspond with Biggs's Joe and Sid).

Karin Field's revelations were carefully studied by intelligence handlers in C11, although there appears to have been little mood or motivation at the Yard, or at the DPP, to take any proceedings against her for perjury. Legal proceedings, were, however, to be initiated from a very different quarter. On 26 October 1964, Tommy Butler received a visit at Scotland Yard from Mr R.C.M. Sykes, a solicitor from the firm of Simmons and Simmons of 14 Dominion Street, London EC2. The firm had been retained and instructed by the *Sunday People* newspaper, who were being sued for libel by Brian Field and eight others involved in the train robbery case: Robert Welch, James Hussey, Thomas Wisbey, Gordon Goody, Miss Gillian Prentergast, Mrs Rene Wisbey, Miss Patricia Copper and Mrs Jean Welch. Sykes discussed 'certain aspects of the affair' and told Butler that he intended to interview Field's father and hoped to travel to Germany to see Field's wife Karin.

The bookworms in C11 would not have to wait too long for another train robbery book to come along. The month after the *Sunday People* serialisation, a book by former Detective Superintendent John Gosling and crime writer Dennis Craig, *The Inside Story of the Great Train Robbery*, was published by W.H. Allen. Despite the claimed 'inside sources', C11 dismissed the book out of hand as 'essentially a work of fiction'. Quick on the heels of the Gosling and Craig book came Ross Richards's *The Great Train Robbery*. Publishers World Distributors Ltd claimed it was based upon the 'off the record words of the police and criminals' and was 'the first, authentic reconstruction of the most outrageous robbery in history'. C11, again, begged to differ – their verdict was that the book 'was based on a subtle blend of fantasy, runaway imagination and press cuttings'.[2]

C11 had known for some time about another book that was in the pipeline, by Peta Fordham, the wife of QC Wilfred Fordham, who had represented Ronald Biggs, John Daly and Gordon Goody at the Aylesbury trial.

In a still closed file, Detective Chief Superintendent Tommy Butler penned a report to Deputy Commander Ernie Millen, outlining that:

On the evening of Friday, 12 February, 1965, information was received in this Office to the effect that serialised excerpts from a book, written by Mrs Peta Fordham, would commence in the 'Sunday Times' dated 14 February 1965.

Mrs Fordham is the wife of Wilfred Fordham of Counsel, who handled the defence of Ronald Arthur Biggs, one of the men convicted of the robbery. She attended the sittings of the Bucks Winter Sessions at Aylesbury every day throughout the trial, and made many notes. Even during the trial period, it was known she was collecting data for a book she intended writing, and had made tentative enquiries of several organs of the Press she thought might be interested in publishing her efforts. In view of this, on Saturday 13 February, 1965, I went to Thomson House, 200 Grays Inn Road, WC1, and interviewed Mr Derek Harris of the Editorial Features Department.

He confirmed that the information we had received was correct. It was therefore pointed out to him that, as three men (Reynolds, White and Edwards), were still wanted by Police for the commission of the offence, a publication such as that envisaged would probably be prejudicial to their fair trial when they are arrested. He was informed that Warrants existed for all three.

He explained that the newspaper was printing excerpts of a book called 'The Robbers Tale', written by Mrs Fordham, which is very shortly to be published by the well-known publishers, Hodder and Stoughton & Co. Ltd. Mr Harris added that everything in the book would of course be examined by the newspaper's legal advisors in the normal course, in addition to the scrutiny doubtlessly made by the legal advisers of the publishers of the complete book.

He said that the problem was one which worried all publishers of printed matter, and one upon which there was very little precedence in Criminal Law. He agreed that the persons named had ample grounds for a libel action and this aspect would doubtlessly be fully considered by his employers, prior to any publication. It was a risk of which every newspaper Editor was fully conscious[3]

The meeting with Mr Harris was, Butler reported, 'quite amicable – he seemingly understanding perfectly the motives prompting it'.

Ronald 'Buster' Edwards later described the book as 'full of childish lies'.[4] Even Fordham herself confessed at the very beginning that 'no one is more conscious than I of the gaps in the story'.[5] This, in the view of C11, was very much an understatement. In their view, the book was 'punctuated with wild guesswork masquerading as received fact'. One of the many examples given of this was the matter of the money dumped in the woods at Dorking:

As to how the money got into Dorking Woods, the explanation was given to me by one of the plotters ... anyone who likes to pursue a game of 'Inspector Scott Investigates' on his own, will find most of the clues in the shorthand transcript of the trial. He will also need maps of the roads by which Brighton is reached from the outer western suburbs of London. If he likes to obtain the relevant copies of the *Der Stern*, he will need only to supply a linking name which, in conjunction with these clues, he should find no difficulty in selecting. One name would be wrong: that of Brian Field.[6]

Written in large letters at the foot of this extract is the comment: 'UTTER NONSENSE!'[7]

The reason for this uncompromising verdict can be found elsewhere in the very same file: undisputed evidence that it was indeed none other than Brian Field, his father Reginald and best friend Gordon Neal who dumped the money, and later made a full confession.[8]

Other paragraphs that warranted the same blunt verdict included the assertion by Fordham that the robbers' convoy was led by a motorbike,[9] and her description of the man she claims was behind the robbery – 'The Mind'[10] – which attracts additional scorn from C11: 'RIDICULOUS'.[11]

Shortly after his arrest in April 1966, Jimmy White's story appeared in the *Sunday People*. It was viewed as anodyne by C11, and attracted the comment: 'There is nothing here which has any bearing on the inquiries.'[12]

It would be another four years before anything else was written by, or on behalf of, anyone connected with the robbery. Ronald Biggs's seventy-sevem pages of transcript certainly gave the bookworms something to get their teeth into in April 1970. They seemed to be primarily interested in comments and aspersions made by Biggs, relating to the conduct of the police:

The main document consists of the story in relation to the planning and execution of the train robbery, the events which followed his arrest, remand in prison, committal, trial, sentence and eventual escape.

The following points occur in the story which involve the police.

Page 14 – para. 3 & 4.V.H.F. used to listen for police messages following raid.

Page 16 – last line. Indications of 'Obliging Old Bill'

Page 18 – last para. 'Old Bill' said to be flying about everywhere following raid.

Page 20 – para. 3. Reynolds guesses correctly police will suspect him and his associates.

Page 20 – para. 5. Ridiculous description of police officers seeking robbers.

Page 21 – para. 4.Inspector Morris of Reigate calls and questions Biggs re Reynolds - tends to discredit ability of Morris and his cursory search of his Biggs' home.

Page 22 – para. 2. Inspector Morris asks Biggs to help trace Reynolds.Whole thing is derogatory and also makes fun of Morris' appearance.

Page 22 – para. 3. Inspector Williams and D/S Moore arrest Biggs.

Page 22 – last para. Biggs recounts interview with D/C/Supt. Butler.

Page 23 – Interview with Butler who indicates that if Biggs does not give the required answer to a questionnaire then Butler will supply the answer he wants. Explains verbals.

Details how wife's school friend told her that a D/C friend at C.C. had informed her that the case against the robbers would be based on fingerprint evidence.

Page 25 – Infers that Goody and Boal were fitted up by paint on shoes of former and door knob in case of latter, which corresponded with paint at farm and on a lorry.[13]

By comparison, the saga of Fred, Sid, Joe and Bert receives little attention, presumably because C11 were already aware of the background to their identities (or at least three of them). C11 did, however, note Biggs's failure to mention that it was actually he that introduced the old train driver.They also took the view that while the narrative was essentially accurate, Biggs had, to an extent, exaggerated his role and involvement in the raid itself.

When, in 1976, Read was first introduced to the robbers at the headquarters of W.H. Allen in Mayfair, it was made clear to him that they would not be saying anything that could incriminate anyone who had not been apprehended or charged at the time. However, tiny clues and small throwaway mentions about the men and their relationships to the others were only of relevance to the police, who knew most of the background anyway, or to those in the criminal fraternity, who were equally in the know. To anyone else reading Piers Paul Read's book, when it was eventually published in 1978, the small, unintentional micro-clues would mean absolutely nothing. They would only do so when lined up against information in police and GPO files, the bulk of which were not to see the light of day until 2010–12.

Of the fifteen men who stopped the train at Sears Crossing, four, as Biggs makes clear in his 1969 manuscript, were never charged. After studying Read's manuscript, C11 were clear that the four aliases used by Biggs correlated with Read's alias and their knowledge as follows:

Fred =	Stan Agate	Identified but not named
Bert =	Alf Thomas =	Harry Smith
Joe =	Bill Jennings	Unidentified
Sid =	Frank Monroe =	Danny Pembroke[14]

Frank Monroe (or Munroe – the spelling was not stipulated by those giving the taped interviews), Alf Thomas and Bill Jennings were aliases created by the robbers when giving their taped accounts. However, the alias 'Stan Agate' was the exception. Read had actually taken it from an earlier 1975 book, *The Most Wanted Man: The Story of Ronald Biggs*, written by Colin McKenzie. This book was based, in part, on McKenzie's tape-recorded interviews with Biggs in Rio de Janeiro on 30 and 31 January 1974, just prior to his arrest on 1 February 1974, with supplementary material taken from *The Sun* newspaper's 1970 serialisation. In his book, McKenzie gives the old train driver the alias 'Stan Agate'. Thirty-five years later, McKenzie revealed that he named the train driver after a real-life Stan Agate, who was a former *Daily Mail* racing correspondent.[15]

While there was nothing in the Read interviews that disclosed information that might directly point to the involvement of Pembroke and Smith in the robbery, or directly link the 'Alf Thomas' alias with Harry Smith, or the 'Frank Monroe' alias with Danny Pembroke, there were several references to matters and relationships the police already knew about that made it significantly easier to identify which aliases were relative to Smith and which to Pembroke. These references would mean nothing to the everyday reader, while those with personal knowledge of the two men would, without too much difficulty, be able to identify the connections.

The main conundrum was not therefore 'Frank' and 'Alf', for the police had known of their involvement in the robbery for over ten years, and had reluctantly reconciled themselves to the fact that it was never going to be possible to charge them, even for possession. Neither was it difficult to match Danny Pembroke with Read's 'Frank Monroe', or Harry Smith with his 'Alf Thomas'. Harry Smith was indeed, as the interviews stated, a tall, well-built man, who had an HGV licence and was a close friend and associate of Jimmy White. Likewise, Danny Pembroke's C11 file showed that he was indeed a friend and associate of both Tommy Wisbey and Bob Welch, had grown up in the same neighbourhood as Wisbey, and had introduced him and Bob Welch to Roger Cordrey. There were also voluminous pages of police and GPO observation records showing him staying at Beaford House with Bob Welch and other associates in September and October 1963.

Likewise, C11 found many of the other aliases given to characters in Read's book relatively easy to identify, due to the explicit and factual references to them and to events they had participated in, most of which were documented in police records:

Mike Prince – George Foreman
Johnny Prince - Freddie Foreman
Bernie Carton – Freddie Foreman
Gus Brown – Jimmy Collins
Joey Gray – Joseph Hartfield
Harry Booth – Terry Hogan
Derek Glass – Billy Green
Godfrey Green – Michael Black[16]

No, the mystery was not about Frank and Alf, or indeed about the old train driver – it was about 'Bill Jennings'. Unlike Frank and Alf, who are mentioned sparingly in the Read interviews, an absolute abundance of information on Jennings is scattered throughout. Why? Why so much information about Jennings? It was almost as if it was a deliberate ploy, the 'too much information' technique to muddy the water.

There was also a suspicion by the bookworms at Scotland Yard that there might be other examples within the manuscript of the same character being given more than one alias. For example, very early in Read's story, a friend of Buster Edwards, who was a partner with him in running the 'Walk-Inn' Club in Lambeth, is referred to as Johnny Prince. Later on in the story, the same man, who is in reality Freddie Foreman, is now referred to as Bernie Carton. C11, therefore, speculated that there could potentially be at least one other instance, if not more, of a character being referred to by different aliases at different stages of the narrative. By this hypothesis, Bill Jennings could equally be referred to by another name at some point or points in the book.

The train robbers, in particular Pembroke and Smith, had probably rightly assumed that while they had been arrested and questioned shortly after the robbery, the long passage of time subsequently must surely suggest that there was no realistic possibility either one of them should believe that the police had any evidence on them that would satisfy a court all these years later. 'Bill Jennings', on the other hand, had never, so far as we are aware, been previously arrested or questioned about the train robbery. He cannot, therefore, have been completely confident that he had either never been previously suspected, or that he might not be in the future, if sufficient information or suspicion came to light.

Having gone through the account with a fine-toothed comb, C11 speculated that 'the man referred to as Bill Jennings is clearly a compendium of several men known to the police'. In fact, the real Bill Jennings might not have been any of the multiple cast of characters paraded in the Read interviews.

One of the pitfalls of intelligence gathering is the temptation to overanalyse and see concealed patterns and coincidences, when frankly there aren't any. One officer, for example, believed that the name Monroe was significant as it is an anagram of Danny Pembroke; another noted that Harry Smith's middle name was Thomas, and hence a link to Alf Thomas. The occurrence of coincidences was of particular interest to Swiss psychiatrist Carl Jung, who developed a theory that remarkable coincidences occur, or are perceived to occur, because of what is called 'synchronicity'. However, this has been opposed by a significant number of mathematicians who argue that from a mathematical perspective, with only twenty-six letters in the English alphabet, the odds of anagrams (intentional or unintentional) occurring within words of certain lengths is statistically quite high. An example is that of mutual birthdays, which shows that the probability of two persons having the same birthday exceeds 50 per cent in a group of twenty-three or more people.

Another hypothesis considered by C11 was less to do with the fact that the interviewees had kicked over the traces so far as Jennings's identity was concerned, and more to do with the important and more relevant question of why. Might, for example, 'Jennings', in the mid-1970s, have been implicated or suspected of other serious offences, that could have been further prejudiced by even the smallest suggestion or suspicion that he might have earlier been implicated in the mail train robbery in 1963?

THREE-CARD MONTE

THE OLD NORTH ROAD, or the Great Cambridge Road, as it was known at one time, was, 400 years ago, a haunt of the highway robber Dick Turpin and a host of other 'Knights of the Road'.

Beginning at London Bridge in the Borough of Southwark, the road proceeded along King William Street, Gracechurch Street and Bishopsgate in the City, before heading north through Hackney and along Shoreditch High Street. It passed Harry Smith's A1 Self Service store on Kingsland High Street, before winding through Stoke Newington and Tottenham. By the end of the 1960s, it was better known to motorists as the A10. For members of Scotland Yard's CID, however, mention of the A10 would, from 1972, have meant something entirely unconnected with a London street map.

On 31 March that year, Commissioner Sir John Waldron retired. There were already several police corruption probes in the Sunday newspapers and these only added to the air of uncertainty that hung over Scotland Yard at the time. The Home Secretary of the day, Reginald Maudling, decided that a new broom was necessary at the Yard, and appointed Sir Robert Mark as the new Commissioner. It was announced at the same time that the old-school Assistant Commissioner, Peter Brodie,[1] who commanded CID, would be retiring the day before Mark's appointment. Mark not only announced a new Assistant Commissioner (Crime), Colin Woods, but also the creation of A10, a new specialist unit to investigate police corruption. Mark immediately proceeded with a root-and-branch campaign against corrupt detectives, telling officers that 'a good police force is one that catches more crooks than it employs'.[2] Among those rooted out were Commander Kenneth Drury, the Head of the Flying Squad, and Detective Chief Superintendent Bill Moody, Head of the Obscene Publications Squad, and ironically responsible for A10's predecessor, the Anti-Corruption Squad.

Both were eventually jailed. Nearly 500 others were dismissed or forced to resign. Mark's view was that CID was, 'routinely corrupt' and said that he would get rid of it altogether if necessary. Asked if he had threatened to put all CID officers back in uniform if that's what it took, Mark responded that: 'I don't regard that as a threat. I look upon it simply as a managerial statement of fact.'[3]

While A10 were primarily concerned with investigating the swarm of current cases being flagged up, they were equally keen to investigate 'cold cases' where contemporary enquires might be linked to past examples of corruption or miscarriages of justice. One former senior Flying Squad officer, Detective Chief Superintendent Frank Williams, who had been a key member of Tommy Butler's Train Robbery Squad, and later Butler's Flying Squad deputy, had already taken retirement by the time Sir Robert Mark became Commissioner. He had regularly been accused of bribery, blackmail and corruption while on the Flying Squad, to such an extent that even Assistant Commissioner Peter Brodie, who was instinctively wary of corruption investigations, as he believed they were bad for CID morale, had been forced to initiate several internal inquiries into Williams's conduct. None of these had, in fact, resulted in any action being taken against Williams and other officers thought to be complicit with him.

By 1976, deeper questions were being asked by A10 as the result of several cases involving a number of high-profile criminals who appeared to have been able, in the not-too-distant past, to effectively buy themselves out of trouble. Information in exchange for cash and favours had been open to controversy for many years, but the type of deals now rumoured to be taking place made them appear small fry by comparison. Williams's 'deals' with criminals had raised eyebrows at the Yard a good decade before Sir Robert Mark and his new broom arrived. This may have been one of the reasons why DCS Tommy Butler had neglected to mention to Commander Millen and Assistant Commissioner Hatherill the machinations behind the two sacks of cash left in the telephone box at Blackhorse Court in December 1963, and the 'deal' with Harry Smith, not to mention the surrender of Buster Edwards in September 1966.

Following the arrest of Charlie Richardson and ten others on 29/30 July 1966, in-depth investigations followed, led by Gerald McArthur, formerly a key member of the train robbery investigation team, and now Assistant Chief Constable of Hertfordshire, commanding No. 5 Regional Crime Squad. These resulted in one of the longest criminal trails in British legal history, lasting from 4 April 1967 to 8 June 1967.

Charlie Richardson alleged in a number of statements that he had been paying police officers sums of money for over ten years. He further added a stroke of irony by asserting that his troubles with the police only began when he stopped paying them, as he no longer saw the point now that he was involved in 'legitimate business'. While the trial ended with Richardson receiving a twenty-five-year custodial sentence, several behind-the-scenes investigations followed into a number of police officers suspected of receiving money from Charlie Richardson. The result of these investigations was that no action was deemed warranted in respect to any of the investigated officers. A file containing information on these investigations was eventually sent to the DPP, which has never been released to the public: 'WILLIAMS, Francis (Detective Superintendent), SMITH, Jim (Detective Inspector) and others: police investigation into allegations against police officers made during enquiries into criminal activities of Charles Richardson. No action.'[5]

While efforts are currently under way to have this file opened under an FOI request, early indications are that this will be resisted. It is therefore not possible, at this point in time, to ascertain the merits or otherwise of the allegations levelled at Frank Williams and other officers in 1967.

Frank Williams retired from the Metropolitan Police in 1971, a year before the creation of A10. However, Sir Robert Mark was of the view that, prior to A10, there had at best been no appetite to root out corrupt officers, and at worst, a blind eye had been turned in some quarters to such activities. While the rise of the super-grass culture, in the advent of the deal struck between armed robber Derek 'Bertie' Smalls and the Director of Public Prosecutions in 1973,[6] was certainly a controversial development, it was a deal, however questionable, that had been officially negotiated and sanctioned by the DPP. The deals done with Harry Smith and Buster Edwards, for example, were very much unofficial, below the radar, and almost always, so rumour had it, involved a generous 'commission' for the officer who brokered it. Sir Robert Mark was convinced that such deals were not only still being done, but were more widespread than ever.

Perhaps the most obvious and large-scale example that came to light during Mark's term as Commissioner involved one James Humphreys, and a host of other porn shop owners in London's Soho district. On 28 February 1976, twelve senior police officers were arrested on corruption charges. Eight had recently retired, while four others, including Commander Kenneth Drury, Head of the Flying Squad, Detective Chief Superintendent Bill Moody, Head of the Obscene Publications Squad, and their overall boss, Commander Wally Virgo, were already under suspension. According to evidence presented in court in March 1977, Humphreys and his associates were paying a mammoth £100,000 per year (£1,250,000 in today's money) to corrupt police officers to enable them to ply their trade. During the trial, Humphreys told the court that in addition to weekly cash payments, he also regularly wined and dined Drury and his wife at top London restaurants, including the Ritz and the Savoy, and paid for gifts and foreign holidays. In fact, he claimed to have become so worried about Drury's excessive appetite and consequent weight gain that he feared this would raise suspicions, and therefore bought Drury an expensive course of slimming drugs and an exercise bike.

With the arrest of Billy Ambrose on 13 August 1976, and the questions that were already being asked about his antecedents and possible connections to the train robbery, A10 too began to take an interest. Who might the 'the third man' have been, and had he possibly avoided arrest as a result of an understanding with one or more police officers?

There were clearly two key questions in relation to the man we shall henceforth call 'Bill Jennings' – in other words, the man originally referred to in Ronald Biggs's 1969 manuscript as 'Joe'. The first and most obvious was, of course, his identity; the second was why there was so little intelligence or even speculation on record about him. What little speculation there was within C11 was to the effect that the 'third man' was either such a small fry criminal that he had been able to remain under the police radar throughout, or alternatively, he was such a big fish as to have avoided arrest by surreptitious means. This second scenario was the one that most vexed A10.

C11 therefore began a thorough review of the intelligence they held, or were aware of, in relation to the 'third man'. They began, ironically, with the file of a man who had the perfect alibi – he was in prison, albeit for a few weeks, at the time of the train robbery. However, his story could, analysts believed, be an important link to Bill Jennings.

His file revealed that one of the first shreds of information that came C11's way pre-dated the train robbery by two months, and at first seemed like a trivial, unimportant scrap of tittle-tattle. In late June 1963, information suggested that there had been much commotion at Lessor & Co., the Newham-based solicitors, who would later represent a number of those charged in connection with the train robbery. The apparent cause of this flurry was the arrest on 21 June of one William Still, and three others – Alexander Brown, Earl Hanslow, and Frederick Smith – who had been stopped in Euston Square by a police officer. He proceeded to search them, and found in their possession explosives, detonators, drills, putty, a pickaxe handle, a jemmy and nylon stockings. They were therefore arrested and taken to Albany Street Police Station, where they were charged with possessing explosives and remanded in custody.

The intriguing thing was that Lessor & Co. were apparently instructed to secure bail for Billy Still, and Billy Still only, at virtually any cost. Vast sums of money were promised to Lessor & Co., so the informant suggested, if they could secure his prompt release. While this snippet of intelligence was somewhat puzzling at the time, it was only flagged when two months later, on 21 August, Mary Manson (also known as Mary McDonald), the wife of Still's business partner, James McDonald,[7] was arrested by Detective Inspector Frank Williams on suspicion of receiving stolen money. This followed a telephone call from the Chequered Flag motor dealership in Chiswick, to the effect that she had accompanied a man, who matched the description of Bruce Reynolds, and purchased an Austin Healy 3000 sports car for the sum of £835, which she paid for in cash.

While Manson was being taken from Scotland Yard, where she had been making a statement, to her home address at 4 Wimbledon Close, Wimbledon, which Williams and Detective Chief Inspector Baldock were about to search, she allegedly told Williams: 'Do you remember me? I was at Judge in Chambers and saw you when Billy Still applied for bail. Do you know he's applied two or three times …? I'm glad he didn't get bail otherwise I knew he would have been on the Aylesbury job with Reynolds.'[8]

This was of great interest to C11; was it indeed the case that Still had been, until his arrest on 21 June, a member of the team planning the train robbery? If so, had he been replaced with another man at that point, or had it been decided to press ahead, one man down? Another source of information suggested that while Still may not have been in on the robbery team, he was possibly the man given responsibility for cleaning up Leatherslade Farm afterwards. Either way, his enforced absence would have put a spoke in the works so far as preparations for the big job were concerned.

Once Ronald Biggs's fingerprints had identified him as a probable participant in the robbery, the view was taken by C11 that his non-appearance on the Hatherill list of suspects was possibly explained by the fact that the informant's knowledge pre-dated June 1963, when Biggs had joined the gang. Alternatively, Biggs may have been the thirteenth person on the Hatherill list – who is referred to as a 'Nondescript man – not named, maybe Jimmy Collins.' This, however, was thought unlikely. Alternatively, could the nondescript man have been Billy Still or even the elusive Bill Jennings? Attention would return to Jimmy Collins in due course.

Still's C11 file listed his associates as:

Ambrose	William D.
Bottom	William C.
Brown	Alexander.
Callaghan	Jeremiah
Daly	John
Daniels	Arthur
Greenwood	Harry
Hanslow	Earl E.
Heywood	Charles F.
Jones	Arthur B.
McDonald	James S.
McDonald	Mary
Morse	Brian
Reynolds	Bruce[9]

Billy Ambrose, apart from being an associate of Billy Still, was also listed as an associate of Bruce Reynolds. According to his C11 file, in 1952, Still was among a number of men arrested and charged with the robbery of 2 million cigarettes from the Leeds warehouse of H. Field Limited. On 29 May, while being taken from Leeds Magistrates Court to Armley Gaol in a prison van:

> with the aid of outside accomplices, he forced open the van door and escaped with three other prisoners. While the other three men were recaptured within 48 hours, Still remained at large for over two years before being arrested by the Irish police in Roscrea, Tipperary on 1 August, 1954.[10]

Billy Ambrose's wife, Elizabeth, had also been charged with being an accessory after the fact in connection with the H. Field Limited cigarette robbery, receiving stolen cigarettes, and conspiracy. She pleaded not guilty; the prosecution offered no evidence against her, and on the instructions of the judge, the jury returned a verdict of not guilty.

Was Billy Ambrose 'the third man'? If so, was there any evidence that had previously been missed to suggest this, and if so, how had his activities remained in the shadows over the past decade? Apart from his Cahill Engineering business in East London, he also operated a bookmaking business in London's Soho. Were there any connections in this respect to other ongoing A10 investigations relating to Kenneth Drury, Wally Virgo and Bill Moody?

Billy Ambrose's name had been sixteenth on Tommy Butler's suspect list of eighteen names. By 1976, Butler had been dead for six years. A man who kept his cards close to his chest, along with his informants, took his secrets to the grave. However, Detective Chief Superintendent Tommy Morrison told A10 that Jimmy Humphreys had been an informer for many years and had been one of Butler's sources at the time of the train robbery.[11] His suspect list had apparently been drawn up from a number of informant sources, including Humphreys, who in 1976 was helping A10 in connection with their investigations of Drury, Virgo and Moody. It was apparent, too, that a number of individuals on Butler's list had been eliminated from further enquiries due to the provision of alibis.

Had anyone on the suspect list later been found to be handing or laundering large sums of money, further enquiries would no doubt have been made. That said, no further enquiries of this kind appear to have been subsequently pursued, and there appear to be no recorded concerns regarding Ambrose between 1963 and his arrest in 1976. However, something had slipped through the net, as early in the Serious Crime Squad's investigation into the fourteen individuals arrested on 13 August 1976, an approach had been made through Interpol for any information that might assist Scotland Yard's investigation. As a result, a number of responses were received, one of which led to a small degree of friction between London and Paris.

The French authorities had reported back that the only information they held was a file on William D. Ambrose and William A. Voss, which they had copied to Scotland Yard back in August 1964. The Yard responded by effectively asking the question, 'What file?' The French reiterated that a copy of the file had been sent to Scotland Yard as a matter of routine and concerned the arrest and conviction of the pair for offences relating to American Express. The Yard denied all knowledge of ever receiving it. While another copy was grudgingly sent from Paris, no record of that file appears to exist today, which is not to say that its contents no longer exist – only that it does not appear to be recorded. Thankfully, however, in May 2021, after much dialogue with the French authorities, the original French file was opened and released by the Paris judicial authorities:

Hearing - 25 July 1964
On behalf of the Public Prosecutor and American Express Company Incorporated, an American company with French Headquarters in Paris, Rue Scribe, represented by their residing MD.

Defendants
William Anthony Voss, born 6 October 1939, London (GB) also known as Terrence Huckfield, of 6 Bewley Close, Bewley Street, London, British. Currently detained and with no other information available.

William Ambrose, born 21 September 1929, London, England. Son of William & Sarah Welsh, resident of 14 Brock Place, Glaucus Street, London. Bookmaker, married with one child and British.

The Case
Possession of Stolen Goods, Use of False Passports, Falsification of Bank documents, Fraud and Attempted Fraud.

Voss & Ambrose together collaboratively:

Knowingly received fraudulent travellers' cheques taken from American Express, committed bank forgery in writing by falsifying stolen traveller's cheques and using them under false pretence.

Using fraudulent means to obtain credit, in this case, by falsifying traveller's cheques, by using fake passports at different banks and obtaining a total of 18,000 francs approximately; and attempting to obtain a further 2,000 francs, the process of which was started but not successful owing to various circumstances outside of their control, and therefore having defrauded or attempted to defraud American Express.

Voss:

By using fraudulent means to establish credit and in this case, by using fake traveller's cheques and a fake passport, also received two shirts and two ties from Maison Gerber.

Using a false passport in a false name.[12]

The file went on to outline the finer points of the proceedings, details of the prosecution's case, and that of the defence. It also outlined the points of law on which Ambrose and Voss were found guilty of the offences of which they were charged. William Voss and Ambrose Williams were both sentenced to eighteen months in prison. Both were also ordered to pay American Express the sum of 19,005 francs, of which 18,970 francs was seized from them on arrest.

The immediate reaction to the 1964 Paris case was its distinct similarity to the offences that Ambrose, Voss and others were now under arrest for in 1976. An obvious question was, how did the file manage to disappear in 1964? Were there any other cases of an international dimension of which Scotland Yard were equally unaware? As the Serious Crime Squad investigation progressed in the autumn of 1976, information suggested that the answer to this could possibly be yes.

Information in the possession of UK sources abroad suggested that there was a link between the case in hand and one Otto Skorzeny, the former Waffen-SS lieutenant colonel who had led the 1943 Gran Sasso raid that, on Hitler's orders, rescued Mussolini from captivity. After the war, Skorzeny settled in Franco's Spain and, in addition to a number of far-right political machinations, set up a property investment company there. The same sources also indicated that train robber Buster Edwards and at least one other person suspected of involvement in the train robbery, possibly the third man, had invested in Skorzeny's property venture. Detectives in London were, as a result, of the view that Skorzeny could be of assistance to the investigation, and preparations were made to send officers to Spain to interview him. Plans to do so were scuppered when it was learnt that he had died from cancer the previous year.[13]

C11 were also aware, through their records on Harry Smith, of several documented connections between Smith and Ambrose. These related initially to 496 Barking Road, E13, which C11 believed:

had been purchased by Harry Smith through Danny Reagan on 7 October 1963 from Richard George Cahill. Cahill (born 20 December, 1924, Silvertown, West

Ham), also known as George Cahill, is the brother of William Cahill (born 19 December 1922, Silvertown, West Ham), whose engineering firm has been headed by Ambrose, since 1964.

As mentioned in Chapter 7, the property was lived in, alternately, by Smith, Ambrose and their respective families from 1963 to the time the Ambrose family moved to Esher in 1975. It had originally been owned by Richard George Cahill, who then moved to 27 St Mary's Avenue, Wanstead.

It was also noted that Richard George Cahill had, in 1964, been a shareholder in the Portsmouth-based company Dales Properties Ltd, which connected him with Danny Regan and the property transactions investigated by Hampshire Police, and outlined in the Harry Smith train robbery file.[14] His elder brother, William, a co-director of William Cahill & Son Engineering Ltd, along with Billy Ambrose, tragically died in a crane accident in Portsmouth on 1 July 1973.

One of the few things C11 were reasonably sure of about the 'third man' was that he was reputedly a close friend and associate of Buster Edwards. Billy Ambrose, was, of course, an associate of Edwards, but then again, so were several others who were considered to be possible candidates for the 'third man'.

Terry Hogan was a case in point. A member of the Billy Hill gang in his early twenties,[15] he was, by the late 1950s, a close associate of Bruce Reynolds. Not long afterwards, he met and began working with Gordon Goody and Buster Edwards. C11 were pretty much convinced that Hogan had participated in the London Airport raid in November 1962, and were equally convinced that he was a member of the train robbery gang from its inception, to around May/June 1963. Word from several informants, some three months later, was that he had bowed out. Views differed as to why; one source claimed he was, by then, making good money from a long fraud, and felt no need to chance his arm. However, the sources were certain that he had no involvement in the train gang after that time. Again, if this is true, was he replaced by another man, or did the gang soldier along without him? C11 were unsure whether 'the third' man had been on the team from the very start, or whether he was a last-minute substitute for Hogan or Still.

Hogan, known to many as 'Lucky Tel', had a reputation for ensuring that he always had a watertight alibi when he most needed one. He certainly had an alibi for the train robbery; not just any old alibi, like some of the other robbers, such as Bobby Welch, who was apparently playing golf in Beckenham on 8 August 1963, or no alibi at all. On Wednesday, 21 August, a week after the discovery of Leatherslade Farm, word came to Hogan's ears that the police were looking for him. He therefore headed to solicitors Lessor & Co., from where he, solicitors' clerk George

Stanley and Mary Manson went to Scotland Yard to make a voluntary statement. Information received suggested that Hogan was in a highly agitated state, and apparently feared a frame-up. If true, this might well back up his claim not to have been involved in any aspect of the robbery. However, Gordon Goody at this time apparently also entertained the same fears.[16]

In his statement, made to Detective Inspector Frank Williams, Hogan told him that he had driven to Cannes on 6 August and had driven back to England on 9 August. He further provided the names of several people he had met at the Martinez Hotel during the short time he was there. He also alluded to a postcard he had sent while there, which was postmarked 8 August 1963. As C11 noted, even if true, it demonstrated that Hogan almost certainly had advance awareness that the robbery was to take place during the period of his absence, hence his carefully timed journey to Cannes. Not unsurprisingly, Detective Chief Superintendent Tommy Butler promptly turned to the French Sûreté Nationale to assist in verifying Hogan's alibi.

C11 was also sure that Hogan had, shortly after Reynolds purchased the Austin Healey sports car, registration number 222 NFC, on 9 August, been with Reynolds when he garaged the car at Cranford Hall Garage, Hayes. Hogan's green Zephyr had also been observed parked nearby.

The police had put out an appeal through the press, asking the public to keep an eye open for the Austin Healey. As a result, James Bryning contacted the police to say he had seen the car in the car park of his block of flats in Ealing. Detective Constable Frank Cowling from Ealing Police Station was sent over to investigate:

> I visited 10 Walpole Lodge, Cunningham Road, Ealing W5, and saw Terence Hogan. I said to him, 'I am making enquiries to trace the owner of an Austin Healey motor car Registration No 222 NFC; this car is believed to have been outside this block of flats recently.' Hogan said, 'I don't know anything about it. I have never had Healey; my car is outside, the Zephyr.' At the time I had no reason to question Hogan further. Outside the flats in Culmington Road, I saw a Green Ford Zephyr motor car, Registration number 591 FGX, which Hogan had pointed out as being his.[17]

At Scotland Yard, Cowling's investigation report was read by Tommy Butler, who immediately recognised the name of Hogan:

> The occupier of 10 Walpole Lodge is Terry Hogan, a friend of Bruce Reynolds. Hogan was, on 19 August, in possession of a green Zodiac, index number 591

FGX, reference to Mr Morris's statement will show that when Reynolds parked the Austin Healey at Cranford Hall Garage, Hayes, he walked along the Bath Road and got into a Ford Zodiac or Zephyr of the latest model which was of a dark colour.[18]

It is only now, nearly six decades after the event, that we know the French Sûreté Nationale were unable to completely verify Hogan's alibi. They certainly succeeded in locating several individuals Hogan claimed to have met while there. However, the Sûreté Nationale stated that they were unreliable witnesses due to their character and record. They further pointed out that the Cannes postcard, which Butler had sent them, was certainly posted in Cannes on the morning of 8 August 1963, but could literally have been posted by anyone; the fact that it was in Hogan's handwriting did not prove that he himself had posted the card.

It is interesting that Hogan was never, at any stage, dismissed as a suspect by C11. This is also evidenced by the fact that his name is still listed as a possible suspect in a Flying Squad report, shared with the Post Office Investigation Branch, dated 12 May 1964.[19]

C11 were also intrigued by the twelfth person on Hatherill's list of seventeen suspects: 'Fair-haired boy 25 years old – well spoken – not named.'[20]

Could this possibly be Terry Hogan? Whether he had dropped out around June 1963 or not, the Hatherill list certainly raises the possibility of someone matching Hogan's general description being in the circle of conspirators at this key time. Identifications and descriptions, even those given of individuals seen from comparatively close quarters, can sometimes be far from reliable. The London Airport job is a case in point, which may yield further clues about the identity of the third man.

TINKER, TAILOR

THE GAME OF THREE-CARD Monte had a long pedigree so far as confidence games went. Some authorities argued that its origins could be traced back to Renaissance Italy. Canada Bill Jones,[1] an English-born confidence trickster, river-boat gambler and card sharp, was considered the uncrowned king of Three-Card Monte in the middle of the nineteenth century in the so-called Wild West of the United States.

The Pinkerton Detective Agency chased him across America. They may have got the better of Jesse James and Butch Cassidy, but they never got to collar Canada Bill. In 1898, the Pinkertons had pursued Soapy Smith, the new king of Three-Card Monte. Smith had 'won' an all-time record haul by playing a Klondike gold miner, John Stewart, eventually depriving him of the entire contents of a sack of gold he had with him. Soapy Smith was killed in a gunfight the following day with a posse raised by the local vigilance committee.

The game, in its full form, is a classic example of a 'short-con'. To play, the dealer places three cards face down on a table (although the street corner version relies on an upturned cardboard box, which provides the ability to set up and disappear quickly). The dealer shows that one of the cards is the target card, and then rear-ranges the cards quickly to confuse the player as to which card is which. The player is then given a chance to choose one of the three cards. If the player correctly iden-tifies the target card, the player wins back their stake, plus the same amount again, otherwise the stake is lost. A common belief is that the dealer may allow the mark to win a couple of bets to draw them in, but this is virtually never the case. In a true Three-Card Monte scam, the mark will never win a single bet, as this is entirely unnecessary. The key to Three-Card Monte is the dealer's sleight of hand and skills of misdirection that prevent the mark from finding the target card.[2]

In the 1960s and '70s, Three-Card Monte teams operated on a daily basis in the West End of London, and on Oxford Street in particular. Every policeman on the beat knew the signs from 100 yards. To the C11 officers reviewing what was known about the possible identity of the 'third man', examining the few threads of intelligence they had seemed disturbingly like the games of Three-Card Monte they'd encountered numerous times as beat officers. Was there a deliberate attempt to misdirect and confuse, or had there been something more sinister at work during the previous decade?

As seen previously in Chapter 5, Micky Ball had allegedly been seen by several witnesses, including Herbert Turner, in the top-floor toilets of Comet House shortly before the wages snatch on 27 November 1962. Ball had truthfully maintained throughout police questioning that he had never set foot in Comet House, being in the blue Jaguar in the car park, outside the main entrance, waiting for the raiders to emerge and make a getaway.

Were the witnesses mistaken, though? Ball had also been identified at a line-up by Denis Walton from the Buck & Ryan tool shop in Euston Road, London, who claimed Ball came in on 23 November asking for 24-inch bolt cutters. Interestingly, Walton's colleague, Frank Alderman, failed to pick out Ball in the same line-up. Both men gave detailed descriptions of the man who came into the shop the following day,[3] which were later used to create a composite Identikit of the man in question. While Walton's and Alderman's descriptions varied slightly, as is often the case in such brief encounters, it struck C11 in 1976 that perhaps Ball had been misidentified. Terry Hogan, whose participation in the airport robbery was verified by several sources, was of a similar height and build to Ball, and critically had light, blond hair and a left-side parting, as Ball did. Hogan was also a close associate of Gordon Goody, who had driven the blond-haired man to Euston Road to buy the bolt cutters. On reflection, the albeit imperfect Identikit bore a closer resemblance to Hogan than to Ball.

A second possibility concerning the blond-haired man was found in a file of unused witness statements given shortly after the train robbery,[4] but was not thought to be of particular relevance or importance at the time. One such statement was made by self-employed motor mechanic Roger Smith on 18 August 1963. Smith had been contracted by Roy James to help maintain his Brabham racing car. In his six-page statement, Smith listed those individuals he had seen at James's garage. Virtually all of them are referred to by their full names, such as Bruce Reynolds, Charlie Wilson, Robert Pelham, Graham Evans, Eric Harris and Ken Simmonds. Some are referred to by nicknames, such as Charlie Wilson's associate 'Waggie' Whitnell. One, however, is simply referred to as 'a blond lad, aged 27, slim build, thin face – he may have come with Charlie Wilson'. This, on the face of it, is a similar description to the unnamed man with blond hair on Commander Hatherill's list of suspects. If this person were Terry Hogan, why did Smith not mention him by name, as he did with most of the others? Hogan was a close associate of a number of those on the list, and would have surely been known to Smith. If, however, the blond man was not Terry Hogan and was not a regular face at the garage, Smith would not, in all probability, have known his name.

Could there, then, be a third blond-haired man involved in the airport robbery – Ball, Hogan, and the unnamed man? C11 thought on balance probably not. The man Roger Smith had seen was most likely Hogan or someone unconnected with the gang, who was a peripheral friend, minor associate or a friend of a friend; but it was, all the same, an open question.

Ronald Harvey, the man who had been at Beaford House with Danny Pembroke, Bobby Welch, Charles Lilley and others in September and October 1963 (and made further visits there in 1964), was the only man who, along with Hogan, was still on the Post Office Investigation Branch's suspect list in May 1964.[5] Interestingly, his name did not appear on either Butler's or Hatherill's list of suspects. Why, then, were the Post Office IB out of kilter? Close study of the voluminous records kept by the Post Office Investigation Branch and the Devon Constabulary on those who had been at Beaford House[6] suggests that he had paid the bill after a visit to Beaford, on 17 February 1964, with 'mouldy' five-pound notes. On that occasion he handed Mrs Wicketts, the owner of Beaford House:

> twenty £5 notes, the numbers of which were duly supplied to the police. One note is within 129 of one of the stolen notes, and unquestionably came from one of the series stolen. This, of course, being alone, is not sufficient for police to interrogate the suspects, for all have close connections with many betting shops in London and the defence which would be forwarded is very obvious.[7]

Equally, his brother, Martin Harvey, had been arrested on 26 September 1963,[8] when £518 of train robbery money was found at his flat at 17 Michaelson House, Bower Drive, Dulwich, when it was searched by police. He made a full confession, and admitted he had been paid £200 for minding the money by a person he refused to name. Had he been minding a lot more than the £518? The sum of £200 seemed rather a large reward for minding £518. By pleading guilty, the matter ended there, but questions about how much money he had received, and from whom, were never to be satisfactorily answered.[9] Apart from the damp money, nothing of value was ever picked up by C11 on Ronald Harvey, and even a decade later, C11's review found nothing new to put Harvey's name further in the frame.

While Commander Hatherill had speculated that Buster Edwards's associate Jimmy Collins might 'possibly' be the nondescript man who was thirteenth on his list of seventeen suspects,[10] this was deemed somewhat unlikely by C11, as Collins was a 'large scouser' and was hardly a match for the term 'nondescript'. More to the point, in light of previous C11 intelligence shortly after the November 1962 raid, suggesting that Collins had been voted out of the airport robbery team for 'losing his bottle', it was considered highly unlikely that he would have been chosen so soon afterwards for an ever bigger job where total trust and reliability were a prerequisite. While he remained in Edwards's circle, he did not appear to have been involved in any further big jobs following his 1962 acquittal at the Old Bailey for the Westminster Bank raid at the Corn Exchange, Mark Lane.[11] The only offence recorded in his CRO file, post-1962, was for a 1967 counterfeiting case in Brussels.[12]

The airport robbery, though, seems to have been seen as one of the most important clues in terms of the 'third man'. While going through the airport robbery investigation files several times over with a fine-toothed comb, another Edwards associate had been noted on one of the two suspect lists. While not arrested in connection with the Westminster Bank raid, he had been mentioned as a possible suspect – his name was Derek Ruddle, nicknamed 'Ding Dong'.[13] While Ruddle had, at various times in the past, given his occupation as a wood log salesman, printer and assistant printer, his principal occupation was believed to be that of a bookmaker in Peckham. In this connection, his name had also been noted as a director of a company set up on 6 September 1962, called Bookmakers Guardian Ltd.

According to information obtained from Companies House, its articles of association stated that its objective was to 'form an association of bookmakers'. The company had a nominal capital of £1,000 in £1 shares and a registered address at 93/97 Regent Street, London W1, which Scotland Yard noted was an 'accommodation address for a multitude of companies'.[14] This information, it should be said, had not come to the attention of the police through any investigation of Ruddle. It had surfaced as the result of Commander Hatherill bringing the Fraud Squad's Detective Chief Inspector Mesher into the train robbery inquiry to investigate the background to the purchase of Leatherslade Farm. This had led subsequently to a separate investigation of solicitors' clerk Brian Field. Mesher's report on Field revealed a history of close involvement in several money laundering and investment ventures, and the fact that in 1959 he had been charged with 'conspiring with Albert Grossman and other persons unknown to cheat and defraud the creditors of Dyne Engineers Company Ltd'.[15]

When Mesher had written to Companies House requesting a list of any companies that Brian Field and John Wheater were in any way connected with, a list promptly arrived on his desk naming a string of companies such as Jiltslade Investments Ltd, Brusteric Investments Ltd, Fusigrand Investments Ltd, Stramquish Investments Ltd, and Trizweeks Investments Ltd.[16] The list went on and on; one name stuck out, however, for the simple reason that it did not appear to be an investment company: Bookmakers Guardian Ltd. In addition to Derek Ruddle, who was listed as the sole company director, the company secretary was Brian A. Field. The shareholders included Field himself, along with solicitor John D. Wheater. According to the documentation, the company's registration papers had been submitted to Companies House by solicitors T.W. James & Wheater of 3 New Quebec Street, London W1, the same firm who had handled the purchase of Leatherslade Farm. It would seem that it was Ronald Edwards who was first represented by the firm when he appeared at the County of London Sessions on 21 November 1961, charged with driving a motor vehicle while disqualified. He was found guilty, given fourteen days' imprisonment, and disqualified from driving for a further two years.[17]

The last, but by no means the least, of C11's shortlist of candidates for the third man was a person who, metaphorically speaking, remained in the shadows. He had, apparently, been one of Frank Williams's network of South London sources, and was referred to by Williams simply as P.W. Williams, according to several former Flying Squad officers, never referred to his sources by name or even nickname, only by letters of the alphabet. These letters did not refer to the individual's own initials, but to a code name Williams had given them. To at least one former Flying Squad colleague, it seemed that P.W. often seemed to know a lot more than the typical source, which suggested to him that P.W. could actually be a direct participant as opposed to an observer or third party in some of the matters that he discussed with Williams. Williams, who often castigated Tommy Butler for playing his cards too close to his chest and for failing to confide in colleagues, was, according to this officer, actually ten times worse than Butler for jealously guarding his sources and for failure to share information with colleagues. P.W. apparently knew an awful lot of detailed information about the train robbery – could P.W. actually be the third man himself, playing Williams at his own game? With nothing more to go on other than suspicion and educated guesswork, C11 could hardly develop a theory any further than that.

Back in 1967, when Frank Williams was the subject of an internal Metropolitan Police investigation about taking bribes from criminals, he had, so the word went, dropped the hint that if any 'unfair' action was taken against him, he knew where the bodies were buried, so to speak, had a written notebook relating to his contacts, and indeed other officers, and would take others down with him. As we know, no action of any kind was taken against Williams in 1967, and the file on that investigation remains closed until 2044. Neither is it known what happened to Williams's 'little black book'. Might it, or indeed the closed police investigation file, tell us some of the answers? If so, we have a very long wait in front of us.

In summary, what little C11 knew about the third man, other than threads of intelligence, was hardly concrete, and was summed up as follows: 'was a close associate of Ronald Edwards, more than likely took part in the London Airport robbery and was averse to taking part in violence'.[18]

In the Piers Paul Read interviews, mention is made of the 1962 wages snatch at the Old Oak Common Railway Maintenance Depot in West London. According to this brief account of the robbery, four men were involved: Buster Edwards, Gordon Goody, Charlie Wilson and 'Bill Jennings'.[19] However, in Bruce Reynolds's 1995 autobiography he refers to the fourth member of the Old Oak Common team as 'Harry Booth' (i.e. Terry Hogan), not 'Bill Jennings'. Puzzlingly, he describes 'Harry Booth' as 'a big boy, about fifteen stone, he couldn't understand all the debate. He took charge and became the physical, if not the cerebral, leader.'[20]

Read also states that shortly after his arrest, following the London Airport robbery, Micky Ball realised that he 'had been mistaken for Bill Jennings who looked something like him'.[21] Interestingly, both Bruce Reynolds in 1995 and Gordon Goody in 2014 seem to corroborate this statement about Bill Jennings's appearance. According to Reynolds's autobiography, the man Goody drives to Buck & Ryan in Euston Road to buy the bolt cutters is Bill Jennings. In Goody's 2014 book, he also states that man he drove to Buck & Ryan was Bill Jennings.[22] Some have commented that a number of recollections in Goody's book appear suspiciously like recycled lifts from Reynolds's earlier book. It may be, therefore, that Goody is simply repeating Reynolds's rendition about the man at Buck & Ryan rather than adding something of his own. Of course, Goody, more than anybody else, should know who it was who went into the Buck & Ryan store, as he himself drove them there and collected them afterwards. Again, as we saw in relation to Goody's recollections about the Ulsterman in Chapter 13, his memory is, for whatever reason, hardly consistent or reliable.

We have heard several descriptions of Bill Jennings from the sources mentioned above. However, there is another description that could well be the only authentic one in existence, so far as the third man is concerned. What's more, it's possibly the only one not emanating from any of the train robbers themselves, but from the lips of someone who more than likely saw him at the scene of the crime, i.e. at Sears Crossing at just gone ten minutes past three on the morning of 8 August 1963. That man was Stanley Hall, who was working in the HVP coach. His description was never called upon as evidence, for the reasons outlined earlier in this book, concerning the way the prosecution chose to present their case in court back in January 1964:

After we had been standing for a few minutes, out of curiosity, I opened the near side leading door – in other words, the left hand door looking towards the train. I was alone at this time and saw some person standing between my coach and the High Value Coach. As I opened the door, the man standing on the permanent way [i.e. standing on the railway track] looked at me. He did not have a mask on and had a roundish face and was wearing glasses. I can't give any idea of age at all, except to say that he was neither very young nor very old. He was bending down most of the time but by the height of the running board I would say he was on the shorter side, of about 5' 6". He was rather thick set. I have got the impression he was wearing a Railwayman's cap, but not a shiny topped one as there was no reflection from the light. He was wearing the blue material type clothing similar to that worn by railway workmen. When I looked out the door the man would be about twelve feet away from me. He did not speak to me; he only glanced in my direction. After a few seconds another man came from under and beneath the two coaches.[23]

Clearly this man, along with the other who appeared from under the coach, were, unbeknown to Stanley Hall, decoupling the HVP coach and the locomotive from the rest of the train.

Of the fifteen robbers present on the track, we know that Ronald Edwards partly resembles the description given by Stanley Hall in terms of height, build and facial appearance. However, we also know that when the train stopped at the red signal and the fireman, David Whitby, climbed down from the cab and went to the line-side telephone, it was Edwards who beckoned him and called to him to 'come here'.[24] It was Edwards who then grabbed hold of Whitby and pushed him down the embankment into the hands of two other robbers. It was also Edwards who then, moments later, headed towards the locomotive and took part in the storming of the cab.

On the basis that the two men Stanley Hall saw around the same time, i.e. just after the train had stopped at the red signal, were busy decoupling the coaches, the man with the 'roundish face' could not have been decoupling coaches while at the same time grabbing Whitby, and then taking part in the assault on the locomotive. All of the robbers' accounts are unanimous in stating that the two men whose job it was to do the decoupling were Roy James and 'Bill Jennings'. There is reasonable agreement where everyone else involved was at this particular time, and their specific role. By a process of elimination, everyone's location is accounted for at Sears Crossing, leaving the 'third man' as the only possible person who could be decoupling the train along with Roy James.

Having eliminated Edwards as the man seen by Hall, and knowing that none of the other robbers matched Hall's description, we are left with the conclusion that C11 reached: that the man Hall saw with the 'roundish face' from only 12ft away was most likely the elusive third man, 'Bill Jennings'.

Coupled with the three threads C11 also referred to – i.e. that the third man was an associate and friend of Edwards, was adverse to taking on a role in the robbery that might involve violence, and had most likely taken part in the airport robbery – the field of vision begins to clear somewhat.

Piers Paul Read's book *The Train Robbers* eventually came out on 1 May 1978. Eighteen days later, at the Old Bailey, Billy Ambrose, having already spent nearly two years on remand, stood in the dock along with the other defendants to finally hear the verdict of the jury. When the case started, more months ago than anyone cared to remember, Mr Kenneth Richardson opened for the Crown, and told the court that 'a long and patient police operation culminated in the arrest of the big fish in the operation'.[25]

Of course, at no point was the involvement of the Security Service mentioned in open court. The case was one of the biggest cases of its kind to come before a court, he told them, and went on to summarise the prosecution's case:

The allegation is that this international organisation was concerned in the pres-entation of forged bank drafts to banks throughout the world with the object of defrauding those banks.

At the time of the arrests, forged bankers' drafts amounting to $9.5 million were found in premises associated with the various defendants, ready to be presented. The Crown would prove that certain banks were defrauded to the extent of hundreds of thousands of dollars. It was a fraud that the Crown say really knew no limit. If it had not been checked, and had gone on, there can be little doubt that this multimillion-pound international banking fraud, could have undermined virtually the entire banking system of the civilised world.[26]

The Crown further alleged that the organisation used 44 St James's Street, Westminster, as its main meeting place for its operations. 'Mr Ambrose was the number one man in England, and was the protector and collector for the group in the UK. As often happened among top people in organisations of this kind, Mr Ambrose kept a low profile, counsel continued.'[27]

Summing up the case against Ambrose at the conclusion of proceedings, the judge, Gerald Hines, went over each and every piece of evidence presented to the jury and the differing interpretations such evidence might suggest. Finally, the jury went away to consider their verdict. The press waited eagerly for their return. The following day, 19 May 1978: 'William Ambrose, a bookmaker and company director in Soho, London was acquitted by the jury at the Central Criminal Court, of being concerned in a multi-million-pound international bank drafts fraud.'[28] Oberlander, though, was found guilty and sentenced to fourteen years. The other remaining defendants, too, were also found guilty and handed down long custodial sentences. Oberlander, however, was destined to complete only eighteen months of his sentence. His lawyers had, during the intervening period, communicated with both the CIA and the FBI in Washington DC, to the effect that he had intelligence that he would only disclose personally. He claimed that the circle of individuals involved in the London case were, in fact, part of a wider international ring of organised crime that was the ultimate recipient of a large proportion of the proceeds. The American authorities therefore had him extradited to the US. Whatever he imparted to the US intelligence community is anyone's guess, but the net result was that he was not to see the inside of an American correctional facility.

The result of Billy Ambrose's acquittal was that the C11 review of any connection that he may or may not have had with the train robbery deflated like a slowly collapsing soufflé. As it was, the view that had emerged was that while he ticked a number of boxes in respect to the third man, he did not entirely fit the character profile. In particular, some weight was given to the intelligence picked up shortly after the train robbery that the third man had been somewhat averse to involving himself in the assault on the HVP coach and had therefore been assigned to decoupling duties. Billy Ambrose, it was felt, was probably not a man who would have shied away from the physical side of the job.

The question remained, however, as to why there had seemingly been a sweeping over of the traces so far as the third man was concerned. What was it about him that warranted such an effort, if indeed such an effort had been made? As with so many similar conundrums, the end often returns to the beginning. Was the third man such a minnow that he was successfully able to evade scrutiny and arrest for the duration of his lifetime, or was the opposite the case?

Sometimes in life, things really are as simple as they might seem at first look. All organisations have minor players, and ironically, they are often the ones who evade accountability. Ronnie Biggs, of course, was without doubt a minor player in the gang, to the extent that most of the robbers maintained that he took little part in the robbery itself, spending most of the time in a Land Rover, minding 'Old Alf' following his failure to move the locomotive. Had Biggs somehow managed to avoid leaving his fingerprints on a sauce bottle, a plate and the Monopoly board, he would, ironically, have ended up, so far as posterity was concerned, another mystery man who got away. No doubt questions similar to those explored in this chapter would have been asked about him in future decades, such as how he had slipped through the net.

With no obvious links to the gang, apart from a tenuous social acquaintanceship with Bruce Reynolds, and not one single informant mentioning his name to either Butler or Hatherill, he would have been home and dry. Biggs would presumably have followed in the footsteps of the 'third man', whose circumstances were remarkably similar, apart from the fact that he kept his gloves on. Biggs's building business was already on the up in 1962–63, and would no doubt have reached even greater heights in the years to come had he been able to invest in more men and capital equipment. In the unlikely event that there were ever rumours voiced in this parallel universe of the future, he would no doubt have retorted resentfully that his prosperity was due in no small part to his honest hard work and enterprise in making a great success of his building business.

But for several unlucky moments at Leatherslade Farm, this would most likely have been Ronnie Biggs's ultimate destiny. Instead, he spent nearly four decades on the run, ironically as the most famous of the train robbers. Indeed, there are some today who actually believe that he was the leader and mastermind of the gang, such is the ease with which history of all kinds is so often distorted with the passage of time.

Who's to say that the third man was not a more careful version of Ronnie Biggs? Was it all really that simple?

Whoever the third man actually was, a number of officers in C11 were certain about one thing: his name was on the list of six.

APPENDICES

METROPOLITAN POLICE STRUCTURE 1963

The Metropolitan Police consisted of four departments, each headed by an Assistant Commissioner:

A Department – Administration
B Department – Traffic
C Department – CID
D Department – Recruitment & Personnel

C Department, the department referred to throughout this book, was in turn subdivided into divisions:

C1 – Murder Squad
C2 – Crime Correspondence
C3 – Fingerprints
C4 – Criminal Records Office
C5 – CID Policy
C6 – Company Fraud Squad
C7 – Laboratory
C8 – Flying Squad
C9 – Provincial Crime Branch
C10 – Stolen Car Squad
C11 – Criminal Intelligence Section

APPENDIX 2

TELEPHONE TAPPING

The earliest records regarding telephone tapping were two fragments from 1937 and 1938 respectively that had originally come from a file that could no longer be located.[1] It would appear that questions were being asked in the spring of 1937 about where responsibility lay for authorising telephone tapping on private lines. The Director General of the Post Office therefore reached an agreement with Sir Robert Russell Scott, the Permanent Under Secretary of State for the Home Office. A note was then written for the file on 2 December 1937 to place these recent developments on the record:

> The position as regards listening in without the knowledge of either party is that until May of this year, the Post Office arranged to listen in at the request of the Police or MI5, and on the specific ad hoc authority of the Director General without a warrant. In practice MI5 only asked for listening in to be arranged in cases covered by Home Office Postal and Telegraph warrants. (See (a) on attached sheet for the form of authority in such warrants.) In May 1937, the Director General agreed with Sir Robert Russell Scott that arrangements for listening in should only be made on Home Office warrant.[2]

It would therefore appear from this that prior to May 1937, if the police or MI5 wished to arrange a phone tap, no formal authorisation or warrant was required; they simply made a request to the Post Office to take the necessary action. Even in this earliest note, there is a strong element of double-speak, as it is implied that while this was the case, MI5, in practice, only made Post Office requests in situations covered by Home Office Postal and Telegraphy warrants.

However, there is much documentary evidence to suggest that in practice, even this liberal regime was merely paid lip service by the secret services. The system of Postal & Telegraphy Warrants had been in existence long before the First World War. We now know that when the secret services were formally set up in 1909, the Post Office had expressed concern about allowing them to intercept and open mail.[3] Hitherto, the Home Secretary had to sign an individual warrant for each and every letter intercepted and opened. Eventually, in 1911, Vernon Kell, the Head of

MI5, had impressed on the Home Secretary, Winston Churchill, the impracticality of such a system and MI5's need to effectively intercept the mail of suspected German spies. As a result, and against the wishes of the Post Office, Churchill made the decision to override this requirement by introducing 'general warrants authorizing the examination of all correspondence of particular people on a list to which additions were continually being made'.[4] This effectively meant that the secret services could have mail intercepted and opened in respect to any person who was on an ever-changing list of their own devising.

Even the Post Office claim that 'in practice MI5 only asked for listening in to be arranged in cases covered by Home Office Postal & Telegraphy warrants' has subsequently been flatly contradicted by MI5's own authorised history, which was published in 2009. This states that 'it was not thought necessary before 1937 to seek Home Office Warrants for telephone calls'.[5]

However, from 1937, Post Office files suggest that the interception of telephone calls could only be made by via a Home Office warrant. How did this work in reality? Within a year of the new understanding between the Post Office and the Home Office, the Post Office themselves were raising questions with the Home Office that, in the fullness of time, would reopen a number of the old telephone tapping loopholes.

On 3 September 1938, the Home Office responded to the Post Office's query:

Dear Gardiner

Your Investigation Branch has asked whether we will issue a warrant authorizing them to tap telephone conversations for the purpose of obtaining information about certain of your sales representatives who are suspected of acting irregularly and getting business from outside firms rather than for the Post Office in return for some bribe.

It seems to me that the general principles governing warrants for tapping telephone conversations are very like the general principles which govern warrants for the opening of letters.

It is impossible to lay down very definite standards as to the degree of mischief which justifies interference with communications for the detection of criminals.

Yours sincerely

A. Maxwell[6]

By implying that the principles governing telephone taps were very like those for opening letters, the Home Office had unconsciously drawn a parallel between individual authorisations and the type of blanket authorisations Churchill had approved in 1911, an approval that still held good in 1938. Whether Maxwell, the author of the Home Office reply, was aware of Churchill's precedent can only be speculated upon. However, it is certain that many in MI5, Special Branch and the CID were.

The elasticity of Maxwell's words about the 'degree of mischief' on the part of criminals to justify telephone tapping, and the impossibility of laying down clear standards, was another hostage to fortune. If this was so difficult to define, in the Home Office's view, why bother approaching the Home Office in the first place? Maxwell's reply seemed to imply that the Home Office was quite relaxed, and indeed agnostic, about telephone tapping.

The Second World War came and went. By implication, the police and the Post Office had been going their own way on telephone tapping for some time, to the blissful ignorance of the Home Office.

Then, in late 1951, the cat was well and truly out of the bag:

Towards the end of 1951, Sir Frank Newsam, the Permanent Secretary at the Home Office, asked the Post Office to attend a meeting in his room to discuss the interception of telephone conversations by the Post Office. His attention had been drawn to the matter through the disclosure by a Sergeant of the Metropolitan Police, of certain general information he had obtained when intercepting conversations in connection with a Post Office theft case.

A meeting took place on 8 January 1952, the Post Office being represented by Sir George Ismay and Sir Clement Hallam, Solicitor to the Post Office.

On the particular question of disclosure mentioned above, Sir Frank Newsam first argued that no disclosure should be made in any circumstances. Sir George Ismay regarded this as inconsistent with the general obligations of servants of the Crown and the issue was narrowed down to the point that a disclosure should take place only with proper authority. The particular case was obscure on this point and it was agreed not to pursue it.

Sir Frank Newsam then raised the question of the legality of interception by the Post Office without a Home Office warrant. Sir George Ismay referred to the past history, but said that the Post Office would welcome reversion to Home Office warrant procedure, provided such requests were dealt with reasonably and expeditiously. Sir Frank Newsam asked that requests should go to him personally with a brief statement indicating the number, and the name of this subscriber of the telephone conversation, that the case was of importance and that it was essential to the proper investigation of it to carry out the interception procedure. He said it would help for speed if the statement was accompanied by a warrant ready for signature. He emphasized that interception should only be asked for in major cases when other resources had been tried and failed. It was agreed by the Post Office to give instructions accordingly.[7]

The fact that Newsam had to raise the issue of the legality of Post Office tapping without a Home Office warrant in the first place is proof, if proof were needed, that such incidents were occurring on more than an occasional basis. It is also telling that Sir George Ismay, with the Post Office Solicitor, Sir Clement Hallam, close to his side, sought to justify this by referring to 'past history'. Equally, the fact that Ismay tried to extricate himself by welcoming 'a reversion to the Home Office Warrant procedure' is admission enough that this had not been happening for some time. It is also significant that Ismay slipped in a proviso, namely that the Post Office would only revert back to the Home Office if 'requests were dealt with reasonably and expeditiously'. This can only imply that, in his view, the Home Office had not always, in the past, been either reasonable or expeditious.

The Post Office/Home Office cat-and-mouse game was, however, to continue well into the 1950s and '60s, despite the Newsam/Ismay summit meeting. Six months later, on 29 July 1952, Sir Clement Hallam's Solicitor's Department was showing no sign at all in its legal advice, that Frank Newsam's tub-thumping had made any lasting impression whatsoever on the Post Office mindset:

> The P.M.G. is not prevented by statute from:
> (1) listening to or recording telephone conversations
> (2) allowing others (e.g. the police) to listen to or record telephone conversations
> (3) disclosing or allowing others to disclose the purport of telephone conversations
> Up to 1937 the PMG authorized listening to and recording of telephone conversations without the consent of either party. Since 1937 such listening and recording has been done only under a Warrant issued by the Home Secretary; if there is need for urgent action in serious criminal cases, action may be taken in advance of the Warrant. The listening and recording are carried out by Post Office staff.
> The PMG is thus free to act as he wishes in this matter, except in so far as he is bound by international convention. When he does act, he does so by virtue of the Royal Prerogative. His refusal to act, except under the authority of a Warrant issued to him from the Home Office or the Governor of Northern Ireland, is a matter of policy, not of law.[8]

More significantly, a further nail was driven home by another piece of legal advice handed down by the Solicitor's Department on 18 August 1953:

The principal Sections relating to the disclosure of telegraphic messages are:

1. Section 45, Telegraph Act 1863 which makes it an offence for a person in the employ of the Postmaster General improperly to divulge to any person the purport of any message.

2. Section 20, Telegraph Act 1868 which makes it an offence for any persons having official duties connected with the Post Office to disclose or make known or intercept, contrary to his duty, the contents or any part of the contents of a telegraphic message.

The view has been taken in the past that the Postmaster General has a discretion under Section 20 of the Telegraph Act 1868 to authorize a disclosure of the contents of a telegraphic message and it has been suggested that the discretion might properly be exercised by a senior member of the Telecommunications Department. Telephone messages may be regarded as telegraphic messages.[9]

In true George Orwell fashion, the Home Office diktat and oversight had now been watered down one step further by a few choice words 'of clarification'. Significantly, it was now considered, by the Solicitor's Department, that the Postmaster-General's discretion under Section 20 could be exercised by 'senior members of the Telecommunications Department'.

Before too long, the Post Office Telecommunications Department were asking the Solicitor's Department if using tape recorders to record telephone conversations, as opposed to taking shorthand, would contravene the agreement with the Home Office. They were asking this in relation to tape recorders assisting in the detection of fraud against the Post Office. On 5 September 1953, following discussions between the Solicitor's Office and the Post Office's Deputy Director General, Sir Ben Barnett, they were told that this would be permissible under the following conditions:

(i) the machine should be set in such a way as not to provide continuous 'listening-in'.

(ii) in no case should the information given on the recording be used as evidence in a prosecution. It should do no more than give an indication of the direction in which fraud was being practiced, and the prosecution of an individual would have to rest on other evidence.

On this basis, Sir Ben agrees that there is no need to consult the Home Office. I hope that what is said in this note will be sufficient for the purposes of drafting the Call Office Group's report, and the only point outstanding is whether we should take any action in regard to the use to be made of the tape recorders we already have. I gather that there are only one or two of them in existence and I suggest that it would be desirable for you to have an informal word with the Regional Directors concerned, bringing to their notice the specific limitations, mentioned above, on the use to be made of these machines.[10]

METROPOLITAN POLICE DISTRICTS AND DIVISIONS

No. 1 District

Division A – Whitehall
Division B – Westminster
Division C – St James's
Division F – Covent Garden
Division T – Kensington
Division V – Wandsworth

No. 2 District

Division D – Marylebone
Division N – Islington
Division S – Hampstead
Division X – Paddington
Division Y – Highgate

No. 3 District

Division E – Holborn
Division G – Finsbury
Division H – Whitechapel
Division J – Bethnal Green
Division K – Stepney
Division TA – Thames

No. 4 District

Division L – Lambeth
Division M – Southwark
Division P – Camberwell
Division R – Greenwich
Division W – Clapham
Division Z – Croydon

APPENDIX 4

THE POST OFFICE SOLICITOR

Postmaster-General Reginald Bevins's worst fears following the train robbery were not confided to the Post Office Investigation Department, or even to his ministerial government colleagues; they were, however, discussed in great detail in an ongoing dialogue with two of his most trusted civil servants. The official record of those conversations and the correspondence that flowed from them were soon to be confined to a manilla folder, which was then tightly tied and knotted with pink ribbon, as was the custom with closed files, and securely stored away in the vaults of the Post Office.[1] The file would not emerge to see the light of day for five decades. By 2019, Bevins had been dead for twenty-three years.

On 13 August 1963, H.N. Pickering, on behalf of the Postmaster-General, wrote confidentially to the Post Office Solicitor:

> Following last week's heavy loss of Bank HVPs, the Postmaster-General has asked whether the Banks concerned could sue us in Common Law for negligence, if in fact we were shown to have been negligent.
>
> Could we please have your advice as to whether the Banks could sue us on this basis or on any other basis.
>
> The salient features of the HVP arrangements with the Banks are set out in the attached note.[2]

Before the Solicitor had the chance to fully research this complex legal conundrum, let alone reply, Pickering wrote again as the result of further panicking on Bevins's part. This time the question was concerning the PMG's fear that Hart & Co., the loss adjusters appointed by the banks, might demand the right to see the TPO coach to inspect its security features. Knowing, as he now did, that these security features were pretty much non-existent, Bevins was clearly in a flap about the prospect.

Eventually, the Solicitor, A.R.C. Griffiths, ventured the following opinion:

In my view the Post Office could not be successfully sued by the Banks for negligence or otherwise in respect of the loss of High Value Packets, except under the Crown Proceedings Act.

The liability of the Post Office in tort is governed by s9 of the Crown Proceedings Act 1947. The HVPs are registered inland postal packets. Proceedings maybe brought against the Crown in respect of the loss of such packets 'in so far as the loss is due to any wrongful act done or any neglect or default committed by a person employed as a servant or agent of the Crown while performing or purporting to perform his functions as such in relation to the receipt, carriage, delivery or other dealing with the packet'. For the purpose of such proceedings it is presumed, unless the contrary is shown, on behalf of the Crown, that the condition in quotation marks above is satisfied. (1947 Act, s.9)[3]

If the Post Office was sued in contract, the defence would be that the acceptance by the Post Office of letters and packets for transmission through the post does not give rise to any contractual relationship. (Triefus & Co. Ltd, v Post Office, 1957 2 QB 352)[4]

Having made the position clear regarding possible legal action against the Post Office, Griffiths then turned his attention to the matter of Hart & Co. and Bevins's fears on that front:

I can think of no ground upon which Messrs. Hart & Co. could obtain an order of the Court to empower them to inspect the coach, unless proceedings were commenced against the owner of the coach or the body in possession of it. If the amount of compensation payable within Post Office regulation has already been paid no such proceedings would lie against the Post Office.

The question whether permission to inspect the coach is granted is, I think, purely one of policy, but it has first to be decided whether the coach is the property of the British Railways Board or the Post Office.

Whoever is the owner, the coach is presumably on the Board's property and is in the custody of the Board. Who does the coach belong to? Who holds the keys of the coach if it is locked up? What arrangements are there between the Post Office and the Board as regards access to the coach? Depending on the answers to these questions, it seems probable that the Board must be brought into the matter and their views obtained; it may be found that they are the proper people to decide whether inspection is to be permitted and, if necessary, to give or refuse permission.[5]

As revealing and cynical as these documents certainly are, they were not the only papers tucked away in the same closed file, for another question had, the following year, been posed to the Post Office Solicitor that would eventually lead Scotland Yard to make a startling, albeit off the record, admission to the Post Office.

The question now posed to the Post Office Solicitor was in relation to the Post Office's offer of a £10,000 reward for information leading to the arrest of those responsible for the train robbery. The new problem Bevins had was that there were now four separate claims to the reward.

The Post Office Solicitor's reply on 30 April 1964 was again a considered one, due to the complex legal issues in play:

> It is probable that where the same information is given by two persons, it is only the first to give it who can claim a reward which has been offered generally, and I think this would apply even under the wording of the Postmaster General's 'Press' notice; for it was said by Alderson B. in Lancaster v. Walsh that according to the proper meaning of the English Language the term 'first information' is a tautologous expression. Information means the communication of material facts for the first time. (See Anson's Law of Contract, twenty-first Edition, page 40, and Lancaster v. Walsh 1838, 4 M. & W. 16). Anson says that according to the nature of the act asked for by the offeror and the circumstances in which the offer is made, an offer may be susceptible of acceptance by only one person or by a number of persons. In the former case the offer is exhausted when once accepted; in the latter it remains open for acceptance by any number of persons. It seems clear that, in general principle, the Postmaster General's offer would not be regarded as one which was open to acceptance by a number of people.
>
> Even on the basis that Mr Maris has a prima facia good claim in law (i.e. on the basis that my view expressed in paragraph 4 above is wrong), he would still, of course, have to establish that it was his information which was the first received which led to the apprehension and conviction of the persons so far convicted as a result of it; and that it was his information, and not some other information, which can fairly be said to have led to the apprehensions and convictions – there must be a reasonable chain of causation. No doubt the IB and the Police can consult on this and advise the Department, as contemplated in paragraph 1 of your minute of 20 April 1964.
>
> It will be gathered from the foregoing that it is possible that other claims may be made (e.g. by persons who may have given information which has led to the apprehension and conviction of persons other than the persons convicted as a result of Mr Maris's information; or by persons who may have given, or who may

give, information leading to the apprehension and conviction of other persons not yet in custody; or, indeed, by persons who may claim that the persons already convicted, or some of them, were apprehended and convicted as a result of information given by them, and not as a result of Mr Maris's information.)

It would be possible legally for the Postmaster General to give public notice withdrawing the offer of reward, and this would avoid any claims arising from information given after the publication of the notice.

A general discussion with the Bucks Police might also be useful; they might tell us how they usually word their reward notices, and how, in practice, they deal with claims to rewards in circumstances such as the present.

The question whether to discuss matters with Messrs Donald Silk & Co. depends upon whether the Postmaster-General is prepared to come to some settlement with Maris. The matter is sufficiently complicated, from the legal point of view, to justify the Postmaster General in saying (if he so wished) that he is unable to decide whether Mr. Maris is the person entitled to the reward, and that the Postmaster-General is not prepared to make any payment except under the award of the Court.[6]

A further legal opinion of the 3 July 1964, is even more revealing:

1. The letter from the Chief Constable dated 26 June is not very helpful, but it is perhaps hardly to be expected that he would commit himself to a definite opinion as to which information led to the apprehension and conviction of any of persons concerned.

2. I gather that Mr Maris's information did not lead to the apprehension and conviction of Cordrey and Boal – presumably Mrs E.E. Clark gave the information leading to their arrest and conviction. If this is so, then as indicated in paragraph (4) of my advice of 30 April last, this alone gives the Postmaster-General grounds to argue that Mr Maris is not entitled in law to any of the reward.

3. It also appears from the Letter of 26 June 1964, that Mr Sheppard may have been the first person to give the information which led to the apprehension and conviction of all those concerned other than Cordrey and Boal. It is not clear from the letter whether it was the information of Mr Sheppard or Mr Maris which the police acted upon and which really led to the apprehension and conviction.

4. I assume, that Mr Ahearn, Mrs N. Hargraves and the other claimants referred to in the penultimate paragraph of the letter of 26 June did not give information which led to the apprehension and conviction of anyone; this could perhaps be verified from the Chief Constable.

Such was the sensitivity surrounding the decision about the allocation of the reward, and what the Post Office felt were vague and 'not very helpful' responses from the police concerning whose information had led them to Leatherslade Farm, a confidential meeting at GPO Headquarters was arranged with Chief Superintendent McArthur on 1 September 1964:

> During the discussion McArthur admitted that Sheppard had been led to believe that he was not the first to mention Leatherslade Farm to them. McArthur stressed that the police would not wish to be publicly associated with the division of the reward, but they would have no objection to the Post Office saying that in reaching their decision they had taken account of information supplied to them by the police.[7]

The form of words put forward by McArthur is carefully crafted, deliberately vague and open to different interpretation: 'He also proposed that if the press queried Sheppard's role, the Post Office could say Sheppard gave information to the police about Leatherslade Farm in the same way as Maris.'

McArthur told the Post Office that the police were not unduly concerned about the possibility of press criticism of the length of time it had taken to discover Leatherslade Farm after the receipt of Sheppard's information. They would not offer to the press any details of the use made of Sheppard's information.

It was agreed that Dennis Wesil of the Postal Services Department would seek a confidential meeting with Sheppard the next day and advise him of the proposed award.

Furthermore, a letter, to be agreed in draft by the Post Office officials, would be sent to Maris's solicitor (Donald Silk), along the lines that: 'No one person meets the requirements of the notices because not all the criminals were apprehended following one person's information. The Post Office is therefore not paying out on the terms of either notice but is making an equitable distribution of the reward.'

The reward would be shared as follows:

Mr Sheppard: £3,000
Mr Maris: £3,000
Mrs Clark: £1,250[8]

If the press asked why had nothing been heard of this Mr Sheppard before, the Post Office could say that they had no occasion to mention his name before. This is the first time the GPO had announced the names of the people to whom the Post Office reward was being paid.

Why was McArthur so adamant that John Maris's telephone tip-off on 12 August had not led them to the possibility that the robbers had chosen a farm? Why had the police denied that the discovery of Leatherslade Farm had led them directly to the men who had planned and carried out the robbery? Why had they insisted on an oath of secrecy from the Post Office about the disclosure of this revelation?

When the Post Office officially informed Maris that he was not, after all, the first person to offer information about Leatherslade Farm, his solicitor immediately smelt a rat and fired off a letter to the Post Office, expressing his incredulity at the proposition that Sheppard had offered anything whatsoever of value to the inquiry.

The Post Office eventually resolved to share the reward among the four claimants. Despite his continued protests, Maris eventually settled for half a loaf, or to be more precise, 20 per cent of the original reward offer, and accepted the sum of £1,000.

Over the next sixty years the myth of Maris, his tip-off and the clues that apparently led to Leatherslade Farm were perpetuated in umpteen books about the Great Train Robbery. Who led the police to Leatherslade Farm? Both Sheppard and Maris claimed their tip-offs were responsible, or were the police already aware of a farmhouse hideaway well before the avalanche of calls from the public descended on the control room at Aylesbury police headquarters?

Was it the Aladdin's cave of clues eventually discovered at Leatherslade Farm that led the police to the identity of the robbers, or did the police already know most, if not all, of the names of those involved before Sheppard and Maris had even picked up their telephones?

THE CAHILL COMPANIES

W. Cahill & Son

The company first appeared in the London telephone directory in 1967 as follows: 'Cahill W. & Son, Machine Buyer, 33 New Barn Street, E13 – ALBrt DK 6397'.

They appeared again in 1968 with exactly the same listing but the new telephone exchange number 01-476-6397. Incorporated 1969.

In 1971 they moved premises to 71 Prince Regent Lane, E13. They retained the above telephone number but acquired a second telephone line, 01-476-5522. They had also changed their services from machine buyers to engineers.

Between 1972 and 1980 the company continued to be listed at 71 Prince Regent Lane, E13, with the same service and the aforementioned telephone numbers.

W. Cahill & Sons (Engineers) Limited

Name: W. Cahill & Sons (Engineers) Limited
   Company number: 00949679
   Company type: private limited with share capital
   Incorporation date: 11 March 1969
   Dissolution date: July 1980 (*London Gazette*)
   Registered address: Pearl Assurance House, 319 Ballards Lane, Finchley, London N12 8LY

Williams Cahill & Sons (Haulage Contractors) Limited

Company number: 01012497
   Incorporation date: 17 May 1971
   Dissolution in 1975 (*London Gazette*)
   Registered address: 319 Ballards Lane, Finchley N12 8LY

William Cahill & Sons (Plant Hire) Limited

GB Dissolved in 1975 (*London Gazette*)
No further company detail.

NOTES

Part 1: Once Upon A Crime

1: Scoop of the Century

1   Wolff, Michael, *The Man Who Owns the News* (Random House, 2008), p.131ff; Preston, John, *Fall* (Penguin Viking, 2021), p.101ff; Roy Greenslade, 'John Brian McConnell Obituary', *The Guardian*, 17 July 2004.
2   Greenslade, 'John Brian McConnell Obituary'.
3   Metropolitan Police File 202/70/654; Ronald A. Biggs, CRO File 40117/45.
4   Ibid.
5   Ibid.
6   Ibid.
7   We now know that the manuscript was typed by Mike Haynes's wife, Jesse, not Charmian Biggs.
8   British Library Newspaper Collection, ISSN 0307-2681: *The Sun*, 20–28 April 1970.
9   Ibid.
10 Metropolitan Police File 202/70/654; Ronald A. Biggs, CRO File 40117/45.
11 Ibid.
12 House of Commons Hansard, 22 April 1970.
13 Ibid.
14 Metropolitan Police File 202/70/654; Ronald A. Biggs, CRO File 40117/45.
15 Statement of the West Cheshire Coroner in ruling that there was no reason to hold an inquest into the death of Jack Mills, who died on 4 February 1970 at Barony Hospital, Cheshire (Ellis, Ellis & Bolton Solicitors, Crewe).
16 Ronald A. Biggs, CRO File 40117/45.
17 Metropolitan Police File 202/70/654; Ronald A. Biggs, CRO File 40117/45.
18 Ibid.
19 Ronald A. Biggs, CRO File 40117/45.
20 Williams, Frank, *No Fixed Address* (W.H. Allen, 1973), p.167.

2: The Mister Men

1   Metropolitan Police File 202/70/654; MEPO 26/282.
2   Frank Monroe, Alf Thomas, Bill Jennings, and Stan Agate.
3   Metropolitan Police File 202/70/654.
4   Ibid.
5   Ibid.
6   Ibid.
7   Ibid.
8   Ibid. Interestingly, there are three versions of this text: Biggs' handwritten, uncensored manuscript; the typed version by Jesse Haynes, who replaced all swearing with ellipses;

and the version published in *The Sun*, where swearing is replaced by underscores. The Met file has Jesse Haynes's version.

9   Ibid.
10 Ibid.
11 Biggs, Ronald, *His Own Story* (Michael Joseph/Sphere Books, 1981), p.70ff.
12 Guttridge, Peter, *The Great Train Robbery* (Crime Archive/The National Archives, 2008), p.106.

3: A Little Cloak and Dagger

1   During the Second World War, Jackson liaised on behalf of the DPP with Special Branch and MI5 in relation to the trial of German spies.
2   Simpson returned to the UK with the idea of introducing parking meters in London. This was not well received by colleagues at Scotland Yard, who feared it would prove unpopular with the public. The idea was, however, adopted by the Minister of Transport, Harold Watkinson, in 1958. The first parking meters were installed in Grosvenor Square, where an hour's parking cost 6s.
3   George Hatherill OBE, Commander of CID; Bill Rawlings, Deputy Commander (MP Districts 1–4); Reg Spooner, Deputy Commander (C1–C8).
4   Jackson, Richard, *Occupied with Crime* (George W. Harrap & Co., 1967), p.121ff.
5   Ibid.
6   Ibid.
7   The Augmentation of the Intelligence Section of the Criminal Investigation Department, MEPO 2/10997.
8   Jackson, *Occupied with Crime*, p.132ff.
9   Ibid., p.116ff.
10 Ibid., p.132ff.
11 Ibid., p.280ff.
12 Ibid., p.252ff.
13 Ibid.
14 Ibid.
15 Ibid., p.121ff.
16 Ibid.
17 Metropolitan Police File 127/61/33; Robberies: Wage Snatches, MEMP 2/10290.
18 Ibid.
19 Ibid.
20 Ibid.
21 Ibid.
22 Michael John Ball, CRO File 47931/52.
23 Ibid.
24 Metropolitan Police File 127/61/33; Robberies: Wage Snatches, MEMP 2/10290.

4: That Riviera Touch

1   Jackson, *Occupied with Crime*, p.283ff.
2   Alfred Robert Gerrard, C11 File.
3   Peter Loughran, C11 File.
4   Ibid.
5   Alfred Robert Gerrard, C11 File.

6   Daniel Pembroke, C11 File.
7   *Nice-Matin*, 25 August 1961.
8   Police & Gendarmerie Record Registers; 29/6/61 to 17/10/61 (0300W 0056 – 3890 to 7396), High Court of Grasse (closed until 2036).
9   Ibid.
10 Ibid.
11 Ibid.
12 Ibid.
13 Correctional Procedure Records; 1/1/62 to 31/12/62 (0307W 0129), High Court of Grasse (closed until 2036).
14 Ibid; Report by Police High Commissioner M. Robert, 22/10/62.
15 Ibid.
16 Ibid.
17 Ibid.

5: An Inspector Calls

1   London Airport was renamed Heathrow Airport in 1966.
2   Robbery with aggravation at London Airport Robbery (Ball M; Goody D; Wilson C), DPP 2/3588; Metropolitan Police File, Robbery at London Airport, 202/62/1376.
3   Ibid.
4   Ibid.
5   Ibid.
6   Ibid.
7   Ibid.
8   Ibid.
9   Ibid.
10 Johnny Haynes is widely regarded as Fulham Football Club's greatest ever player. He made 594 appearances for the club between 1952 and 1970, and won fifty-six England caps between 1954 and 1962. He was captain of the national side between 1960 and 1962, and led them through the 1962 World Cup tournament in Chile. Shortly after returning to England from Chile, he was badly injured in a car accident, and never regained his place in the England team. Twenty-seven years old at the time of the accident, he had been expected to captain England in the 1966 World Cup tournament.
11 Robbery with aggravation at London Airport Robbery (Ball M; Goody D; Wilson C), DPP 2/3588; Metropolitan Police File, Robbery at London Airport, 202/62/1376.
12 Ibid.
13 Ibid.

6: The Big Job

1   This was the same locomotive, Class 40 Diesel, No. D326, that would, eight months later, be used for the Travelling Post Office train that was robbed on 8 August 1963.
2   *Daily Express*, 21 February 1963, p.1.
3   Hertfordshire Constabulary Report, 22 February 1963 (Bedfordshire Police).
4   *Daily Express*, 21 February 1963, p.1.

5 Hertfordshire Constabulary Report, 22 February 1963 (Bedfordshire Police).
6 For further details of the London–Brighton line train robberies, see Cook, Andrew, *The Great Train Robbery: The Untold Story from the Closed Investigation Files* (The History Press, 2013), p.20ff.
7 MEPO 2/10575.
8 POST 120/95.
9 MEPO 2/10575.
10 Ibid.

Part 2: Fish Off the Hook

7: Night Owls

1 'Hugh' was a name chosen at random. The real 'Hugh' is now in his 70s and lives in the south-east of England.
2 Harry Fenton was, in the 1970s, a high street 'off the peg' chain of men's tailors. It made its name in the sixties, specialising in suits and shirts for a Mod clientele.
3 From a handwritten note by 'Hugh'.
4 Kirby, Dick, *You're Nicked!* (Robinson, 2007), p.30ff; Metropolitan Police File 253/76/1177.
5 Ibid, p.34ff.
6 Ibid.
7 POST 120/95.
8 William David Ambrose, CRO File No. 21598/52.
9 MEPO 2/10060; DPP 2/3060.
10 Ibid.
11 Ibid.
12 Ibid.

8: Doing a Deal

1 Metropolitan Police File 202/70/654.
2 DPP 2/3718, 2 of 6.
3 Henry Thomas Smith, CRO File No 1551/47.
4 Ibid.
5 Ibid.
6 Metropolitan Police File 202/63/943; MEPO 2/10571; DPP 2/3911.
7 Ibid.
8 Ibid.
9 Ibid.
10 Williams, *No Fixed Address*, p.72ff.
11 Ibid., p.73ff.
12 Metropolitan Police File 202/63/943; MEPO 2/10571; DPP 2/3911.

9: Safe as Houses

1   Metropolitan Police File 202/63/943; MEPO 2/10571.
2   Ibid.
3   Ibid.
4   Ibid.
5   Ibid.
6   Ibid.
7   Ibid.
8   Ibid.
9   Ibid.
10 Ibid.
11 Ibid.; POST 122/15959.
12 Ibid.
13 Metropolitan Police File 202/63/943; MEPO 2/10571.
14 Ibid.
15 Ibid.
16 Ibid.
17 Ibid.
18 Ibid.
19 Ibid.
20 Ibid.

10: X Marks the Spot

1   An advertisement for Beaford House, 1963.
2   Metropolitan Police File 202/63/943; MEMP 2/10571.
3   Ibid.
4   DPP.
5   Ibid.
6   Metropolitan Police File 202/63/943; MEMP 2/10571.
7   Ibid.
8   For further details about train robberies on the London–Brighton line, see Cook, *The Great Train Robbery*, p.20ff.
9   POST 120/448.
10 Ibid.
11 Metropolitan Police File 202/63/943; MEMP 2/10571.
12 Ibid.
13 Ibid.
14 Ibid.
15 Ibid.
16 Ibid.
17 Ibid.
18 Ibid.
19 Ibid.
20 Ibid.

11: A Sound Investment

1 Richardson, Charlie, *My Manor* (Pan Books, 1992), p.140ff.
2 Ibid., p.167ff.
3 MEPO 2/11024 to 11027; DPP 2/4291 to 4294; Pretoria National Archives: The state versus Lawrence Bradbury 184/66 & 17/7/22/1759.
4 Ibid.
5 Ibid.
6 Ibid.
7 Sir Noel Dryden (1910–70), actor, best remembered for the films *The Three Witnesses* (1935), *Late at Night* (1946) and *ITV Television Playhouse* (1955).
8 *The Times*, 11 August 1962, p.4; 20 October 1962, p.5.
9 POST 120/95; Metropolitan Police File 202/63/943.
10 MEPO 2/11024 to 11027; DPP 2/4291 to 4294; Pretoria National Archives: The state versus Lawrence Bradbury 184/66 & 17/7/22/1759.
11 Ibid.
12 *Sunday Express*, 12 February 1967.
13 POST 120/95.
14 MEPO 2/11024 to 11027; DPP 2/4291 to 4294; Pretoria National Archives: The state versus Lawrence Bradbury 184/66 & 17/7/22/1759.
15 Ibid.
16 Ibid.
17 Ibid.
18 Ibid.
19 Ibid.
20 Ibid.
21 Oakhurst was a production company in which both Baker and Deeley had an interest.
22 Letter, Film Finances Ltd to Oakhurst Productions Ltd, 1 February 1967 (Film Finances Archive).
23 *The Times*, 10 April 1967, p.3.
24 Gerald Wilson was interviewed for the 2015 Studio Canal/Network re-release of the *Robbery* movie on DVD and Blu-ray.
25 Sussex County Council Planning Committee; planning application references A62/276 and A70/680, discussed at meetings on 29 September 1970 and 20 October 1970.
26 Corbett, Ronnie, *High Hopes: My Autobiography* (Ebury Press, 2000), p.96ff.
27 Corbett, *High Hopes*, p.77ff.
28 Foreman, Freddie, *The Godfather of British Crime* (John Blake, 2008), p.152ff.

12: There for the Taking

1 Ministry of Justice, J 297/35.
2 Ibid.
3 Ibid.
4 Ibid.
5 Ibid.
6 Ibid.
7 Ibid.

8   Ibid.
9   Ibid.
10 Ibid.
11 Ibid.
12 Ibid.
13 Ibid.
14 Ibid.
15 Ibid.
16 Ibid.
17 James Thomas Spinks, CRO File No 1132/46; MEPO 2/10290.
18 Ministry of Justice, J 297/35.
19 Ibid.

13: The Insider

1   Goody, Gordon, *How to Rob a Train* (Milo, 2014), p.179ff; *The Great British Train Robbery: A Tale of Two Thieves* (Kowalski & Scallie Filmworks, 2014).
2   Ibid.
3   Read, Piers Paul, *The Train Robbers* (W.H. Allen, Secker & Warburg, 1978), p.39ff.
4   *The Great Train Robbery: The Hidden Tapes*, Truenorth TV/Channel 4, 12 August 2019.
5   Ibid.
6   POST 120/95; POST 120/445.
7   Ibid.
8   POST 120/95.
9   Ibid.
10 Ibid.
11 Ibid.
12 Reynolds, Bruce, *Crossing the Line: The Autobiography of a Thief* (Virgin, 2003), p.255ff.
13 POST 120/95.
14 Ibid.
15 Papers of Percy Hoskins.

14: The Outsider

1   HO 287/1496.
2   Frank Dewhurst was the Post Office official in charge of the HVP coach.
3   DPP 2/3718, 2 of 6.
4   Ibid.
5   Millan, Ernest, *Specialist in Crime* (George Harrap & Co. Ltd, 1972), p.2070ff.
6   MEPO 2/10571.
7   POST 120/95.
8   Ibid.
9   POST 120/132.
10 MEPO 2/10571.
11 Read, *The Train Robbers*, p.281ff.
12 Ibid., p.269ff.

Part 3: Will the Real Bill Jennings Please Stand Up

15: The Bookworms

1 Hansard, House of Commons, 8 May 1957.
2 John Gosling retired from Scotland Yard in 1957 and died two years after the book was published. It is thought that the bulk of the book was the work of his co-author Dennis Craig, a writer of crime fiction. Of the nine chapters in the Gosling/Craig book, only one, Chapter 9, has any reference at all to 'inside information'. This turns out to be the story of a character called 'Johnny Rainbow', supposedly an ex-army officer who had 'an unblemished' record, and who left the army in 1957. 'Rainbow' is apparently the ringleader of the gang and plots the robbery with military precision. It was not a story that stood comparison to the reality of the intelligence C11 had. The remainder of the book is a simple but accurate retelling of the train robbery story, using contemporary published press stories as the main source.
3 Metropolitan Police File 202/63/943, MEMO 2/10571.
4 POST 120/104.
5 Fordham, Peta, *The Robbers' Tale* (Hodder and Stoughton, 1965), p.7ff.
6 Ibid., p.81ff.
7 Metropolitan Police File 202/63/943, MEMO 2/10575.
8 Ibid.
9 Fordham, *The Robbers' Tale*, p.59ff.
10 Ibid., p.26ff.
11 Metropolitan Police File 202/63/943, MEMO 2/10571.
12 Ibid.; POST 120/102; POST 120/138; POST 120/139; POST 120/140.
13 Metropolitan Police File 202/70/654.
14 Ibid.
15 Author's interview with Colin Mackenzie, 8 September 2010.
16 Metropolitan Police File 202/70/654.

16: Three-Card Monte

1 Assistant Commissioner Peter Brodie was the favourite to be appointed Commissioner, and was apparently expecting to be so appointed on Waldron's retirement. Reginald Maudling, like his Labour predecessor as Home Secretary, James Callaghan, and indeed Sir Philip Allen, the Permanent Secretary at the Home Office, felt that the established tradition of appointing Commissioners who had spent most, if not their entire, careers within the Metropolitan Police should be broken.
2 Mark, Sir Robert, *In the Office of Constable: An Autobiography* (Collins, 1978), p.126ff, and p.248ff.
3 Ibid.
4 DPP 2/4243 to 4244; DPP 2/4237 to 4242; CRIM 1/4648 to 4669.
5 DPP 2/4470, closed until 2044.
6 In 1972, the Director of Public Prosecutions, Sir Norman Skelhorn, gave bank robber Bertie Smalls, Britain's first super-grass, immunity from prosecution in light of the amounts of testimony and detail he had provided in Queen's Evidence. This testimony

convicted twenty-one individuals for a total of 302 years' imprisonment. However, the Law Lords later expressed the view that this 'arrangement' was 'an unholy deal'.

7   MacDonald ran two antiques businesses: Mac's Antiques at 69 Portobello Road, London W11, and at Skrine Hall, 18 Thornton Road, Wimbledon, SW19.

8   DPP 2/318, 1 of 6, part 2.

9   William Still, C11 File No. 11815/38.

10 Ibid.

11 J 82/4017; Root, Neil, *Crossing the Line of Duty* (The History Press, 2019), p.114ff.

12 Archives de Paris (archives de la Cour d' Appel de Paris), Enregistre a Paris – 4 Civil, 17 September, 1964, F 502902.

13 Kirby, *You're Nicked!*, p.39ff.

14 Metropolitan Police File 202/63/943; MEPO 2/10571.

15 POST 120/93; POST 120/443.

16 DPP 2/3719; Terence Hogan CRO File No. 38593/45.

17 Ibid.; DPP 3/3718/1.

18 Ibid.

19 POST 120/95.

20 Ibid.

17: Tinker, Tailor

1   William Jones, born in York, England, 1820, died of TB in Reading, Pennsylvania, 1877.

2   In 1994, American illusionist John Lenahan gave a basic explanation of the secret behind Three-Card Monte on BBC TV's *How Do They Do It?* programme. The following day he became the first person in eighty-five years to be expelled from the 'Magic Circle'.

3   Metropolitan Police File 202/62/1376; DPP 2/3588 – Denis Walton had actually phoned Albany Street CID shortly after the man wanting to buy the bolt cutters had left the shop, as he thought he was 'up to no good'. 'I was suspicious of the man and his intentions with the bolt croppers. I was suspicious because although he was wearing a blue boiler suit under his jacket, which appeared to be of an expensive cut, he did not appear to be a workman.'

4   DPP 2/3719, part 2.

5   POST 120/95.

6   POST 120/448; Metropolitan Police File 202/63/943; MEPO 2/10571.

7   Metropolitan Police File 202/63/943; MEPO 2/10571.

8   DPP 2/3718/1.

9   Martin Harvey was sentenced to twelve months' imprisonment for receiving stolen money.

10 POST 120/95.

11 *Daily Express*, 18 July 1962, p.1; *The Times*, 20 October 1962, p.5.

12 James Collins, CRO File No 26404/44 – Collins was given a two-year sentence for counterfeiting on 3 November 1967 in Brussels.

13 'Ding Dong' as in Ding Dong Dell.

14 DPP 2/3735; Metropolitan Police File 202/63/943; MEPO 2/10571.

15 BT 31/765560; 765633; 765634.

16 ASSI 13/658; DPP 2/3735.

17 POST 120/104.

18 Metropolitan Police File 202/62/1376.

19 Read, *The Train Robbers*, p.19ff.

20 Reynolds, *Crossing the Line*, p.145ff.

21 Ibid., p.27ff.
22 Ibid., p.171ff; Goody, *How to Rob a Train*, p.74ff
23 DPP 2/3718/ part 1 of 6.
24 DPP 2/3718.
25 J 82/4075/1.
26 Ibid.
27 Ibid.
28 Ibid.

Appendix 2: Telephone Tapping

1 Extracts from Post Office File 12 of P16339/38 (substantive file no longer in existence).
2 Post Office TCP 66/1-2; General Post Office, Disclosure of Information Concerning Telephone Calls & Telephone Tapping Policy Papers; 1952–86 (previously closed, opened 2019 but unclassified at time of writing).
3 *The Security Service (MI5) 1908–1945* (Public Record Office, 1999), p.68.
4 Winston Churchill to Sir Edward Grey, 22 November 1911, CCAC Churchill MSS, CHAR 13/1/25.
5 Andrew, Christopher, *The Defence of the Realm: The Authorized History of MI5* (Allen Lane, 2009), p.147.
6 Post Office TCP 66/1-2; General Post Office, Disclosure of Information Concerning Telephone Calls & Telephone Tapping Policy Papers; 1952–86 (previously closed, opened 2019 but unclassified at time of writing).
7 Ibid.
8 Ibid.
9 Ibid.
10 Ibid.

Appendix 4: The Post Office Solicitor

1 Post Office 2017/30; item 8414, Travelling Post Office – Train Robbery (Miscellaneous), previously closed, opened 2019 but unclassified at time of writing.
2 Ibid.
3 Ibid.
4 Ibid.
5 Ibid.
6 Ibid.
7 Ibid.
8 Ibid.

BIBLIOGRAPHY

Andrew, Christopher, *The Defence of the Realm: The Authorised History of MI5* (Allen Lane, 2009)

Biggs, Ronnie, *Keep on Running* (Bloomsbury, 1995)

Biggs, Ronnie, *Odd Man Out* (MPress, 2011)

Biggs, Ronnie, *His Own Story* (Sphere, 1981)

Butler, R.A., *The Art of the Possible* (Hamish Hamilton, 1971)

Clarkson, Wensley, *Killing Charlie* (Mainstream Publishing, 2006)

Coates, Tim, *The Great British Train Robbery* (self-published, 2003)

Cook, Andrew, *The Great Train Robbery: The Untold Story from the Closed Investigation Files* (The History Press, 2013)

Cook, Andrew, *1963: That Was the Year That Was* (The History Press, 2013)

Corbett, Ronnie, *High Hopes: My Autobiography* (Ebury Press, 2000)

Delano, Anthony, *Slip-Up* (Coronet, 1986)

Dorril, Stephen, *MI6: Fifty Years of Special Operations* (Fourth Estate, 2000)

Ferguson, Niall, *Empire: How Britain Made the Modern World* (Allen Lane, 2003)

Fewtrell, Malcolm, *The Train Robbery* (Arthur Barker, 1964)

Fido, Martin & Skinner, Keith, *The Official Encyclopedia of Scotland Yard* (Virgin Books, 1999)

Fordham, Peta, *The Robbers' Tale* (Hodder & Stoughton, 1965)

Foreman, Freddie, *The Godfather of British Crime* (John Blake, 2008)

Goody, Gordon, *How to Rob a Train* (Milo, 2014)

Gosling, John & Dennis, Craig, *The Inside Story of the Great Train Robbery* (W.H. Allen, 1964)

Gutteridge, Peter, *The Great Train Robbery* (Crime Archive/National Archive, 2008)

Hall, Sheldon, *Robbery* (Network, 2015)

Hatherill, George, *A Detective's Story* (Andre Deutsch, 1971)

Hoskins, Percy, *Two Men Were Acquitted* (Secker & Warburg, 1984)

Hoskins, Percy, *No Hiding Place* (Daily Express Publications, 1952)

Jackson, Richard, *Occupied with Crime* (George W. Harrap & Co., 1967)

Kirby, Dick, *You're Nicked!* (Robinson, 2007)

Kirby Dick, *The Guv'nors* (Wharncliffe True Crime, 2010)

Kirby, Dick, *London's Gangs at War* (Pen & Sword, 2017)

Kirby, Dick, *The Sweeney: The First 60 Years: 1919–1978* (Pen & Sword, 2019)

Lapping, Brian, *End of Empire* (Granada Publishing, 1985)

Lee, Colin, *The Men Who Robbed the Great Train Robbers* (Matador, 2014)

Mackenzie, Colin, *The Most Wanted Man* (Hart-Davis, MacGibbon, 1975)

Macmillan, Harold, *Pointing the Way* (Macmillan, 1972)

Marchetti, Victor & Marks, John, *The CIA and the Cult of Intelligence* (Dell Publishing, 1974)

Mark, Sir Robert, *In the Office of Constable: An Autobiography* (Collins, 1978)

Millen, Ernest, *Specialist in Crime* (George Harrap & Co., 1972)

Morton, James, *Bent Coppers* (Little, Brown, 1993)

Moss, Alan & Skinner, Keith, *The Scotland Yard Files* (The National Archives, 2006)

Omand, David, *How Spies Think: Ten Lessons in Intelligence* (Penguin Viking, 2020)

Pickard, Chris & Reynolds, Nick, *The Great Train Robbery 50th Anniversary Edition* (MPress Media, 2013)

Preston, John, *Fall: The Mystery of Robert Maxwell* (Penguin, 2021)

Read, Leonard, *Nipper* (MacDonald, 1991)

Read, Piers Paul, *The Train Robbers* (W.H. Allen, 1978)

Reynolds, Bruce, *Crossing the Line: The Autobiography of a Thief* (Virgin Books, 2003)

Reynolds, Bruce, *Autobiography of a Thief* (Bantam Press, 1995)

Richards, Ross, *The Great Train Robbery* (Consul Books, 1964)

Richardson, Charlie, *My Manor* (Pan Books, 1992)

Richardson, Eddie, *The Last Word* (Headline, 2006)

Root, Neil, *Crossing the Line of Duty* (The History Press, 2019)

Rozenberg, Joshua, *The Case for the Crown* (Thorsons Publishing, 1987)

Russell-Pavier, Nick & Richards, Stewart, *The Great Train Robbery: Crime of the Century* (Weidenfeld & Nicolson, 2013)

Ryan, Robert, *Signal Red* (Headline, 2010)

Sandbrook, Dominic, *Never Had it So Good: 1956–63* (Little, Brown, 2005)

Sandbrook Dominic, *White Heat: 1964–70* (Little, Brown, 2006)

Shirley, John & Short, Martin, *The Fall of Scotland Yard* (Penguin Books, 1977)

Slipper, Jack, *Slipper of the Yard* (Sidgwick & Jackson, 1981)

Summers, Anthony, *Official and Confidential* (Putnam, 1993)

The Security Service (MI5) 1908–1945 (Public Records Office, 1999)

Thomas, Donald, *Villains' Paradise* (John Murray, 2005)

Wheen, Francis, *The Sixties* (Century, 1982)

Williams, Frank, *No Fixed Address* (W.H. Allen, 1973)

Wolff, Michael, *The Man Who Owns the News* (Random House, 2008)

INDEX

References to images are in *italics*.

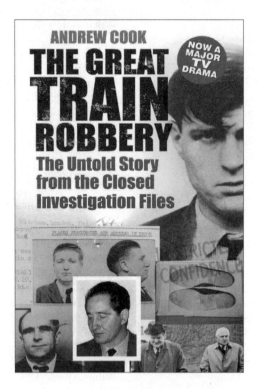

ANDREW COOK

THE GREAT TRAIN ROBBERY

NOW A MAJOR TV DRAMA

The Untold Story from the Closed Investigation Files

978 0 7524 9981 9

The Great Train Robbery of 1963 is one of the most infamous crimes in British history, but fifty years of selective falsehood and fantasy has obscured the reality of the story behind the robbery. In *The Great Train Robbery: The Untold Story from the Closed Investigation Files*, Andrew Cook uses FOI requests to piece together what really happened.

The History Press   The destination for history
www.thehistorypress.co.uk